For my grandchildren, Cruz Amelia and Caspian Jan,
for whom I tried to make a better world

The
LIBERTARIAN
INSTITUTE

What Social Animals Owe to Each Other
Sheldon Richman

First Edition, 2020

Edited by Scott Horton

Cover picture: "Market of Athens"
by J. Buhlmann

Cover design by TheBumperSticker.com

Published in the United States of America by

The Libertarian Institute
612 W. 34th St.
Austin, TX 78705

LibertarianInstitute.org

ISBN-13: 978-1-7336473-3-5
ISBN-10: 1-7336473-3-3

Contents

Introduction

These essays, written over the past 20 years, have a single underlying theme: namely, that we human beings, as *social* animals, need individual freedom to fully flourish. The equation is simple: individual freedom = social cooperation = individual and social flourishing. Many corollaries follow. To pick one, the freedom to choose with whom we will cooperate entails competition among those who wish to cooperate with any given individual. So the imagined conflict between cooperation and competition is a misjudgment. They are two sides of the same coin.

It ought to be uncontroversial to assert that when people are free to cooperate, much of that activity will occur in the marketplace. And that means we cannot fully appreciate cooperation without understanding key features of markets: trade, competition, entrepreneurship, profit, prices, scarcity, coordination, marginal utility, subjective value, the law of cost, "natural" resources, and so on. I address those issues throughout this book with the aim of showing that the free market — unmolested, that is, by force-wielding politicians and bureaucrats — is indispensable to the well-being of all.

Another phenomenon that cries out for understanding is spontaneous, or unplanned, order. Simply put, when we individuals go about the business of making better lives for ourselves and our families, we generate a large, highly complex, and beneficent order *that was no part of our intention*. This order, since it is unplanned, enables each of us to carry out our own mission — achieving the good life — in ways we can barely appreciate without investigating economics and social philosophy. But our lives depend on it. Nevertheless, people, some of whom even have good intentions, constantly propose ways to restrict and even incapacitate it in favor of a top-down planned society. The idea of unplanned order is very old, so it is sad that in the 21st century, most people still don't get it.

I must beg the reader's indulgence. Since these essays were written over a long period, mostly under the running title *The Goal Is Freedom*, for various organizations and my own blog *Free Association*, they overlap and repeat several key points. Except for an instance or two, I decided to let this go. Since these points come up in different contexts, I thought it best to leave the essays largely as they originally appeared online and on paper. I've done some tweaking and a bit of updating, but they are pretty much intact.

Needless to say, my perspective on display in these essays evolved over many years, beginning in the late 1960s, through reading, attendance at lectures, and conversations with learned people from the many interrelated disciplines: economics, politics, philosophy, history, etc. The list of people to whom I am indebted is too long to reproduce here; many of their names and the titles of their writings will be found in the essays. Also needless to say, any errors of fact or interpretation are mine alone.

The title may sound familiar. The classical-liberal sociologist William Graham Sumner collected some of his essays under the title *What Social Classes Owe to Each Other* and T.M. Scanlon wrote a book called *What We Owe to Each Other*. I am familiar with the first, but not the second. The meaning of the title will be clear in the first chapter, from which the book's title was taken.

Chapter 1.
What Social Animals Owe to Each Other

If I were compelled to summarize the libertarian philosophy's distinguishing feature while standing on one foot, I'd say the following: every person owes it to all other persons not to aggress against them. This is known as the nonaggression principle.

What is the nature of this obligation — for that's what it is, an obligation?

The first thing to notice is that it is unchosen. I never agreed not to aggress against others. Others never agreed not to aggress against me. So if I struck you and you objected, you would not accept as my defense, "I never agreed not to strike you."

Even an explicit agreement rests on an unchosen obligation. Let's say you lent me five dollars, I refused to repay the loan, and when you demanded repayment, I said, "Why am I obligated to repay the money?" You would probably reply, "Because you agreed to repay me." If I replied, "True, but when did I agree to abide by my agreements?" what would you say? If you said that failure to repay constituted aggression and I replied that I never agreed not to aggress against you, we'd be back where we started.

Of course this would point the way to absurdity — an infinite regress of agreements to keep my agreements. We would get nowhere. There has to be a starting point.

If I were to ask, "*Why* do we owe it to others not to aggress against them," what would you say? I presume some answer rooted in facts would be offered because the alternative would be to say this principle has no basis whatsoever, that it's just a free-floating principle, like an iceberg. That would amount to saying the principle has no binding force. It's just a whim, which might not be shared by others. In other words, if a nonlibertarian demands to know why he is bound by the unchosen nonaggression obligation, libertarians will have answers. Their answers will differ — some will be more robust than others — but they will have answers. At least I hope so.

Now if we have an unchosen obligation not to aggress against others and that obligation is rooted in certain facts, this raises a new question: might the facts that impose the unchosen obligation not to aggress also impose *other* obligations? If one unchosen obligation can be shown to exist, why couldn't the same foundation in which that one is rooted produce others?

To the question "Why do we owe it to others not to aggress against them," I would respond along these lines: because we individually should treat other persons respectfully, that is, as ends in themselves and not merely as means to our own ends. But some libertarians would reject that as too broad because it seems to obligate us to more than just nonaggression. They might answer the question this way: "Because one may use force against another only in defense or retaliation against someone who initiated the use of force." But this can't be sufficient because it amounts to a circular argument: to say that one may use force *only* in response to aggression is in effect merely to restate the nonaggression obligation. One shouldn't aggress because one shouldn't aggress. But the principle could hardly justify itself.

So we need a real justification, and the one I've offered seems like a good start. Nonaggression is an implication of the obligation to treat persons respectfully, as ends in themselves and not merely as means. Of course this also requires justification. Why should we treat other persons not only justly but respectfully?

Many libertarians, though certainly not all, approach the question of just conduct — specifically, as it relates to the use of force — from egoistic considerations, such as those provided by Ayn Rand. They say we should never aggress against others because doing so would be contrary to our self-interest: the dishonesty required by a life of injustice would be psychologically damaging, and eventually we'd run out of victims.

Socrates and Plato saw a problem with the first part of this answer. If one could act unjustly toward others while *appearing* to be just, could unjust conduct serve one's self-interest? Egoistic libertarians can be asked the same question. What if you could lead an unjust life with a guarantee of the appearance of justice? Must dishonesty be psychologically damaging? The same people who would say yes to that question, however, would also say that a person who spins a complicated web of lies to keep the Nazis from learning he is harboring Jews in his attic *won't* suffer such damage. If that person can escape harm, why not the unjust liar? Saying that one set of lies is for a good cause doesn't strike me as an adequate answer. How would a good cause save someone from the harm of "faking reality"?

So it seems that a simple self-interest model doesn't take us where we want to go: to the unchosen obligation to respect people's freedom, or more broadly, to treat persons as ends and not merely as means. I would be a little uneasy if a libertarian told me that it is only his self-interest that prevents him from clubbing me on the noggin and making off with my wallet.

And yet self-interest still might provide an answer. Roderick T. Long tackles this problem in his monograph *Reason and Value: Aristotle versus Rand*. What Long shows, to my satisfaction at least, is that Rand's notion of self-interest as expressed in her nonfiction essays is too flimsy to support the libertarian prohibition against aggression and the general injunction to treat people respectfully. To be more precise, Long shows that Rand's explicit writings on ethics are a tangle of at least three different and inconsistent defenses of the nonaggression obligation (one of them Kantian).

Before we get to this, however, I must invoke an important distinction that Long emphasizes: instrumental versus constitutive means to an end. An instrumental means is external to the end. A constitutive means is intrinsic to the end; we can't imagine the end without it. Long uses the example of a man dressing up for an evening out (where "dressing up" includes a necktie). Shopping for a tie is an instrumental means. Wearing the tie is a constitutive means — it is part of what we mean by "dressing up." One can dress up without shopping for a tie, but one cannot dress up (by stipulation) without wearing a tie.

We can look at justice, which includes respect for other persons' rights, in both ways. Does respect for their rights serve our self-interest *merely* because we would earn good reputations and others will cooperate with us? (This is Thomas Hobbes's position.) Or is respecting their rights also a *constituent* of living a good human life, of flourishing? The answer is crucial. In the first case, one's self-interest could be served by acting unjustly so long as one could *appear* to be just. In the second, one could not flourish by acting unjustly even if one could go undetected. As Socrates suggested, it is preferable to live justly with a reputation for injustice than to live unjustly with a reputation for justice.

Long shows that Rand has both instrumental and constitutive elements in her nonfiction writing on ethics; in some places she says a person's goal should be survival, while in other places she speaks of survival "qua man." It isn't entirely clear whether individuals should aim at the longest possible life regardless of the *type* of life or at a particular *type* of life regardless of its length. (Her novels appear to take the latter position — suicide is even contemplated by heroic characters.) If it's the first, then violating someone's rights might occasionally be to one's self-interest. Imagine that at 4 a.m. you pass an alley in a deserted part of town where a man is passed out and a hundred-dollar bill is sticking out of his pocket. The chances of getting caught are zero. Do you take the money? If not, why not? An instrumental model of justice should say to take the money. A constitutive model would not.

It might be said that a rational person acts on rational *principles* even if in particular cases his or her self-interest is not served. But Long points out that such "rule egoism" ends up being no egoism at all because the rule is followed regardless of its consequences. This approach is deontological (rule-bound), not teleological (objective-bound) as Rand would seem to want it. So the reply is inadequate.

What are the grounds for accepting the constitutive model of virtue, including justice? Turning to Aristotle, Long writes,

For Aristotle, a human being is essentially a *logikon* animal and a *politikon* animal. ...

To be a rational animal is to be a language-using animal, a conversing animal, a discursive animal. And to live a human life is thus to live a life centered around discourse.

Our nature as *logikon* is thus closely allied with our nature as *politikon*. To be a *politikon* animal is not simply to be an animal that lives in groups or sets up governments; it is to cooperate with others on the basis of discourse about shared ends. ...

Being *politikon* is for Aristotle an expression of being *logikon*; just as logikon animals naturally conduct their private affairs through reason rather than through unreflective passion, so they naturally conduct their common affairs through public discourse and rational persuasion, rather than through violence. ...

Thus, Long adds, "To violate the rights of others, then, is to lessen one's humanity. ... To trample on the rights of others is never in our self-interest, because well-being cannot [quoting Aristotle] 'come about for those who rob and use force.'"

One's goal is to flourish by achieving excellence in those things that make one human — Aristotle says that "the task of man is a certain life, and this an activity and actions of soul with *logos*." One cannot flourish if one lives in a nonhuman way. If this sounds like Rand, it's because her fictional characters understand it, even if her nonfiction essays do not express it unambiguously.

Long concludes,

A truly human life, then, will be a life characterized by reason and intelligent cooperation. (Bees may cooperate after a fashion, but not on the basis of discourse about shared ends.) To a *logikon* animal, reason has value not only as an instrumental means to other goals but as an intrinsic and constitutive part of a fully human life; and the same holds true for cooperation. The *logikon* animal, insofar as it genuinely expresses *logos*, will not deal on cooperative terms with others merely because doing so makes others more likely to contribute instrumentally to the agent's good; rather, the agent will see a life of cooperation with others as an essential part of his own good.

Aristotle's book on friendship in the *Nicomachean Ethics* beautifully elaborates this point.

If this is right, we owe respect to others' humanity, via respect for their rights, because the activity manifesting that respect is a constituent of our own flourishing as *logikon* and *politikon* animals. We owe it to ourselves to owe it to others. This Aristotelian insight points to an interpersonal moral realm in which the basic interests of others meld in important ways with our own. "To the extent that we are *logikon* animals," Long writes, "participation in a human community, together with a shared pursuit of the human good, is a constitutive part of a truly human life."

But does this show that we owe anything *more* than nonaggression? It seems so. We abstain from aggressing against others because, as *logikon* and *politikon* animals, we flourish by engaging the humanity of other individuals. Clearly, abstaining from aggression is not the only way to engage their humanity, just as aggression is not the only way to deny their humanity. Thus these Aristotelian considerations entail the obligation broadly to treat others respectfully.

One last question remains: Is this obligation broadly to treat other persons as ends and not merely as means a *libertarian* matter? It is at least in this way: the obligation broadly to treat other persons as ends and not merely as means is *validated by the same set of facts that validate the nonaggression obligation*. Nonaggression is simply one application of respect. Thus a libertarian society in which people generally thought that nonaggression was *all* they owed others would be a society that should fear for its future viability qua libertarian society.

Finally, I'm sure libertarians do not have to be reminded that nonaggressive affronts against persons may be responded to only in nonaggressive ways. Neither governmental nor private force may be deployed to counter nonviolent offenses. Why not? Because the rule of proportionality dictates that force may be used only to meet force and only in proportion to the aggression. In other words, some obligations are en*force*able, and others are not.

Future of Freedom Foundation, April 18, 2014

Chapter 2.
Is Freedom a Radical Idea?

The answer to the question "Is freedom a radical idea" is: no and yes. Let me explain.

Starting with the "no": Most children grow up learning the libertarian, or nonaggression, ethic. Parents say: "Don't hit, don't take other kids' stuff without asking, and don't break your promises." Nothing radical — in the sense of out of the mainstream — there. It neatly translates into: respect life, liberty, and property, and be good to your word.

Most people carry these principles with them into adulthood. They avoid common-law offenses against persons and property, not because they are afraid of the cops, but because such behavior conflicts with their living the lives they want to live.

Libertarianism can be seen therefore as merely a plea for the consistent application of these rules to and for everyone. It's Spencer's Law of Equal Liberty: "each has freedom to do all that he wills provided that he infringes not the equal freedom of any other."

Now let's move on to the "yes." In the political realm, throughout history freedom has been a radical idea indeed, the exception. There the rules are different. The state — that is, certain special individuals — may "legitimately" do what you and I may not do. If you or I kill when our lives are not in serious danger, it is called murder. When the state does it, it is called war, or counterinsurgency, or capital punishment, or justifiable homicide by the police. If you or I, threatening force, demand money from our neighbors for their protection or to do good works, it is called robbery. When the state does it, it's called taxation. If you or I force someone into service, it's called slavery. If the state does it, it's called conscription or national service. Etc. Etc. Etc.

Why these differences? Many reasons have been offered throughout the millennia. The state was once said to be a deity's earthly agent. (Some still believe this.) It was later said to embody the general will. And it was also said to operate by the consent of the governed. (Who remembers giving consent?)

Regardless of the rationalization, the state, by a process of moral alchemy, or moral laundering, claims to turn bad things into good. By this ideology, rulers have kept the idea of freedom tightly constrained, when it is in effect at all.

Thus throughout history, and with only the rarest of exceptions, freedom has been far removed from the center of political events — even during that ostensibly exceptional period, say, 1776–1901. This is not to say the idea of freedom played no role whatever (the Declaration of Independence was a gleaming embodiment of the idea), but most of the time it did not play the fundamental role that we tend to believe.

Contrary to popular sentiment, for example, freedom was not the driving force along the road to the Constitution, which has been fairly called a counterrevolution. (See my *America's Counter-Revolution: The Constitution Revisited.*) We need only remind ourselves that the Constitution came *after* the Articles of Confederation, which (for all its faults) had deprived the national quasi-government of both the *power to tax* and the *power to regulate trade.* (Can you imagine?) Those omissions, which Madison, Hamilton, and other leading founders regretted so badly, were "corrected" at the Constitutional Convention in Philadelphia in 1787. (The libertarian Albert Jay Nock called it a coup d'état.) The warnings of the prophetic Antifederalists were ignored, and except for Jeffersonian respites now and again, we've lived with the predictable consequences ever since. John Taylor of Caroline and others complained about big government in the early 1800s!

As historian Merrill Jensen put it, the "founding fathers who wrote the Constitution of 1787 were quite a different set of men from those who signed the Declaration of Independence in 1776."

The U.S. government of course sanctioned chattel slavery for Africans until 1865 (with lesser oppressions later); the Indians were brutalized; and the rights of women and others were not recognized. These things and substantial economic intervention by the states kept freedom from its rightful place. And what of the period from 1870 to whenever the Progressive Era started? "War is the health of the state," Randolph Bourne wisely wrote. That would cover civil wars too. Abraham Lincoln came to power filled with enthusiasm for the Whig Henry Clay's American System: internal improvements, protective tariffs, and central banking. Intellectual monopoly (patents and copyrights), business subsidies, and land grants to cronies were cut from the same cloth. Add the Civil war, the income tax (which later expired), the veterans pension program, and you have the makings of one big government. The benefits of a big business-big government relationship were not lost on those with power and influence. (As was said at the time, "The tariff is the mother of trusts." Was the tariff repealed? No. Instead, government power was augmented through antitrust laws.)

Here's how historian Arthur A. Ekirch Jr. summed up the touted golden age of freedom in his not-to-be-missed classic, *The Decline of American Liberalism*:

[I]n the America of the [eighteen] eighties and nineties, doctrines of laissez faire and of the limited state were being twisted and distorted from their original meaning. Businessmen and judges took up the individualism of Jefferson and [Herbert] Spencer and converted it into a rationale for materialist exploitation. Resisting public intervention or government regulation when it confined or restrained special interests, the business community, however, could see no inconsistency in an acceptance of the stream of subsidies and tariffs, of which Henry George and other individualists complained.

It turns out that most business people in that period were like most in any period. If you can gain some shelter from competition through the state, why not? Advantage-seekers exist at all times, and rulers happily oblige them. (Jonathan R.T. Hughes's *The Governmental Habit Redux* is instructive. See also the perceptive August 1984 *Freeman* article by Edmund Opitz, "The Robber Barons and the Real Gilded Age.")

Undeniably, material conditions improved for most Americans throughout this time. A degree of freedom goes a long way, and entrepreneurship found ways around the powers that be. But in a fully competitive economy, living standards would have risen — but without the distortions of state monopoly (as identified by libertarian writer Benjamin Tucker), trade protection, and subsidies (most egregiously and consequentially in transportation, i.e., the subsidized railroads) — *and* with more opportunity to make a living independent of corporate hierarchy. (Yet who would not accept a slower acceleration in living standards as the price for a greater degree of freedom and independence?)

What does this tell us about freedom? It tells us that the good old days still lie ahead.

Foundation for Economic Education, October 29, 2010

Chapter 3.
One Moral Standard for All

Libertarians make a self-defeating mistake in assuming that their fundamental principles differ radically from most other people's principles. Think how much easier it would be to bring others to the libertarian position if we realized that they already agree with us in substantial ways.

What am I talking about? It's quite simple. Libertarians believe that the initiation of force is wrong. So do the overwhelming majority of nonlibertarians. They, too, think it is wrong to commit offenses against person and property. I don't believe they abstain merely because they fear the consequences (retaliation, prosecution, fines, jail, lack of economic growth). They abstain because they sense deep down that it is wrong, unjust, improper. In other words, even if they never articulate it, they believe that other individuals are ends in themselves and not merely means to other people's ends. They believe in the dignity of individuals. As a result, they perceive and respect the moral space around others. (This doesn't mean they are consistent, but when they are not, at least they feel compelled to rationalize.)

That's the starting point of the libertarian philosophy. (I am not a calculating consequentialist, or utilitarian, but neither am I a rule-worshiping deontologist. Rather, I am comfortable with the Greek approach to morality, *eudaimonism*, which, as philosopher Roderick T. Long writes, "means that virtues like prudence and benevolence play a role in determining the content of justice, but also — via a process of mutual adjustment — that justice plays a role in determining the content of virtues like prudence and benevolence." In this view, justice, or respect for rights, like the other virtues, is a *constitutive*, or internal, means [rather than an instrumental means] to the ultimate end of all action: flourishing, or the good life.)

Libertarians differ from others in that they apply the *same* moral standard to all people's conduct. Others have a double-standard, the live-and-let-live standard for "private" individuals and another, conflicting one for government personnel. All we have to do is get people to see this and all will be well.

Okay, I'm oversimplifying a bit. But if I'm close to right, you'll have to admit that the libertarian's job now looks much more manageable. Socrates would walk through the agora in Athens showing people that they unwittingly held contradictory positions on justice, virtue, etc. By asking them probing questions, he nudged them into adjusting their views until they were brought into harmony, with the nobler of their views holding sway. (Does this mean that agoraphobia began as a fear of being accosted by a Greek philosopher in a public place?)

So it remains only for libertarians to engage in a series of thought experiments to win others over to their position. For example, if I would properly be recognized as an armed robber were I to threaten my neighbors into giving me a percentage of their incomes so that I might feed the hungry, house the homeless, and provide pensions for the retired, why aren't government officials similarly recognized? If I can't legally impose mandates on people, why can members of Congress do so? If I can't forbid you to use marijuana or heroin or cocaine, why can DEA agents do it?

Those officials are human beings. You are a human being. I am a human being. So we must have the same basic rights. Therefore, it follows that what you and I may not do *they* may not do. The burden of rebuttal is now on those who reject the libertarian position.

Undoubtedly the nonlibertarian will respond that government officials were duly elected by the people according to the Constitution or hired by those so elected. Thus they may do what is prohibited to you and me. This reply is inadequate. If you and I admittedly have no right to tax and regulate others, how could we delegate a nonexistent right to someone else through an election? Obviously, we can't.

That's the nub of the libertarian philosophy right there. No one has the right to treat people merely as means — no matter how noble his end. *No one*. The implication is that if you want someone's cooperation, you must use persuasion (such as offering to engage in a mutually beneficial exchange), not force. That principle must be applicable to all human beings on pain of contradiction.

This argument should have particular appeal for advocates of equality — for what better embodies their ideal than the libertarian principle, which establishes the most fundamental equality of all persons? I don't mean equality of outcome, equality of income, equality of opportunity, equality under the law, or equality of freedom. I mean something more basic: what Long calls equality of *authority*. You can find it in John Locke's *Second Treatise of Government*, chapter 2, §6:

> Being all equal and independent, no one ought to harm another in his life, health, liberty or possessions. ... And, being furnished with like faculties, sharing all in one community of nature, there cannot be supposed any such subordination among us that may authorise us to destroy one another, as if we were made for one another's uses.

"Unless it be to do justice on an offender," Locke continued, no one may "take away, or impair the life, or what tends to the preservation of the life, the liberty, health, limb, or goods of another."

Long traces out a key implication of this idea: "Lockean equality involves not merely equality before legislators, judges, and police, but, far more crucially, equality *with* legislators, judges, and police."

One moral standard for all, no exceptions, no privileges. That's a fitting summation of the libertarian philosophy. The good news is that most people are more than halfway there.

Future of Freedom Foundation, November 15, 2013

Chapter 4.
Property and Force:
A Reply to Matt Bruenig

My article "One Moral Standard for All" (in this volume) drew a curious response from Matt Bruenig, a contributor to the Demos blog, *Policy Shop*. His article "Libertarians Are Huge Fans of Initiating Force" overlooks the fact that the aim of my article was not to defend the libertarian philosophy, but to show that most people live by it most of the time. The problem is that they apply a different moral standard to government personnel.

Mr. Bruenig's article, which will satisfy only those of his readers who know nothing firsthand about libertarianism, charges libertarians with failing to understand that the concept "*initiation of force*" must be defined in terms of a theory of entitlement. It is that theory which reveals who, in any particular violent interaction, is the aggressor and who is the defender. Thus, he says, an act that a libertarian would call aggression would look different to someone working from a different theory of entitlement. (Strangely, he believes he can validate taxation by this reasoning.)

That Mr. Bruenig thinks this is news to libertarians indicates how much research he did before writing his article. I know of no libertarian who would be surprised by his statement. But Mr. Bruenig goes further and accuses libertarians of circular reasoning in defining entitlement and the initiation of force, or aggression. Is he right? Let's see.

To be fair, I will quote him at length.

> Suppose I walk on to some piece of ground that a libertarian claims ownership over. Suppose I contend that people cannot own pieces of ground because nobody makes them. In my walking on the ground, I do not touch the libertarian or threaten to touch him in any way. Nonetheless, the libertarian proceeds to initiate force against me or calls the police to get them to initiate force against me. Libertarians are fine doing this and therefore libertarians are huge fans of initiating force. The initiation of force or the threat to initiate force is the mechanism that underlies all private property claims.
>
> Now a libertarian will see this and object. They will say that, in fact, violently attacking me for wandering on to some piece of ground is not the *initiation* of force. It is *defensive* force. Aimlessly wandering on to

ground is actually the initiation of force. I am the force initiator because, despite touching and threatening nobody, I set foot on some piece of the world that the libertarian believes belongs to him.

I must stop here. As I understand libertarianism, a property owner has no right to violently attack someone merely for aimlessly wandering on his land. The means of defending oneself and one's property must be morally *proportionate* to the rights violation. *Aggression* and its synonyms are terms of art that apply to a large range of actions, from the trivial to the lethal, and these terms do not imply that violence or deadly force may be used in response to any and all violations. Any uninvited crossing into another person's moral sphere counts as an invasion, no matter how slight or nonviolent. But since the sole permissible objective of defense is to terminate the invasion and obtain compensation for damages (if any occur), one may use only the minimum force required to accomplish those goals. Any greater use constitutes aggression in itself.

As Auburn philosopher Roderick T. Long formulates the *Principle of Proportion*: "If S violates O's boundary, O (or O's agent) has the right to invade S's boundary in whatever way is necessary to end S's violation of O's boundary, so long as O's (or O's agent's) invasion of S's boundary is not disproportionate to the seriousness of S's violation of O's boundary."

Mr. Bruenig shamefully tries to inflame his readers with images of libertarians beating up or shooting — with impunity — free spirits who harmlessly stroll onto private property.

He continues,

> But at this point, it's clear that when the libertarians talk about not initiating force, they are using the word "initiation" in a very idiosyncratic way. They have packed into the word "initiation" their entire theory of who is entitled to what. What they actually mean by "initiation of force" is not some neutral notion of hauling off and physically attacking someone. Instead, the phrase "initiation of force" simply means "acting in a way that is *inconsistent* with the libertarian theory of entitlement, whether using force or not." And then "defensive force" simply means "violently attacking people in a way that is *consistent* with the libertarian theory of entitlement."

> This definitional move is transparently silly and ultimately reveals a blatant and undeniable *circularity in libertarian procedural reasoning*. Libertarians like Richman claim that they think we can determine who is entitled to what by looking towards the principle of non-aggression (i.e., the principle of non-initiation of force). But then they define "non-aggression" by referring to their theory of who is entitled to what.

> So in the case of the libertarian in the hypothetical who attacks me, here is how the libertarian line goes. *The reason the libertarian is entitled to that piece*

of land is because they are being non-aggressive. The reason the libertarian's attack on me is non-aggressive is because he is entitled to that piece of land. So their claims of entitlement are justified by appealing to non-aggression and their claims of non-aggression are justified by appealing to their claims of entitlement. It is truly and seriously as *vacuously circular* as that. [Emphasis added.]

We stand charged with circular reasoning. How do we plead? Not guilty.

First, note that Mr. Bruenig presents no evidence for his charge; he quotes no libertarian at all, let alone me. (I'm not claiming that no libertarian ever argued the way Mr. Bruenig describes, only that such an argument does not inherently underlie the libertarian philosophy.)

Next, what's idiosyncratic about the libertarian idea? It's the way most people think about these issues, which was the point of my article. To use an old example from economist and political philosopher Murray Rothbard, if you see a person seizing a watch from someone, in judging who is the aggressor and who is the victim, it makes a world of difference *who owns the watch.* Likewise if someone peacefully walks onto private property or into a home uninvited. Most people would agree with the libertarian view.

As for the charge of circularity, I (and the libertarians I know) do *not* justify entitlement in terms of the noninitiation of force. We justify entitlement in terms of the conditions under which human beings, in light of their nature and the nature of reality, may flourish in a social setting. Justice and rights theory are aspects of morality. "Morality as I conceive of it has both personal and interpersonal dimensions (which are … inextricably linked): it is concerned with personal flourishing and with what we can reasonably be said to owe others," legal philosopher Gary Chartier writes in *Anarchy and Legal Order: Law and Politics in a Stateless Society.*

To be sure, it is a marker of entitlement that no initiation of force occurred in the acquisition of goods, but that simply means that no one else had previously satisfied the conditions bestowing entitlement and hence the acquisition violated no other person's rights. Fundamentally, one is entitled to a parcel of land as the initial appropriator not because force was not used in its acquisition, but because the land was unowned when one mixed one's labor with (transformed) it and brought it into one's sphere.

Where's the circularity, Mr. Bruenig? There is indeed a close relationship between the concepts *entitlement* and *aggression,* but as Long wrote in private correspondence, "Master and slave are interdefined; so are parent and child. It's not circular because we can define the whole relationship."

Let's go at Mr. Bruenig's argument in another way. In a follow-up post, "The Libertarian Bizarro World," he writes,

> If you are a libertarian who believes justice requires the following of a certain liberty-respecting process, you have to explain how anything can come to be owned in the first place. That initial move is, by any coherent

account, the most violent extinction of personal liberty that there ever can be.

> On a fairly traditional account (e.g., Hobbes' account), liberty and freedom are defined as: being free of bodily restraint. Being able to walk about the world freely and without people stopping you and saying you can't go here or there is a fairly appealing notion of liberty. This is what things are like (analytically speaking) prior to ownership. Prior to anyone owning things, you should presumably be free to move about the world however you see fit. And if someone were to come up to you and physically restrain you from moving about the world, you would rightly understand that as a restriction on your liberty.

> But physically restraining you from moving about the world is exactly what property ownership does. Whereas before ownership you have full liberty to walk about the earth as you'd like, after ownership, you don't. Should you try, someone (the person claiming ownership of, for instance, a piece of land) will physically restrain your body.

It is true that in the libertarian (and in most people's) view, the lives and property of each person represent restraints on the *physical* freedom of everyone else. That's what it means to respect other people, to treat them as ends and not merely as means. But Mr. Bruenig's conception of freedom entails the freedom to disregard the lives and interests of others. Observe this exchange from the comments section of the blog:

> Me: So a valid account of freedom would entail everyone's being able to walk through anyone's home at any time.

> Matt Bruenig: Yes. Now maybe you have some good reasons for why we should violently destroy that freedom. But that's what they are: reasons for violently restricting people's liberty.

Apparently the homeowner's status as an end in himself does not count as a good reason to restrict (not necessarily violently) the intruder's "liberty" to use the homeowner as a means to his own ends.

Of course, libertarians don't define freedom in merely physical terms, as Mr. Bruenig does. Libertarians don't talk about freedom in a vacuum, focusing on one isolated person's ability to move anyway he chooses. Rather, they advocate the freedom of *all* persons in society. If everyone is to be free, freedoms cannot conflict; they must be "compossible." Smith's freedom cannot *morally* include the freedom to enter Jones's house uninvited, or the freedom to thrust his fist against Jones's head. It doesn't much matter if you call these prohibitions limitations on freedom or exclusions from the concept *freedom*. In the end, Mr. Bruenig is making a trivial point.

Even when pressed, Mr. Bruenig stuck to his physical, amoral, and relativist notion of freedom. When he wrote that a purported trespasser is an aggressor only if you think the "victim" owns the property, I commented, "And a rapist is aggressive only if you think the woman owns her body." I received no reply.

Why should persons be free of bodily restraint, able to walk about the world freely? The likely answer is that each owns himself or herself, body and mind, and thus has a right to autonomy. But if that is so, they may not ignore the equal freedom of others — otherwise *all* are not free — and they *should* not do so because a fully human life consists of a social life of reason, not force.

But how do we get from the right to one's body to the right to one's (justly acquired) possessions, including land? A person's possessions are extensions of his life and labor. (Mr. Bruenig says no one made the land, but labor can make it productive.) Flourishing requires the use of physical objects, including shelter and other uses of land, in an environment of respect for and from others. Thus to violate a person's property is to violate that person. (Again, violations can be trivial and the response must be proportionate.) Nothing in libertarian theory, however, rules out nonstate public property or common-law easements. (Nobel laureate Elinor Ostrom's work on nonstate management of common-pool resources is relevant here.)

The details of a property system will surely be determined by custom and could well differ from place to place. But the centrality of property in a proper human community cannot be denied. In *A Treatise on Human Nature* (Book III, Part II, Section VI), philosopher David Hume referred to "the three fundamental laws of nature, *that of the stability of possession, of its transference by consent,* and *of the performance of promises,*" noting that:

> 'Tis on the strict observance of those three laws, that the peace and security of human society entirely depend; nor is there any possibility of establishing a good correspondence among men, where these are neglected. Society is absolutely necessary for the well-being of men; and these are as necessary to the support of society.

Finally, I must point out that defending property rights in theory does not obligate libertarians to defend all particular property holdings in a given society. Land and other forms of wealth are often obtained through government privilege, that is, through theft from their rightful owners or through preemption of homesteading. A sound libertarian theory of property does not regard such property as justly held. As social philosopher/welder Karl Hess wrote in "What Are the Specifics?": "The truth, of course, is that libertarianism wants to advance *principles* of property but that it in no way wishes to *defend*, willy nilly, all property which now is called private."

Future of Freedom Foundation, November 22, 2013

Chapter 5.
The Moral Case for Freedom Is the Practical Case for Freedom

If I say that a government activity — "public" schooling perhaps, or the war on selected drug merchants and users — helps turn inner cities into hellholes and makes people's lives miserable, is that a moral or practical (utilitarian or generally consequentialist) objection?

Some libertarians are inclined to say it's a practical objection, but I've long been uncomfortable with this answer. For one thing, valid or not, utilitarianism is a moral theory, so utilitarian propositions cannot be excluded from the realm of moral propositions.

Leaving that aside, we must inquire whether libertarian concerns are really divisible into a concern with duties (deontology), say, regarding individual rights, and a concern with consequences. This is an unfortunate feature of many libertarians' thinking, but it's not confined to libertarians. In this bifurcated view of the human world, there is a list of moral dos and don'ts that are not directly related to "practical" matters, specifically, the conditions under which human beings can prosper. That strikes me as odd if for no other reason than that the "moral" side appears to outrank the "practical" side: success is nice, but the ethical test has priority. Some libertarians often say they would favor freedom even if it did not promote good things like prosperity because people have a right to freedom that is unrelated to its consequences. (Of course, they don't believe that freedom could have bad consequences. But is that just a happy coincidence? More on this below.)

I'm hardly alone in my uneasiness with this separation of the moral and the practical. In my camp is no less a personage than Adam Smith. Look at this passage from *The Wealth of Nations*:

> The happiness and perfection of a man, considered not only as an individual, but as the member of a family, of a state, and of the great society of mankind, was the object which the ancient moral philosophy proposed to investigate. In that philosophy, the duties of human life were treated of as subservient to the happiness and perfection of human life. But when moral, as well as natural philosophy, came to be taught only as subservient to theology, the duties of human life were treated of as chiefly subservient to the happiness of a life to come. In the ancient philosophy, the perfection of virtue was represented as necessarily productive, to the

person who possessed it, of the most perfect happiness in this life. In the modern philosophy, it was frequently represented as generally, or rather as almost always, inconsistent with any degree of happiness in this life; and heaven was to be earned only by penance and mortification, by the austerities and abasement of a monk, not by the liberal, generous, and spirited conduct of a man. Casuistry, and an ascetic morality, made up, in most cases, the greater part of the moral philosophy of the schools. By far the most important of all the different branches of philosophy became in this manner by far the most corrupted.

In commenting on this passage, libertarians Tibor Machan and David Brown wrote in "The Self-Imposed Poverty of Economics:"

Smith saw that when morality, or ethics, is conceived along lines that would be fully realized in the work of Immanuel Kant — who denied that anything done to advance one's own cause can have moral significance — moral thinking cannot embrace the virtue of prudence, or practical wisdom. (Nor can *any* moral virtue be construed or justified, however broadly, in relation to the acting agent's own well-being and flourishing.) But prudence — recognized as a prominent virtue indeed in the ethics of Socrates and Aristotle — would make plenty of room for an ethical conception of most economic activity. ... With prudence expelled from the moral realm, however, all the economists can do to render commerce and business respectable is to collapse them, along with the rest of life, into expressions of near-bodily functions à la Hobbes.

As we see, division of human life into the moral and practical is of recent vintage. Smith's reference to "ancient philosophy" is a reference to Socrates, Plato, and Aristotle, for whom this chasm would be unfathomable. Moral inquiry for them was essentially an investigation into the art of living as a reasoning, language-using *social* being. The concern of ethics, according to Aristotle, is to learn how such a being must think and act in order to flourish individually and as a member of society; the object of consideration is "the practical life of man as possessing reason." That's why prudence (or practical wisdom) finds a place on his list of virtues. In *Rational Man: A Modern Interpretation of Aristotelian Ethics*, philosopher Henry B. Veatch elaborated on why ethics may be regarded as the art of living, although, to be sure, it is an art unlike any other.

So I, for one, don't accept the division of the case for freedom into "the moral" and "the practical." It's a mistake, not to mention harmful to the cause. But does this mean I am a consequentialist, a utilitarian? Heavens no! The consequentialist case for freedom is too insecure. How would you feel if someone said, "I will respect your rights to life, liberty, and property so long as I calculate that doing so will produce the greatest good"? The classic monkey wrench in the utilitarian machine is the question whether one person

19

may morally be killed so that his harvested organs may save the lives of five others?

Practically speaking, how would a utilitarian go about netting out the good and bad consequences when interpersonal comparisons of subjective utility are by their nature ruled out? Moreover, as legal philosopher Gary Chartier emphasizes in his book *Anarchy and Legal Order*, the components of well-being are disparate and incommensurable — irreducible to an underlying homogeneous element.

One response is along these lines: Yes, *act, or direct, utilitarianism*, in which each action is to be evaluated according to whether it will produce the greatest good/happiness/pleasure, is indeed problematic. Therefore let us substitute for it *rule, or indirect, utilitarianism*, à la libertarian Henry Hazlitt's *The Foundations of Morality*, according to which it is *rules*, not acts, that are to be judged according to their tendency to create the greatest good by maximizing social cooperation.

This seems like a promising approach, but as Auburn philosopher Roderick T. Long points out, there's a problem: "It has often been claimed that indirect utilitarianism is unstable, and must collapse either into direct utilitarianism on the one hand or into 'rules fetishism' on the other." In other words, a hardy rule utilitarian will follow a rule even when it is expected *not* to maximize good consequences — if he did otherwise, he'd be an act utilitarian. But then *following the rule*, not maximizing the good, becomes the overriding objective (regardless of why the rule was adopted initially) — and this is no longer utilitarianism. It is rule-bounded deontology.

Thus utilitarianism is fatally flawed. Rejecting it, however, does not obligate one to embrace deontology. In the Aristotelian (eudaimonist, or virtue-ethics) approach, a concern with consequences is obviously justified — remember, we're interested in "the practical life of man as possessing reason" — but that concern figures in the very formulation of the virtues, just as considerations of virtue, such as justice (including respect for rights), figure in our formulation of what constitutes good consequences. Long writes in "Why Does Justice Have Good Consequences?":

> On this view, human welfare (whether individual or general) and justice are conceptually interrelated, with neither concept being basic but each depending in part on the other (and all the other virtues) for its content, just as Aristotle defines virtue and human flourishing in terms of one another.

Finally, both sides of the artificial moral-practical divide need each other if the strongest case for freedom is to be proffered. Long writes:

> Most people are unlikely to find the deontological case for a given course of action compelling so long as they believe it would have terrible

consequences; likewise, they are equally unlikely to find the consequentialist case compelling so long as they believe that the action violates human dignity, or equality, or liberty.

But Long believes there's more to this than strategic considerations:

In real life, one rarely finds members of either camp relying solely on a single set of considerations. It is a rare moral or political polemic indeed that does not include both consequentialist and deontological arguments. …

Whatever they may say officially, most consequentialists would be deeply disturbed to discover that their favoured policies slighted human dignity, and most deontologists would be deeply disturbed to discover that their favoured policies had disastrous consequences.

This "suggests that most professed deontologists and consequentialists are actually, to their credit, crypto-eudaemonists," Long writes elsewhere.

This is a big subject about which much has been written. Thus lots more could be said. I hope I've said enough for now to justify seeing the moral and practical cases for freedom as one and the same.

Future of Freedom Foundation, December 27, 2013

Chapter 6.
The Consequences of Liberty

Consistent free-market advocates — and not just professional economists — are not only enthusiastic about their preferred system of political economy; they are very enthusiastic about it. At least part of that enthusiasm is fueled by a well-grounded conviction that the general level of prosperity would be unprecedentedly high if people were free to engage in peaceful production and exchange without forcible interference by the state or freelance aggressors.

This enthusiasm is found in two broad categories of radical free-market advocates, or libertarians: those who regard themselves as consequentialists (or utilitarians), that is, those who think moral acts are acts that *maximize* some good like pleasure or happiness or well-being, and those who regard themselves as deontologists, or advocates of doing one's moral duty (say, respecting other people's rights) as good in itself, without reference to consequences.

In chapter 1 of legal philosopher Gary Chartier's *Anarchy and Legal Order*, he explains certain fundamental problems with consequentialism.

> There is no underlying *thing* that well-being *is*. "Well being" or "welfare" or "flourishing" or "fulfillment" should simply be seen as a summary label for all the different aspects of a life that goes well. There is no quantity, no substance, that underlies all dimensions of well-being qua dimensions of well-being. And the absence of such a substratum, a definable common element, means that the various aspects of well-being are *incommensurable* — that there is no way of measuring them in relation to each other. ... Similarly, particular instances of the various aspects of well-being are *non-fungible*: there is no objective basis for trading one off against another.

If this is true, utilitarianism, which implores us to *maximize social well-being*, must be a nonstarter.

I ignore for now a third kind of libertarian, the *eudaimonists*, or virtue ethicists, with whom I identify. Eudaimonist libertarians are also enthusiastic about free markets in part because of the prospect for a high level of general prosperity. (See in this volume "The Moral Case for Freedom Is the Practical Case for Freedom.")

It's no surprise that consequentialists would embrace free markets on grounds that they will produce general prosperity. In their view, they would be touting the (supposed) maximization of a good, which is what interests them. And we can understand a deontologist's joy at the prospect of high general prosperity. Why not rejoice that one's moral duties yield good consequences even if yielding good consequences is not their objective?

But this raises a question: what if we suspended disbelief and supposed that free markets could reasonably be expected to impoverish most people while benefiting only the few? What then?

I would still favor freedom, but I don't mind confessing I'd have decidedly less enthusiasm for it. Why wouldn't I be less than thrilled by the prospect of human suffering? On the other hand, prosperity is not the only important thing in life. The ability to be self-directed counts for a lot in my book. Money, to be sure, can enhance self-directedness by expanding options, but it's better to be poor and free than poor and unfree. Those who would suggest a third alternative — unfree and wealthy — have entirely too much faith in the state.

Some deontologist free-marketeers may insist that their enthusiasm for markets would go on even if most people faced poverty. I have trouble believing that: I would suspect secret disappointment. For one thing, I doubt that this type of libertarian is as pure a deontologist as claimed. Philosopher Roderick Long has something to say on this matter:

> In real life, one rarely finds members of either camp [deontologist and consequentialist] relying solely on a single set of considerations. It is a rare moral or political polemic indeed that does not include both consequentialist and deontological arguments. ...

> Whatever they may say officially, most consequentialists would be deeply disturbed to discover that their favoured policies slighted human dignity, and most deontologists would be deeply disturbed to discover that their favoured policies had disastrous consequences.

Fortunately, this discussion is purely hypothetical. We know that a radically freed market would create a high level of prosperity even for the "poorest." But before getting into the reasons for that, there is a point worth putting on the table. Sometimes the question posed to deontologists is different: what if free markets increased income inequality (not poverty)? The switch from poverty to income inequality is sometimes unnoticed, but it is significant. Increasing "market inequality" (as opposed to what I call "political-economic inequality," which results from government privilege) is consistent with dramatically rising prosperity for all.

It is entirely possible for the poorest in a society to become richer even as the gap between the richest and poorest grows. Imagine an accordion-like elevator that is rising as a whole while being stretched out, putting the floor further from the ceiling.

I don't think a shocking income gap is likely in an increasingly prosperous freed market, but the scenario is not logically absurd. At any rate, I am not concerned about the prospect of growing market inequality the way I would be about mass poverty if I thought a freed market would produce it. My view accords with that of libertarian Benjamin Tucker: "Equality if we can get it, but Liberty at any rate!"

As I say, this discussion is hypothetical. Freedom (or justice) can be counted on to produce good outcomes, in a eudaimonistic way, for everyone. But is this just a lucky break? Or is there a more solid explanation? It's long seemed obvious to me that good should be expected to come from abiding by natural law (including respect for natural rights). This is a fairly general statement, however, and it would be better to have a detailed explanation of why this is the case.

Fortunately, we have one — from Roderick Long in his paper "Why Does Justice Have Good Consequences?" I recommend reading this paper in its entirety. Here I will only hit the highlights. Long first shows "the concurrence of deontological and consequentialist criteria" by arguing that, as Socrates, Plato, Aristotle, and the Stoics taught, the contents of the individual virtues reciprocally determine one another. This is part of what is meant by the "unity of virtue." For example,

> What courage requires of me [in a given instance] cannot be determined independently of what prudence [which is concerned with consequences] requires of me, and vice versa. ... This does not make justice a consequentialist notion, since the direction of determination runs both ways; *what counts as a beneficial consequence will be partly determined by the requirements of justice.* ... Aristotle defines virtue and human flourishing in terms of one another. [Emphasis added.]

Because "justice and benefit are conceptually entangled," it's no mere "happy coincidence" that justice has good consequences.

This is Long's "unity-of-virtue solution" to the puzzle of why justice is beneficial. But he can't leave it at that because his "solution gives us no reason ... to expect any concurrence between the prima facie contents of justice and benefit, before they have been mutually adjusted." After all, if the *pre-adjusted* prima facie contents can be mutually adjusted to each other, *that* cannot be explained via the unity of virtue.

Here I can only summarize Long's answer. He finds that the prima facie content of justice, "considered apart from consequentialist considerations," is represented by libertarianism, that is, the principle that each person is an end in himself and therefore is equal in authority to everyone else. On the other hand, "the prima facie subjectivist content of benefit, considered apart from justice," would entail the long-run satisfaction of people's preferences.

The social theorists of the Austrian school have shown, on praxeological (human-action) grounds, how a libertarian social order constitutes an economic democracy, in which consumer preferences direct the productive resources of society through the imputation of value from consumer goods to producer goods. Hence justice, as it would be conceived prior to adjustment, does a reasonably good job of producing beneficial consequences, as those would be conceived prior to adjustment. Whether one thinks that the alterations to be produced in these two concepts after adjustment would be great or small, the fact remains that there is a rough concurrence prior to adjustment, and this rough concurrence seems to require explanation.

That explanation, Long says, is to be found in the work of the Austrian economists.

> If the Austrians are right, and I think they are, then a solution to our problem may be in sight. The fact that a libertarian social order tends to satisfy consumer preferences is not a contingent empirical fact; the Austrians argue at length … that this concurrence can be established by conceptual analysis.

> But if this is so, then the concurrence requires no explanation. It makes sense to ask why there are four shrimp on my plate instead of five, because the alternative is all too conceivable. But it doesn't make sense to ask why two plus two equals four instead of five, because the alternative is incoherent. Nothing could count as two plus two equaling five, so "Why don't two and two make five?" is no more coherent a question than "Why isn't MOO?" If the praxeological approach is sound, then demanding to know why the laws of social science are as they are is equally incoherent. That whose alternative is inconceivable requires no explanation.

It may be an interesting exercise to imagine how we'd feel about freed markets if the consequences were generally bad, but we need lose no sleep over the question. And now we know why.

Future of Freedom Foundation, January 30, 2015

Chapter 7.
Market, State, and Autonomy

In *The Future of Liberalism* (2009), Alan Wolfe writes that the true heirs to the liberalism of John Locke, Adam Smith, and Thomas Jefferson are not today's classical liberals (libertarians), but rather the other kind of liberals, those who would use government power to assure autonomy and equality for all. Such "modern liberalism," for Wolfe, is simply an updating of the original: in the 18th century, political power crushed autonomy and equality, requiring a free market as the antidote; now private corporate power under "capitalism" does the same, but this time the remedy is active government.

Early in his book Wolfe writes:

> The core substantive principle of liberalism is this: *As many people as possible should have as much say as is feasible over the direction their lives will take.* Expressed in this form, liberalism, as in the days of John Locke, is committed both to liberty and to equality. [Emphasis in original.]

> With respect to liberty, liberals want for the person what Thomas Jefferson wanted for the country: independence. Dependency, for liberals, cripples. … When we have no choice but to accept someone else's power over us, we fail to think for ourselves, are confined to conditions of existence resembling an endless struggle for survival, are unable to plan for the future, and cannot possess elementary human dignity. The autonomous life is therefore the best life. We have the potential, and are therefore responsible for realizing it, to be masters of our own destiny.

This sounds pretty good, no? Being subject to another's arbitrary will clashes with the liberal spirit, which projects the ideal of mastery of one's destiny even as one cooperates with others for mutual benefit.

I also agree with Wolfe that *equality* is a core value of classical liberalism, but not as he means it. True liberal equality is not income equality; nor is it merely equality of liberty or equality under the law. The first would require continuous violent state interference with voluntary exchange, while the other two are inadequate in themselves. By equality, I mean what Roderick Long calls, per Locke, "equality of authority." For Locke a state of equality is one in which "all the power and jurisdiction is reciprocal, no one having more than another, there being nothing more evident than that creatures of the same species and rank ... should also be equal one amongst another, without subordination or subjection."

But now I must part ways with Wolfe because he has an utterly self-defeating idea of how to secure everyone's mastery over their own destiny: the welfare state. Judging by the history and nature of the state, we must conclude that Wolfe's program would lead not to liberation but rather to subjugation of the individual. Wolfe has things turned topsy-turvy:

> To advocate today what Smith advocated yesterday — a free market unregulated by government — is to foster greater, rather than lesser, dependency and less, rather than more, equality. ... [I]n the highly organized and concentrated forms taken by capitalism in the contemporary world, removing government from the marketplace does not allow large numbers of people to become entrepreneurs in ways that enable them to set the terms by which their lives will be led; it instead allows firms to reduce their obligations to their employees and thereby make them more dependent on the vagaries of the market.

The latter part of the quote has some validity, but before I get to that, let's look at the general point. I take Wolfe to be saying that one is less autonomous when subject to impersonal market forces than when subject to political forces ostensibly designed to ensure autonomy and equality. This strikes me as entirely wrong.

Admittedly, in a freed economy no one person or group would control what we call market forces (the law of supply and demand, and so on) to which we all must adjust as we carry out our plans. That would seem to impinge on our autonomy. But these forces are called *impersonal* precisely because they are not the product of any single will or directed at any chosen objective. Rather the term *market forces* simply refers to the spontaneous, orderly, and essential process (the price system) generated by other people's freedom to choose what to buy and sell. In other words, each individual's autonomy is bounded by each other individual's autonomy. While we all must take prices and other people's choices into account as we make our plans, we each have great leeway in the marketplace with which we can minimize our vulnerability to the arbitrary will of others. If one person won't deal with you, someone else most likely will, so the prospect of being victimized by, say, invidious discrimination shrinks. ("Money talks.") Thus the maximum degree of individual autonomy is fully compatible with life in the marketplace, especially as the extent of the market expands. (Of course this is not to suggest that *all* of life is lived in the marketplace.)

The market is not only compatible with autonomy; it's also essential to it. In contrast to the market, Wolfe's alternative, the state, uses force (or the threat thereof) to work its will. If you don't like what one set of politicians decrees, you can't simply select another. And there's no opting out. What we have is an inequality of authority.

Wolfe is naïve about the democratic state. Because they lack both the requisite knowledge and incentives, government officials are not responsive to average people beyond the superficial gestures politicians have to make to obtain and retain power. No one vote counts, and the governmental apparatus is inevitably captured by well-organized interest groups, predominantly associated with big business, that have the time, wealth, and motivation to have the system rigged to their advantage through exploitative, anticompetitive interventions. (Majority rule would be no better, for what would happen to minorities.) Any "welfare" for low-income people is more in the nature of hush money to prevent civil strife. Wolfe's belief that the state can be the protector of the autonomy and equality of regular people is puzzling because government action — rooted in coercion — *by its very nature* undermines autonomy and fosters dependency.

Wolfe is right to be concerned about "the highly organized and concentrated forms taken by capitalism in the contemporary world." That system does indeed undermine autonomy and equality. Where he goes wrong is in equating the "capitalist" economy with the free market. Thus he is guilty of what Kevin Carson calls "vulgar liberalism" and Roderick Long calls "left-conflationism": attributing the evils of corporatism to its antithesis, the freed market. (It's the mirror image of the view, "vulgar libertarianism," that defends business conduct in the corporate state on the grounds that the free market wouldn't permit such conduct if it did not efficiently serve consumers.)

Contrary to Wolfe, fully "removing government from the marketplace" — that is, abolishing privileges as well as regulations — would not foster dependency. Rather, it would eliminate the myriad government-maintained barriers to competition from worker-managed firms, partnerships, and self-employment. Those barriers *increase* people's dependency on the arbitrary will of others. Freeing the market would end the monetary manipulation and bailout authority that encourage banks and other firms to take undue risks that subject workers to business cycles and prolonged unemployment. In sum, a freed market would mean the end to all the privileges that produce the evils to which Wolfe rightly objects but misattributes to market forces.

"Man in any complex society," F.A. Hayek wrote in "Individualism: True and False,"

> can have no choice but between adjusting himself to what to him must seem the blind forces of the social process and obeying the orders of a superior. So long as he knows only the hard discipline of the market, he may well think the direction by some other intelligent human brain preferable; but, when he tries it, he soon discovers that the former still leaves him at least some choice, while the latter leaves him none, and that

it is better to have a choice between unpleasant alternatives than being coerced into one.

If the alternative we face is between grappling with market forces and trusting a ruling elite to orchestrate just social outcomes, anyone concerned with autonomy and equality should choose the market. A benevolent, peaceful state is not on the menu.

Foundation for Economic Education, August 10, 2012

Chapter 8.
Social Cooperation

A giant in the modern literature of freedom and free markets is Ludwig von Mises's magnum opus as *Human Action*, first published in 1949. That was not the title he first had in mind. Mises's original title was *Social Cooperation*.

That title is significant, and it prompts a question: would the libertarian, or modern classical-liberal, movement have been perceived differently by the world if Mises, a leading light among liberal scholars, had used the original title? Phrased so narrowly, the answer to that question is probably no. So let's broaden it: would the movement have been perceived differently if its dominant theme were social cooperation rather than (rugged) individualism, self-reliance, independence, and other synonyms of which libertarians are so fond?

Maybe.

There's no mystery why that other title occurred to Mises. I haven't tried to make a count, but I would guess that "social cooperation" is the second most-used phrase in the book. The first is probably "division of labor," which is another way of saying "social cooperation." (A friend who counted the phrases confirms my guess.) *Human Action* is about the benefits of social cooperation or it isn't about anything at all. The first matter Mises takes up after his opening disquisition on the nature of action itself is ... cooperation. He begins, "Society is concerted action, cooperation. ... It substitutes collaboration for the — at least conceivable — isolated life of individuals. Society is division of labor and combination of labor. In his capacity as an acting animal man becomes a social animal."

It is through cooperation and the division of labor that we all can live better lives. Naturally, Mises laid great stress on the need for peace, since the absence of peace is the breakdown of that vital cooperation. This put Mises squarely in the pacifist classical-liberal tradition as exemplified by Richard Cobden, John Bright, Frédéric Bastiat, Herbert Spencer, and William Graham Sumner. Mises wrote in an earlier book, *Liberalism* (1927):

> The liberal critique of the argument in favor of war is fundamentally different from that of the humanitarians. It starts from the premise that not war, but peace, is the father of all things. ... War only destroys; it cannot create. ... The liberal abhors war, not, like the humanitarian, in

spite of the fact that it has beneficial consequences, but because it has only harmful ones.

Given Mises's orientation, it is unsurprising to see him attach so much importance to what he calls the Ricardian Law of Association. This is known as the law of comparative advantage (or cost), which states that two parties can gain from trade even if one is absolutely more efficient at making every product they both want.

The key is opportunity cost. A $500-an-hour lawyer who is also the fastest, most accurate typist in the world will most likely find it advantageous to hire a $20-an-hour typist. Why? Because every hour the lawyer spends typing instead of practicing law would implicitly cost $500 minus $20. The typist faces no such opportunity cost. So lawyer and typist both benefit by cooperating. This is true of groups (such as countries) too. Guiding by prices, people will tend to discover the benefits of specializing in what, comparatively, they make most efficiently (or least inefficiently) and trading with others. As a result more total goods will be produced — to the benefit of all.

This law is an important part of the argument for free international trade as well as domestic trade because it answers the objection that a national group which can't make anything as efficiently (absolutely) as others will be left out of the world economy.

Mises understood that the law of comparative advantage was merely an application of the broader *law of association*. As he wrote in *Human Action*:

> The law of association makes us comprehend the tendencies which resulted in the progressive intensification of human cooperation. We conceive what incentive induced people not to consider themselves simply as rivals in a struggle for the appropriation of the limited supply of means of subsistence made available by nature. We realize what has impelled them and permanently impels them to consort with one another for the sake of cooperation. Every step forward on the way to a more developed mode of the division of labor serves the interests of all participants. ... The factor that brought about primitive society and daily works toward its progressive intensification is human action that is animated by the insight into the higher productivity of labor achieved under the division of labor.

This seemingly simple idea leads to counterintuitive conclusions. As a result of expanding cooperation, human beings, unlike lower animals, compete to *produce*, not to *consume*. Mises expressed this with my favorite sentence in *Human Action*: "The fact that my fellow man wants to acquire shoes as I do, does not make it harder for me to get shoes, but easier." The expansion of cooperation also means dealing with strangers at great distance — a further incentive for world peace and harmony.

Unfortunately the emphasis on cooperation is not what many people are likely to "know" about free-market economics and the normative freedom philosophy. They are more apt to associate these with "rugged individualism" than "social cooperation." I have no doubt that a major reason for this is that critics of the market order *want* the public to have a distorted sense of the genuinely liberal worldview. When President Bill Clinton declared (disingenuously) in his 1996 state of the union address that "the era of big government is over," he followed up by saying: "We can't go back to the era of fending for yourself." But human beings have always been social/political animals. There was no era when men and women fended for themselves. The choice isn't between cooperation and a Hobbesian war of all against all, but between free and forced association.

Of course, free-market advocates typically emphasize the importance of the division of labor. Nevertheless they are partly responsible for the public misperception. Their rhetoric too often implies atomism, however inadvertently. (The appropriate individualism is what I've dubbed molecular individualism, or "*Adamistic*" individualism, in reference to Adam Smith, whose *Wealth of Nations* is a paean to social cooperation.) I understand the value of the terms "individualism," "self-reliance," and "independence," but we should realize that they can easily lead to undesirable caricatures. Let's not encourage anyone to think that the libertarian ideal is Ted Kaczynski minus the mail bombs.

We all grapple with an uncertain future. Social cooperation unquestionably makes that task easier than if we attempted to fend for ourselves alone. That's why individuals before the advent of the welfare state created mutual-aid (fraternal) organizations. Besides camaraderie, these groups provided what the welfare state feebly and coercively supposes to provide today: islands of relative security in a sea of uncertainty.

If people support the welfare state, we shouldn't be puzzled. It's because they cannot see a better voluntarist alternative. That's where libertarians come in.

We libertarians might have an easier time persuading others if we emphasized that freedom produces ever-more innovative ways to cooperate for mutual benefit and that when government dominates life, social cooperation is imperiled.

Foundation for Economic Education, October 26, 2011

Chapter 9.
Social Cooperation, Part 2

Mises was no maverick in his conception of social cooperation. Interest in social cooperation pervades the best classical-liberal and libertarian thought. Paradoxical as it sounds, it is at the heart of the philosophy of individualism. If opponents of the freedom philosophy base their criticism on an atomistic — instead of an Adamistic — model of the individual, it's largely because too many libertarians overlook their heritage and emphasize that side of the coin to the neglect of the social side.

Leading thinkers in the liberal tradition have sought a synthesis of individualism and "socialism." In *Social Statics* (1850), Herbert Spencer discussed the "tendency to individuation," which is most pronounced in the human race:

> [The person] is self-conscious; that is, he recognizes his own individuality. … [W]hat we call the moral law — the law of equal freedom — is the law under which individuation becomes perfect, and that ability to act up to this law is the final endowment of humanity. … The increasing assertion of personal rights is an increasing demand that the external conditions needful to a complete unfolding of the individuality shall be respected. Not only is there now a consciousness of individuality and an intelligence whereby individuality may be preserved, but there is a perception that the sphere of action requisite for due development of the individuality may be claimed, and a correlative desire to claim it. And when the change at present going on is complete — when each possesses an active instinct of freedom, together with an active sympathy — then will all the still existing limitations to individuality, be they governmental restraints or be they the aggressions of men on one another, cease. Then none will be hindered from duly unfolding their natures.

But, crucially, in the next section Spencer wrote:

> Yet must this higher individuation be joined with the greatest mutual dependence. Paradoxical though the assertion looks, the progress is at once toward complete separateness and complete union. But the separateness is of a kind consistent with the most complex combinations for fulfilling social wants; and the union is of a kind that does not hinder entire development of each personality. Civilization is evolving a state of

things and a kind of character in which two apparently conflicting requirements are reconciled.

Thus Spencer foresaw "at once perfect individuation and perfect mutual dependence." He continued:

> Just that kind of individuality will be acquired which finds in the most highly organized community the fittest sphere for its manifestation, which finds in each social arrangement a condition answering to some faculty in itself, which could not, in fact, expand at all if otherwise circumstanced. The ultimate man will be one whose private requirements coincide with public ones. He will be that manner of man who, in spontaneously fulfilling his own nature, incidentally performs the functions of a social unit, and yet is only enabled so to fulfill his own nature by all others doing the like.

For Spencer, to violate the law of equal freedom — "that vital law of the social organism" — is to assault society itself. It sounds as though Spencer is saying that we need society not only for economic exchange and security but something more: our very nature requires it.

Despite some differences this reminds me of Aristotle. (Fred D. Miller, Jr., finds classical-liberal themes in Aristotle.) In *Politics* Aristotle stated that a polis is not merely a collection of individuals seeking gains from trade and safety. It "is a community of families and aggregations of families in well-being, for the sake of a perfect and self-sufficing life. ... The end of the [community] is the good life."

Aristotle famously identified the human being as a social/political animal, a concept inseparable from the capacity to reason, use language, and engage in discourse. In Aristotle's view a human being can live like a human being only in society. We need other people to be fully human because we can't know what we need to know or do what we need to do except through interaction in a community. "For each individual among the many has a share of virtue and prudence," Aristotle wrote.

Likewise in the *Nicomachean Ethics* he wrote,

> For the final and perfect good seems to be self-sufficient. However, we define something as self-sufficient not by reference to the "self" alone. We do not mean a man who lives his life in isolation, but a man who also lives with parents, children, a wife, and friends and fellow citizens generally, since man is by nature a social and political animal.

Auburn University philosopher Roderick T. Long (to whom I am indebted for his discussion of Aristotle in *Reason and Value: Aristotle versus Ayn Rand*) emphasizes Aristotle's view that we can't know very much without help from society. Discussing Aristotle's theory of knowledge and belief, Long notes that for the Greek philosopher *endoxa*, or "reputable beliefs," are critical to the individual. No one builds up her knowledge from scratch on a bedrock foundation. We are born into a particular context and are taught many things, some true and some false. It would be impossible to start over, and fortunately there is no need to. We can begin with the beliefs we have and move forward making adjustments as we find inconsistencies and learn new information. This is necessarily a social process. Long writes: "But Aristotle thinks I will have good reasons for including the endoxa of others — the collective wisdom of mankind, as it were — among my endoxa or phainomena. The pursuit of knowledge is a cooperative endeavor, and will be more successful if everyone is allowed to make a contribution."

Aristotle says, "For each man has something personal to contribute toward the truth… ." For him, society is not just a bridge to the good life, it is constitutive of the good life.

I could also invoke Ludwig Wittgenstein (no classical liberal), who drew attention to the intrinsically public nature of language (and hence thought) itself. Wittgenstein, like F.A. Hayek, underscored the communality of rules. "The word 'agreement' and the word 'rule,'" Wittgenstein wrote, "are related to one another, they are cousins [as were Wittgenstein and Hayek]. If I teach anyone the use of the one word, he learns the use of the other with it."

Only individuals value, choose, and act, of course, but in an important sense the resulting social whole is greater than the sum of its individual parts. Thus the defense of personal liberty is the defense of society. Let's hear liberalism's opponents criticize that.

Foundation for Economic Education, November 30, 2011

Chapter 10.
Government Undermines
Social Cooperation

I should know better than to take seriously the insipid words of presidential speechwriters, especially those who composed an inaugural address. Still, I can't let some of the words Barack Obama read at his 2013 inauguration pass without comment.

For example, Obama said this:

> Preserving our individual freedoms ultimately requires collective action. For the American people can no more meet the demands of today's world by acting alone than American soldiers could have met the forces of fascism or communism with muskets and militias. No single person can train all the math and science teachers we'll need to equip our children for the future, or build the roads and networks and research labs that will bring new jobs and businesses to our shores. Now, more than ever, we must do these things together, as one nation, and one people.

Here is the standard false alternative beloved by politicians seeking to justify their own violence-based power. The fallacy is clear when stated this way: since individuals acting in isolation aren't capable of doing many things they want done, the government should take charge and see that they are done.

What's left out? The "collective action" of voluntary civil society, which includes the market as well as all peaceful noncommercial activities (such as mutual-aid associations). To listen to Obama, you'd never know there was community life apart from the state, which, let us never forget, is founded on the power to inflict force on nonaggressors. (The power to tax — the appropriation of private property under threat of violence — is the fundamental power without which no government power can exist.)

Politicians say such things hoping the average person is too dulled by the government's schools and the slavish news media to notice the missing piece. The liberal (libertarian) vision of the free society never posited the isolated individual as the source of progress. Not wanting the government to manage human affairs does not imply the absence of social cooperation. Quite the contrary! Social cooperation lies at the very heart of the classical-liberal vision. It's found in every liberal thinker from Adam Smith — who underscored the division of labor and the "propensity to truck, barter, and exchange" — to today's libertarian thinkers.

Indeed, Ludwig Mises's chapter eight of *Human Action*, "Human Cooperation," begins,

> Society is concerted action, cooperation. … The total complex of mutual relations created by such concerted actions is called society. It substitutes collaboration for the — at least conceivable — isolated life of individuals. Society is division of labor and combination of labor. In his capacity as an acting animal man becomes a social animal.

Mises of course was a hard-core advocate of laissez faire. Government would have barely been noticeable in his ideal society. The thought of raising living standards through individual isolation would have struck him as absurd. Human beings progress through cooperation and only through cooperation. He explicitly broadened David Ricardo's law of comparative advantage and dubbed it the "law of association." The principle explains not only why free trade benefits all participating countries, but also why individuals do better by working together than by acting alone:

> The law of association makes us comprehend the tendencies which resulted in the progressive intensification of human cooperation. We conceive what incentive induced people not to consider themselves simply as rivals in a struggle for the appropriation of the limited supply of means of subsistence made available by nature. We realize what has impelled them and permanently impels them to consort with one another for the sake of cooperation. Every step forward on the way to a more developed mode of the division of labor serves the interests of all participants. In order to comprehend why man did not remain solitary, searching like the animals for food and shelter for himself only and at most also for his consort and his helpless infants, we do not need to have recourse to a miraculous interference of the Deity or to the empty hypostasis of an innate urge toward association. Neither are we forced to assume that the isolated individuals or primitive hordes one day pledged themselves by a contract to establish social bonds. The factor that brought about primitive society and daily works toward its progressive intensification is human action that is animated by the insight into the higher productivity of labor achieved under the division of labor.

One of the stalwarts of the liberal tradition, the 19th-century French economist Frédéric Bastiat, made quite a big deal of this point in the opening chapter of his economics treatise, *Economic Harmonies* (1850). Noting the average person's access to a vast array of goods in mid-19th-century France, Bastiat observed:

> It is impossible not to be struck by the disproportion, truly incommensurable, that exists between the satisfactions this man derives

from society and the satisfactions that he could provide for himself *if he were reduced to his own resources.* I make bold to say that in one day he consumes more things *than he could produce himself* in ten centuries. [Emphasis added.]

What makes the phenomenon stranger still is that the same thing holds true for all other men. Every one of the members of society has consumed a million times more than he could have produced; yet no one has robbed anyone else.

Like all advocates of individual liberty, Bastiat understood that the choice is *not* between isolated action and government social engineering.

So when Obama said "the American people [cannot] meet the demands of today's world by acting alone," he attacked a straw man. Who proposes such a thing? Note the ambiguity in the sentence. By "acting alone," does he mean individuals acting in isolation with no division of labor? Or does he mean people acting cooperatively, by consent, and without government involvement? If the second, then he is simply wrong. People acting cooperatively through the market can indeed "meet the demands of today's world." The clumsy bureaucracy and the "private sector" cronies it serves need only leave us alone.

But Obama apparently meant individuals literally acting alone because he immediately added, "No single person can train all the math and science teachers we'll need to equip our children for the future, or build the roads and networks and research labs that will bring new jobs and businesses to our shores."

Who wrote that nonsense? Who among Obama's critics thinks that a "single person" could do any of those things? Does Obama (or his speechwriters) even know what opponents of government social engineering stand for? They must think they can distract people from the libertarian alternative with a false picture of the choice we face. Get people to think the choice is between government social engineering and literal individual self-sufficiency, and the libertarian ideal of voluntary social cooperation through the freed market will present no threat to the privilege-laden status quo.

Here is the irony: government intervention undermines social cooperation in myriad ways. To name just one, privileges for favored producers drive a wedge between entrepreneurs and consumers by distorting relative prices and eroding the market's ability to coordinate supply and demand over time. In general, government "welfare" activity crowds out private solutions that are far more amenable to freedom and cooperation.

Politicians pose as the great advocates of "collective action," but in fact their schemes increasingly replace mutually beneficial social cooperation with top-down special-interest-driven decrees.

Future of Freedom Foundation, January 25, 2013

Chapter 11.
Immigration and Social Engineering

Immigration brings out the social engineers and central planners across the political establishment. We see this clearly in the debate over Donald Trump's support for legislation that would cut legal immigration in half while tilting it toward well-educated English-speakers and against low-skilled non-English-speakers.

Even establishment opponents of Trump's position believe "we" must update the immigration system to better serve "the economy." But they disagree on particulars. Trumpsters think the economy needs only scientists and inventors (preferably future Nobel Prize winners, I suppose), while Republican and Democratic anti-Trumpsters counter that the economy also needs *some* unskilled workers to pick crops in the hot sun and do menial work in luxury resorts, which Americans apparently don't want to do.

But what is this thing they call "the economy," which has needs? Social engineers of all parties and persuasions talk as though an economy is some kind of mechanism to be centrally fine-tuned and overhauled occasionally according to a plan. Even those who style themselves free enterprisers display the central-planning mentality when it comes to immigration.

Contrary to this establishment view, the economy is not a mechanism. It is, rather, hundreds of millions of American producers and consumers, who also happen to be embedded in a global marketplace. Why can't they be trusted, without the direction of politicians, to decide for themselves what they need and to engage in social cooperation — that is, among other things, to trade goods and services — to obtain it?

It is we whom the social engineers wish to manipulate. In the process they would cruelly keep poor people in perpetual misery and political oppression by locking them out of America. Why? Because the economy doesn't need them.

Like all central planners, the immigration planners exhibit what F.A. Hayek called "the pretense of knowledge." Do these presumptuous frauds know what specific skills will be demanded in the future? To know that, they would have to know what products will be demanded in the future. But we don't know what we'll want because lots of things have not been invented yet. And we can't predict who will invent them. People who today have few skills and who speak no English will be among those who make our lives better. Let them come here to make better lives for themselves. That's their right, which is justification enough. But we will benefit too.

Notice, also, that advocates of immigration control — progressive and conservative — often say the economy doesn't have enough jobs for the people already here. So how can we let more in? This assumes the "size" of the economy is fixed and that more people would result in smaller shares for everyone. But if we stop thinking of the economy as a mechanism and start thinking of it as an unending series of exchanges between people seeking their betterment, we can see through this fallacy. Newcomers are both producers and consumers. Therefore their entry into our society presents new opportunities on both the supply and demand sides. In a freed economy this would portend higher living standards for everyone.

Resources are not fixed, as evidenced by the fact that seven billion people are far wealthier today than much smaller world populations were in previous ages.

In fact, resources — that is, useful materials — are not even natural. As the great economist Julian Simon taught us, what we call *natural resources* are merely useless things and even detriments until someone exercising intelligence — "the ultimate resource" — discovers how we may use them to make our lives better. Not so long ago, you would have paid dearly to remove crude oil from your land. Then a chemist distilled kerosene from it. Kerosene was better and cheaper than whale oil for lighting lamps; and so, suddenly, finding oil — "black gold, Texas tea" — on your land turned you into Jed Clampett.

We indeed live in a world of scarcity, but that doesn't mean total wealth does not grow, making everyone richer. Because of human intelligence, we get more and more output from less and less input. A growing population makes us not poorer but richer — if we are free. My favorite line in economist Ludwig von Mises's *Human Action* is: "The fact that my fellow man wants to acquire shoes as I do, does not make it harder for me to get shoes, but easier." What did he mean? "Because many people or even all people want bread, clothes, shoes, and cars, large-scale production of these goods becomes feasible and reduces the costs of production to such an extent that they are accessible at low prices."

Let's also dispense with the nonsense that current immigrants are a subversive element in society because they have their own cultures and speak their own languages. That nonsense was spoken about every immigrant group throughout American history. We will thrive when people are free to live in any peaceful way they choose. The nationalists are simply wrong. Attempts to plan society must come to grief.

If we Americans value freedom, we will dismiss the social engineers, open the borders, and liberate ourselves.

Libertarian Institute, August 4, 2017

Chapter 12.
In Defense of Extreme Cosmopolitanism

Cosmopolitanism is under assault from across the political spectrum, both in the United States and abroad. Just yesterday President Donald Trump's chief strategist, alt-right leader and self-described economic nationalist Steve Bannon, told the Conservative Political Action Conference that "the center core of what we believe [is] that we're a nation with an economy, not an economy in some global marketplace with open borders, but we're a nation with a culture and a reason for being," This is a false alternative of course, but Bannon's preference for nationalist tribalism is revealing.

The rejection of cosmopolitanism is bad for liberty, peace, and prosperity because they all go hand in hand. The link between liberty and cosmopolitanism is more than conceptual. Of course freedom includes the freedom of individuals to associate peacefully with anyone anywhere of their choosing, which in turn generates peaceful interdependence and prosperity. But the link is also existential: rising generations, no matter what they have been taught by their elders, naturally will be curious about other people and their ways of living, their cultures. They naturally will question what has been presented to them as sacred (even if "secular") tradition. This will inevitably lead to cultural and material exchanges and hence further social evolution. The "ideal" of a culture insulated from change is a chimera, especially these days; it would be unachievable even if it were desirable — which it most assuredly is not. Even totalitarian states struggle in vain to shut out "subversive" foreign influences, as the old Soviet Union demonstrated.

We may not go so far as Aristophanes and say that "Whirl is king," but unforeseen change is inevitable and also reasonably assimilable in normal circumstances. In a freed society most change occurs at the margin — the world does not start afresh each day — because no central authority has the power to make society-wide decisions. But with freedom, the cumulative effect of change is dramatic and largely benign.

Original cosmopolitan liberalism, what we call libertarianism today, embodies this fact of life. It embraces it with gusto. Liberty and the prosperity it produces enable us to grapple with — and indeed relish — the uncertain future that, being the product of human action but not human design, *spontaneously* unfolds before us. Serendipity happens. We can therefore view liberalism as occupying the ground between conservatism/traditionalism and rationalism/Jacobinism.

As Nobel laureate F.A. Hayek wrote in "Why I Am Not a Conservative": "As has often been acknowledged by conservative writers, one of the fundamental traits of the conservative attitude is a fear of change, a timid distrust of the new as such, while the liberal position is based on courage and confidence, on a preparedness to let change run its course even if we cannot predict where it will lead."

Hayek's openness to change may seem in conflict with the apparent conservatism of *The Constitution of Liberty* (1960) and his final book, *The Fatal Conceit* (1988). (The fatal conceit lies in believing that our principles of moral conduct were originally the product of reason rather than of spontaneous social evolution as people grappled with reality in search of better lives.) But no actual conflict in Hayek exists. ("Why I Am Not a Conservative" is the postscript to *The Constitution of Liberty.*) In the absence of good cause to depart from traditional practices, one tends to accept those practices because, among other reasons, their longevity may be an evidence of their value. (Longevity is no guarantee of this.) The case for such "conservative" deference dates back at least to Aristotle. (See philosopher Roderick T. Long's discussion of the importance of *endoxa*, "the credible opinions handed down" [*Stanford Encyclopedia of Philosophy*], in his *Reason and Value: Aristotle versus Rand*. Long's essay suggests that cultural innovation reasonably begins with defeasible received wisdom as opposed to wholesale rejection of it.) But the good sense in defaulting to credible opinions provides no case for freezing traditions in place, for this would imply an unjustifiable hubris regarding the current state of our knowledge. After all, today's traditions were once new: how do we know there aren't hitherto undiscovered better ways to accomplish our ultimate objective, namely, the flourishing of individuals in society? Why would we want to deprive ourselves of the opportunity to learn of such knowledge? And on what grounds do we assume that anything worth knowing is to be found within our national borders? Hence liberal cosmopolitanism, from the Greek suggesting "citizen of the world." (I'm reminded of Adam Smith's observation that "the division of labor is limited by the extent of the market.")

Apparent efforts to romanticize tradition and cultural preservation (aka stagnation) have a way of teaching a different lesson. Think of the beloved musical *Fiddler on the Roof*, based on the Yiddish stories by Sholem Aleichem. The protagonist, Tevye the dairyman, opens the show by celebrating the tradition that has enabled him and his neighbors (and their forebears) to keep "our balance for many years." As he explains, "Because of our tradition, everyone here knows who he is and what God expects him to do." (At the same time he confesses: "You may ask, 'How did this tradition get started?' I'll tell you. I don't know. But it's a tradition.") At sundown on the Sabbath, Tevye and his wife pray that God will keep their five daughters "from the strangers' ways."

Yet almost immediately the traditional structure that Tevye believes he can't survive without begins to crumble at the margin, and he is powerless to prevent it. When he agrees to marry off his eldest daughter, Tzeitel, to the much older butcher, as arranged by the village matchmaker, she begs her father not to force her to go through with the marriage. A year earlier she and her childhood friend, now the village tailor, had secretly agreed to wed as soon as he could afford a sewing machine. (Aside: when the tailor Motel Kamzoil gets his sewing machine he boasts that from now on clothes will be made quickly and perfectly — no more handmade things. There's an economic lesson in that for another day.) Now under pressure from the matchmaker, Tzeitel asks her father for permission to marry the man she loves. Tevye at first is furious at her impertinence, but when he looks in his daughter's eyes as she stands by her beloved, he can't help but relent. His daughter's happiness outranks tradition. (Before this scene we saw Tevye celebrating the marriage agreement with the butcher by participating in a Russian dance with Russian gentiles in the local tavern, indulging, it would seem, in the strangers' ways.)

Tzeitel's break with tradition is only the beginning. Tevye's second daughter, Hodel, then falls in love with Perchik, a poor young radical teacher from Kiev, the big, strange, distant city. This was the same young visitor whom villagers had denounced as a "radical" for saying that girls should be educated and for dancing with a female (Hodel) at Tzeitel's wedding. The "attack" on tradition kicks up a notch when Hodel and Perchik decide to marry: they do not ask Tevye for his permission — only for his blessing. He is scandalized at this further blow to the structure, but in one of his trademark dialogues with God, Tevye acknowledges that "our ways also once were new" — a subversive thought for one who wishes to keep his children from the strangers' ways. Again he relents and gives his blessing (and his permission), explaining to his wife, "It's a new world, Golde," one in which people marry for love. He then alarms his wife, whom he had met only on their wedding day, by asking, "Golde, do you love me?" Tevye is clearly warming up to the new world.

But Tevye finally draws the line when his third daughter, Chava, marries a young Russian she has fallen in love with. As he is packing to move his family out of their *shetl*, Anatevka (from which the tsar has expelled the Jews), he relays his blessing to Chava and her new husband. It is noteworthy that Tevye, like Sholem Aleichem himself, moves to "New York, America" not Palestine. (Tevye's brother had previously moved to Chicago.)

So even insular little Anatevka could not shield itself from change and the outside world. Was Sholem Aleichem a subversive? If so, many people seem to have missed it. But how can you celebrate traditionalism while showing the virtually inevitable erosion of particular traditions at the hands of the young and free seeking only to be happy? There's a lesson here for all of us, especially those who seek to "make America great *again*."

Whirl is king, despite one's wishes and efforts. Of course this does not mean that all change is good, but attempting to prevent all change in order to prevent *bad* change is futile and self-defeating. Moreover, change that one person sees as bad another person may see as good. People should be free to shield themselves against change they do not like, but coercive power must be kept out of the picture.

The history of original liberalism overflows with acknowledgments that openness to change, which is the essence of cosmopolitanism, is vital to flourishing. The free and competitive marketplace of ideas, like the market for goods and services, was championed by early liberals precisely because it was the way to dispel ignorance not just in how we think but in how we live. Thus they showed an appropriate humility — a recognition of the limits of knowledge — in their praise for the free marketplace of ideas.

John Stuart Mill's *On Liberty* (1859) is well-known in this regard, so I'll limit myself to one quotation:

> That mankind are not infallible; that their truths, for the most part, are only half-truths; that unity of opinion, unless resulting from the fullest and freest comparison of opposite opinions, is not desirable, and diversity not an evil, but a good, until mankind are much more capable than at present of recognising all sides of the truth, are principles applicable to men's modes of action, not less than to their opinions. As it is useful that while mankind are imperfect there should be different opinions, so is it that there should be different experiments of living; that free scope should be given to varieties of character, short of injury to others; and that the worth of different modes of life should be proved practically, when any one thinks fit to try them. It is desirable, in short, that in things which do not primarily concern others, individuality should assert itself. Where, not the person's own character, but the traditions or customs of other people are the rule of conduct, there is wanting one of the principal ingredients of human happiness, and quite the chief ingredient of individual and social progress. [Emphasis added.]

To take an earlier example from across the Channel, Charles Dunoyer, a pioneering French radical liberal and one of the originators of class analysis (which Marx explicitly borrowed and distorted), criticized the socialism of Henri de Saint-Simon precisely because it failed to recognize the value of the competitive marketplace of ideas. Dunoyer wrote in 1827 that the Saint-Simonians' "complaints against what they call the *critical system*, that is to say, against a general and permanent state of examination, of debate, of competition, attacks society in its most active principle of life, in its most efficacious means of development." They don't want to "leav[e] society to itself," letting it develop "by the free competition of individual efforts." Yet they contradict themselves by conceding that "free discussion is necessary" sometimes. But if that's true, Dunoyer asked, what can be the case against freedom?

Dunoyer continued: "Is there, in the course of centuries, a single instant where society does not tend, in a multitude of ways, to modify its ideas, to change its manner of existence? To accuse liberty of what remains of confusion in moral and social doctrines is to see evil in the remedy, and to complain precisely of what tends to make the confusion cease."

Thus he concluded that

> the error of the organic school [Saint-Simonians] is the belief that liberty is only a provisional utility. ... It is ... in the nature of things that liberty of examination will be perpetually necessary. Society which lives chiefly by action, acts, at each instant, according to the notions that it possesses, but, to act better and better, it needs to work constantly to perfect its knowledge, and it is only able to succeed by means of liberty: research, inquiry, examination, discussion, controversy, such is its natural state, and such it will always be, even when its knowledge has acquired the greatest certainty and understanding.

In pursuit of this life-enhancing knowledge, the political program based on liberal cosmopolitanism — libertarianism — centers on unconditional free trade and freedom of movement, that is, open borders for people, capital, producer goods, and consumer goods. This program represents not merely an adherence to an abstraction, *liberty*. Rather it embodies the understanding that the flourishing of flesh-and-blood individual human beings, like the division of labor, is limited by the extent of society and that therefore the boundaries of society should be expanded through peaceful voluntary exchange and movement to include the entire world. The current popular nationalist, tribalist program is thus exposed as a threat to human flourishing.

Libertarian Institute, February 24, 2017

Chapter 13.
Does the Market Exhibit Cooperation?

The *American Heritage Dictionary* defines the verb *cooperate* as "to work or act together toward a common end or purpose" and "to form an association for common, usually economic, benefit." Note that these definitions seem to require awareness about some joint effort to achieve a common objective.

This would seem to leave little room for the social cooperation that libertarians emphasize when describing what Adam Smith called the "system of natural liberty." Indeed, economist F.A. Hayek stressed that what goes on in the market is precisely *not* the striving for common goals and that individual awareness of all the goals aimed at need not be — and in fact never is — present.

In volume 2 of *Law, Legislation, and Liberty* (1976), Hayek wrote,

> It is often made a reproach to the Great Society and its market order that it lacks an agreed ranking of ends. This, however, is in fact its great merit which makes individual freedom and all it values possible. The Great Society arose through the discovery that men can live together in peace and mutually benefiting each other without agreeing on the particular aims which they severally pursue.

Hayek went on to say,

> In the Great Society we all in fact contribute not only to the satisfaction of needs of which we do not know, but sometimes even to the achievement of ends of which we would disapprove if we knew about them. We cannot help this because we do not know for what purposes the goods or services which we supply to others will be used by them.

Considering that the market order itself is not a conscious collaboration on behalf of a unitary set of social ends, may one speak literally of social cooperation? George Mason University economics professor Daniel Klein thinks not. In his provocative book, *Knowledge and Coordination: A Liberal Interpretation*, Klein acknowledges that advocates of the market going back to Adam Smith in the 18th century used the language of cooperation:

> Adam Smith said the day laborer obtains his woolen coat by virtue of "assistance and co-operation of many thousands," an *expansive notion* of cooperation reiterated by Thomas Hodgskin and Richard Whately, but

when Smith observes that man "stands at all times in need of the co-operation and assistance of great multitudes," he says, "while his whole life is scarce sufficient to gain the friendship of a few persons," suggesting that it isn't simply cooperation that yields him the woolen coat. [Emphasis added.]

Many other thinkers, Klein notes, spoke in terms similar to Smith's, including Edward Gibbon Wakefield (who distinguished deliberate "simple co-operation" from unintended "complex co-operation"), Frédéric Bastiat, Henry George, Philip Wicksteed, H.C. Macpherson, and Milton and Rose Friedman. Ludwig von Mises should be on the list. Indeed, he almost called his grand treatise on economics *Social Cooperation* rather than *Human Action*.

In contrast, Klein writes, "Karl Marx rightly emphasized that the capitalist system, *in the whole*, was not cooperation — and ultimately he condemned it for that. '[A]ll labour in which many individuals cooperate necessarily requires a commanding will to coordinate and unify the process … much as that of an orchestra conductor.'"

I'm not sure why Marx should be taken as authoritative on the meaning of *cooperation*. For that matter, I'm not sure whether Marx here was referring to the free market or the mercantilist/corporatist system that has historically been called *capitalism*.

At any rate, Klein prefers to "define cooperation as entailing mutual consciousness among the cooperators." But why, if the word has been used more expansively since at least the 18th century? *Social cooperation* is no neologism. Indeed, Klein quotes Max Hirsch's 1901 book, *Democracy versus Socialism*, which stated,

The co-ordination of efforts may, however, take place consciously or unconsciously. … While conscious co-operation utilises only an insignificant part of the intelligence of the co-operators, unconscious co-operation utilises the whole sum of their individual intelligences. The latter, therefore, is a higher and more efficient form of co-operation, and its product must be superior to that of the former.

All of this prompts Klein to ask,

Is it semantically legitimate to regard Wakefield's "complex cooperation" or Hirsch's "unconscious cooperation" as cooperation at all? In defending the presumption of liberty, classical liberals need to distinguish mutual and concatenate coordination, so as to clarify the meaning of cooperation. If they wish to praise the free enterprise system as a system of cooperation, if they wish to talk like Hodgskin, Whately, Bastiat, George, Wicksteed, and the Friedmans, they had better be prepared to explain how two people who have no mutual consciousness, who know nothing of each other, can be said to be cooperating.

Fair enough. Clarity is a virtue. There is certainly a difference between the cooperation that goes on within a firm and the cooperation that goes on among distant strangers within a catallaxy, or market. When necessary we may qualify the term with words like *conscious* or *implicit*. But I see no case for watering down the market-as-cooperation theme by saying, as Klein wishes to do, that it is "allegorical." When I describe the market order as a grand cooperative process to nonlibertarians, I encounter no confusion.

But perhaps I've conceded too much to Klein. While there is surely a difference between the cooperation in a firm and the cooperation in a catallaxy, they may not be quite as different as I've allowed. To be sure, parties to a transaction are not united to further a *common* end, but they *are* united (if temporarily) to help each other further their separate ends. "I'll help you if you help me" sounds like cooperation. Since the market is a series of such exchanges, there's no reason for people not to see themselves as engaging in mutually beneficial activities — that is, cooperating with strangers for purposes they may never know. As Klein himself writes, "They are potentially made aware that they are taking part in mutually coordinated action."

Going further, there is no reason why people can't figure out that the catallaxy, "in the whole" — the division of labor, the price system, etc. — provides a framework for cooperation, in which persons who differ over the value of particular goods realize through their trading that, at a deeper level, they have a *common interest* in the system of private property and free exchange. If such thoughtful men as Bastiat and Leonard Read could arrive at this truth, so can all thoughtful people. It doesn't require highly technical information.

Still, Klein is uneasy at a forthright assertion that "the free economy [is] a system of cooperation." Why? Because "it entails *myriad instances* of cooperation, but it also entails myriad instances of competition. It entails myriad instances of deception and misrepresentation. It entails a lot of things, not just instances of cooperation."

I am surprised by this response. The presence of deception and misrepresentation doesn't refute the insight that the market order, in the whole, is a form of cooperation. As for competition, it's the complement, not the opposite, of cooperation. Competition is what you have when people are free to choose with whom they will cooperate.

Dictionaries are descriptive, not prescriptive; they reflect usage. The word *cooperate* may predominantly (though as we've seen, not exclusively) be used in the sense given in the *American Heritage*, but this does not mean there isn't enough of a "family resemblance" (Ludwig Wittgenstein's term) between explicit cooperation and what goes on in the market to justify our application of the term to the catallaxy.

In the end I'm not sure it matters whether *social cooperation* is an "allegorical kind of cooperation," an analogy, or a reasonable (and seasoned) extension of the concept. To me, it seems much more than an allegory, and I disagree with Klein that unless we fess up to allegory we will 1) "cut off [our] inquiry," 2) be unable to "handle ... challenges to our talk of communication and cooperation," and 3) appear "unattuned to the social." But if *social cooperation* is "only" allegorical, what is it an allegory for? If you were to describe the referent, I don't see how you could escape sounding as though you were describing a form of cooperation.

Future of Freedom Foundation, February 8, 2013

Chapter 14.
The Market Is a Beautiful Thing

Market advocates tend to respect the intellect of their fellow human beings. You can tell by their reliance on philosophical, moral, economic, and historical arguments when trying to persuade others. But what if most people's aversion to the market isn't founded in philosophy, morality, economics, or history? What if their objection is aesthetic?

More and more I've come to think this is the case, and I believe I witnessed an example some years ago at a lecture I gave at St. Lawrence University in Canton, New York. During the Q&A a woman asked, in all sincerity, I believe, why society couldn't do without money since so many bad things are associated with it. She also suggested that cooperation is better than market competition. I replied that since money facilitates exchange and exchange is *cooperation*, it follows that money facilitates *cooperation* — a lovely thing, indeed. Government, I added, corrupts money.

I also said that competition is what happens when we are free to decide with whom we will cooperate. I don't know if my response prompted her to rethink her objections to the market, but I am confident her objection was aesthetic. For her, money and competition are ugly. Perhaps I didn't respond on an aesthetic level; it's something I have to work on. But I tried, and so must we all when we encounter these sorts of objections.

Like that nice woman, many decent people dislike markets because they find them unattractive. And they associate markets with other things they find unattractive besides money and competition: (rugged, atomistic) individualism, "selfishness," and profit. F.A. Hayek noticed this, writing in "Individualism: True and False," "the belief that individualism approves and encourages human selfishness is one of the main reasons why so many people dislike it." If that's the case, philosophical, moral, economic, and historical arguments may fall on deaf ears. The objections must be met on an aesthetic level.

In other words, advocates of free markets must demonstrate that markets are things of beauty. Fortunately, that is not hard to do.

The free market is a political-legal setting in which people are at liberty to peacefully pursue their plans. This activity generates, unintentionally, an undesigned order that facilitates cooperation and coordination among even distant strangers, making each person's pursuit more effective and efficient than otherwise. The price system is the primary means by which this is accomplished. To many people, the price system seems impersonal and cold, but it's the key to the market's beauty, for it is what gives the market its *coordinative and corrective power*, which, although generated by individuals' purposive action, transcends them. The market is beautiful not because it lives up to some mathematically elegant equilibrium model — but because it does not! Its beauty lies in its power to coordinate activities and correct errors. And it does this work without compulsion or authoritarian central direction. As a result, when truly free — no privileges, no arbitrary restrictions — the market gives all a better chance at living in any peaceful way they wish. How lovely!

That is where our emphasis should be placed. The 19th-century French liberal economist Frédéric Bastiat knew what he was doing when he called his (unfinished) magnum opus *Economic Harmonies*. His purpose throughout was to show that the market setting harmonizes people's deepest interests and enables them to further their own causes by cooperating with others through exchange. For him a central feature of the market is its inexorable transfer of wealth from the private to the "communal domain," as technological innovation and competition increasingly substitute the gratis services of nature for arduous human labor. As a description of this harmony, his book is a work of art — as is Ludwig von Mises's *Human Action*, which is dedicated to showing that markets are social cooperation. (That nearly was the title of the work).

To most people the quintessential market "force," the law of supply and demand, seems sterile and cold, but it is the market's beauty in action, and we must find ways to communicate it in that way. Adam Smith saw it. Indulge me as I quote from *The Wealth of Nations* (bk. 1, chap. 7):

> The market price of every particular commodity is regulated by the proportion between the quantity which is actually brought to market, and the demand of those who are willing to pay the natural price of the commodity, or the whole value of the rent, labour, and profit, which must be paid in order to bring it thither. Such people may be called the effectual demanders, and their demand the effectual demand; since it may be sufficient to effectuate the bringing of the commodity to market. ...

> When the quantity of any commodity which is brought to market falls short of the effectual demand, all those who are willing to pay the whole value of the rent, wages, and profit, which must be paid in order to bring it thither, cannot be supplied with the quantity which they want. Rather than want [do without] it altogether, some of them will be willing to give more. A competition will immediately begin among them, and the market price will rise more or less above the natural price. ...

> When the quantity brought to market exceeds the effectual demand, it cannot be all sold to those who are willing to pay the whole value of the

rent, wages and profit, which must be paid in order to bring it thither. Some part must be sold to those who are willing to pay less, and the low price which they give for it must reduce the price of the whole. The market price will sink more or less below the natural price. ...

If at any time it [quantity] exceeds the effectual demand, some of the component parts of its price must be paid below their natural rate. If it is rent, the interest of the landlords will immediately prompt them to withdraw a part of their land; and if it is wages or profit, the interest of the labourers in the one case, and of their employers in the other, will prompt them to withdraw a part of their labour or stock from this employment. The quantity brought to market will soon be no more than sufficient to supply the effectual demand. All the different parts of its price will rise to their natural rate, and the whole price to its natural price.

If, on the contrary, the quantity brought to market should at any time fall short of the effectual demand, some of the component parts of its price must rise above their natural rate. If it is rent, the interest of all other landlords will naturally prompt them to prepare more land for the raising of this commodity; if it is wages or profit, the interest of all other labourers and dealers will soon prompt them to employ more labour and stock in preparing and bringing it to market. The quantity brought thither will soon be sufficient to supply the effectual demand. All the different parts of its price will soon sink to their natural rate, and the whole price to its natural price.

The natural price, therefore, is, as it were, the central price, to which the prices of all commodities are continually gravitating.

This metaphorical "mechanism" operates for all goods and services simultaneously. So when the market price of a good falls below the level sufficient "to bring it thither," some producers will move to the production of other goods for which the market price is *above* the level required "to bring it thither," setting in motion a lowering of the market price. The preferences of consumers — reflected in prices — tell producers: "We have enough of good X, but we need more of good Y." And producers have an incentive to respond cooperatively and produce more of good Y. All this and more — the division of labor, for example — go on without command — if the market is free.

What could be lovelier!

Bastiat commented: "We should be shutting our eyes to the facts if we refused to recognize that society cannot present such complicated combinations in which civil and criminal law play so little part without being subject to a prodigiously ingenious mechanism."

Not just prodigiously ingenious, monsieur. Beautiful!

Future of Freedom Foundation, April 12, 2013

Chapter 15.
Love the Market?

Libertarians are sometimes accused of being "market fundamentalists," and there's a sense in which I will plead guilty to the charge. Libertarians certainly have great esteem for "the market" — but our esteem is rooted in reason and history, not faith.

This esteem, granted, is often misunderstood. As I see things, it need have nothing to do with hyper-consumerism, shallow materialism, or single-minded acquisitiveness. (This is not to condemn the desire for material comforts of course.) Nor does it indicate a wish to see *everything* located within the cash nexus or the for-profit world. "The market" is better understood as much more than those things, though the boundary between it and the nonmarket parts of civil society (which include families and noncommercial associations of various kinds) may be hard to locate. Let's just leave it at this: the market takes in a good portion, though not all, of the voluntary relationships in society; it's an important part of the voluntary sector, and so it is decisively different from the state, or coercive, sector.

If the market isn't worth esteeming solely for material reasons, what is its big attraction for libertarians? Many volumes could be (and have been) written on that subject, so I will have to keep my ambitions realistic here.

A fundamental attraction lies in the market's role as a facilitator of social cooperation, permitting a degree of peace, harmony, and interpersonal coordination that could not be achieved by other means. To be sure, such cooperation is partly instrumental; it is a key path to material well-being. But it is more than that: as social beings we value cooperative interaction as an *end*, or as a constitutive means to our ultimate end, as well as an instrumental means.

The market (though not just a physical place) is where people meet in peace to engage in mutually beneficial exchanges of all kinds, material and nonmaterial. As such, it makes possible a host of wider values that we take for granted. For example, free exchange generates prices that are indispensable for economic calculation and coordination among producers and consumers, as economist Ludwig von Mises famously taught. Without true market prices, we wouldn't know what to produce, how much to produce, and by what methods. This is no trivial thing. In a world of scarce means and abundant ends, the need to make trade-offs is pervasive. We can't have everything we want at the same time, and we don't want the (subjectively) less important at the expense of the (subjectively) more important. It is good that there's a way for us to minimize waste and maximize efficiency in achieving our ends. Only the market can achieve that.

Markets and market prices permit extensive specialization and division of labor, which have value far beyond the satisfaction of material needs. Without a division of labor or with only a primitive one, people would have to spend time inefficiently producing many things for personal consumption, time that could be spent enjoying leisure, the "higher" pursuits, and social activities. With a division of labor, one has a better chance to develop one's unique talents and skills.

Moreover, to the extent the market is free and competitive, the division of labor and economies of scale push prices down, making a unit of labor more valuable and further freeing individuals for noncommercial activity or for the production of art and literature. As Mises wrote, "Because many people or even all people want bread, clothes, shoes, and cars, large-scale production of these goods becomes feasible and reduces the costs of production to such an extent that they are accessible at low prices. The fact that my fellow man wants to acquire shoes as I do, does not make it harder for me to get shoes, but easier."

This is part of the answer to those who long for a "gift economy" in which people produce for the community without expectation of direct reciprocity. While such an arrangement can work within the family or other small groups, or in circumstances where the range of choice is strictly limited, it is difficult to imagine how a large and prosperous society could arise or endure without free exchange and money prices. Even if one thinks it would be nicer for people to give their products as gifts, expecting that they will be able to take what they "need" from the common store, I see no getting around the fact that this arrangement would lack information (provided by prices) indispensable to the kind of decision-making on which everyone's material and nonmaterial well-being depend.

Another benefit, which grows out of the first, is that the market facilitates constructive interaction with strangers and hence promotes peace across broad geographical areas, even globally. What deeper compliment could one pay to a social system? A money-based division of labor brings people together for mutual advantage, expanding the array of goods and fostering goodwill among individuals who might otherwise view one another with fear and suspicion. Instead of fighting or hiding, they are producing valuable things for exchange and relating to each as equals, and the resulting cultural cross-fertilization has untold beneficent consequences.

Some will say that the market is a cold and calculating place, where people do good only in order to do well. Remember Adam Smith's observation that we rely on the self-interest, not the benevolence, of the butcher, baker, and brewer for our dinner. But (as Smith well understood) this leaves a good deal out of the picture. While it is true that people enter the market to acquire goods and services, and their providers seek their own (and their families') well-being in serving others, that does not prevent the emergence of benevolence and even friendship in the course of market transactions. At a personal level, people understand that other individuals are ends in themselves, not only means, and that realization colors market relationships. Have you never asked a store clerk with whom you've had repeated commercial encounters how he was feeling or how his kids were doing? Moreover, we are capable of realizing and taking satisfaction in the *general good* produced by the market order.

If there is deep value in the market as an institution, then logically there is value in those things without which the market could not exist, such as private property. Those who harbor a moral or aesthetic aversion to the market typically dislike private property too — or at least they think they do. Actually, their anti-property attitude is often belied by other stated positions. For example, if one believes — and finds offensive — that labor is deprived of its just product in some social systems, isn't that a pro-property concern?

Property makes autonomy possible by creating a zone of freedom around each of us, leaving us at liberty to pursue the plans by which we define ourselves. And being free in one's justly acquired possessions averts violent conflict. Far from insulating individuals from one another, property fosters peaceful cooperation through free association and exchange.

No doubt *property* has gotten a bad name over the centuries due to its unfortunate association with slavery and the expropriation of peasants by idle ruling classes. These will be understood as *perversions* of the concept when one realizes that property logically proceeds from *self*-ownership. (The American abolitionist movement perceptively labeled slavery "man-stealing.")

In defending private property, I do not mean to imply that nonstate public property or voluntary community management of common pool resources (à la Nobel laureate Elinor Ostrom) are anti-market. On the contrary, those exist within, not in conflict with, the larger market economy

Finally, it should be noted that much opposition to the free market (and that on which it is founded) stems from its misidentification with the current corporatist economy and its many attendant evils. Richard Cobden, the towering advocate of peace and free trade in 19th-century England, once said, "They who propose to influence by force the traffic of the world, forget that affairs of trade, like matters of conscience, change their very nature if touched by the hand of violence; for as faith, if forced, would no longer be religion, but hypocrisy, so commerce becomes robbery if coerced by warlike armaments."

Likewise, when the market and the institution of property are touched by the hand of violence — that is, by the state — their very essences change. It makes no sense to judge the free market by the nature and record of (state) capitalism.

Future of Freedom Foundation, November 16, 2012

Chapter 16.
In Praise of Profit

I've sought to present a defense of key libertarian concepts — *market, private property, and competition* — in a way intended to make them palatable to people who believe in individual liberty yet have something like an aesthetic aversion to the market economy.

Now Let's examine *profit*, another concept that has an unpleasant taste for some people who might otherwise be attracted to libertarianism. We've all heard the exhortation "people before profits." My goal here is to show that in a freed market (not our corporatist economy), there need be no conflict between treating people well and earning profit. On the contrary, profitability in the market would depend on being sensitive to what people want.

We first must recognize that the pursuit of profit, or gain, is the defining feature of *all* purposeful human action, as economist Ludwig von Mises taught. It makes action what it is. Whenever one acts — whenever one chooses an end and the means to achieve it — one seeks to improve one's condition, that is, to replace one state of affairs with another that the acting person prefers. If I am hungry (or anticipate soon becoming hungry) and I prepare a meal, I take steps to create a state of satisfaction because I prefer that condition to the one that would have come to pass had I not acted.

All action is of that nature. The actor replaces situation B with situation A. The end sought may be egoistic, altruistic, or anything else. What counts is that for whatever reason the person *wants* the end realized. This applies to Mother Teresa as much as to an acquisitive materialist. They want different things, but *they* want them, and so they act. (This is not to be confused with psychological egoism, the idea that we are all self-interested. The point is logical not psychological.)

It is already implicit in what I've said that if an action is successful — if the end is achieved — the actor experiences a profit. How so? Assuming the person has not made a mistake (which is always possible), he or she prefers the end to whatever was given up, or forgone, to obtain it; what's given up is the price, or the opportunity cost. Mises called this gain, or surplus, "psychic profit." We are not talking about market transactions only. Alone on an island, when Crusoe decides to make a net so he can catch more fish than he can with his hands, the "price" he pays includes anything else he would have achieved with his time and resources, including indulging in leisure.

By nature, then, all action aims at profit, and all successful action is profitable. No one would undertake an action expecting to give up what one prefers in exchange for what one does not prefer. In fact, one *can't* do it. To act is to demonstrate one's preference under the circumstances. (Thus, Mises held that the analysis of the features common to all human action is a conceptual, or a priori, matter.)

Those who condemn profit as an unjust gain need to reevaluate their position in light of the foregoing. Remember, in analyzing profit I am assuming a freed market, that is, an environment based on individual liberty and free enterprise without special privileges from the government. The conclusions drawn here cannot be automatically applied to the current corporatist economy in which people are able to make profits that would be unavailable in a freed market.

For example, if a corporation is highly profitable because it sells drones to the government, we shouldn't applaud the company for its competence in the marketplace. The corporation's activities are not aimed at pleasing consumers making free choices, but rather at pleasing government officials who obtain their revenue by force (taxation).

In free-market transactions, just as with individual actions, the parties each seek a state of affairs that they prefer over others they might achieve with their resources. If Olivia gives an orange to Alexander in exchange for his apple (assuming no coercion or fraud), we must conclude that they evaluate the products differently. Olivia prefers the apple to the orange, and Adam prefers the orange to the apple. Both profit — though the gain cannot be measured or quantified because it is subjective and represents an immeasurable value-ranking. Presumably, no one would condemn this dual profit. By the way, note the win-win, positive-sum situation.

When goods are exchanged for money, however, some people see the situation differently. For one thing, only the receiver of money is said to profit. But that is wrong. If Olivia buys the apple from Alexander for a dollar, we still must conclude that she prefers the apple to whatever else she could have bought with the dollar. That gain is her profit.

Nothing is changed if we imagine that Adam paid only 75 cents for the apple. Olivia still prefers the apple to her other alternatives for the money. She of course would like to pay less, just as Alexander would like to charge more. But the agreed-on price satisfies both parties — or else it would not have occurred. There are no grounds for criticizing Adam for his profit. (If Olivia insists on paying less, Alexander might find someone who is willing to pay a dollar. If Alexander insists on charging more, Olivia might find someone who is willing to charge only one dollar. Hence the importance of free competition.)

Mises and his student Israel Kirzner used the term *entrepreneurial profit* for the gains made from spotting price discrepancies in the market. If an alert person sees that apples are selling for 75 cents in one part of the market and one dollar in another part, that person can profit by buying in the former and selling in the latter. The profit is the reward for alertness and action; there was nothing to stop anyone else who noticed what the entrepreneur noticed from doing the same. But note that the profit will be fleeting. Buying apples in the cheap market will drive up the price there, while bringing additional apples to the dear market will drive down the price there. Soon there will be one price and no entrepreneurial profit.

The story is the same with more complicated enterprises. If consumers are willing to pay more for an item than it costs to gather the factors of production and assemble it, some part of the return for some period will be pure entrepreneurial profit resulting from that formerly unnoticed price discrepancy. That abnormal profit will attract competitors until the return is more in line with other industries.

Price discrepancies can be seen as knowledge errors: resources are undervalued with respect to their potential. Entrepreneurial activity consists in spotting and correcting such discrepancies. Profit is the reward for that service, but after the error is corrected, the profit disappears.

The upshot is that in the absence of government privilege, profit — psychic or monetary — is legitimate and praiseworthy. In a freed market, profit is an inducement to serve others and a sign that they are being well served.

Future of Freedom Foundation, November 30, 2012

Chapter 17.
The Virtues of Competition

Competition deserves its own discussion.

Differing attitudes about market competition divide people needlessly. An appreciation of what competition makes possible could prepare the ground for a convergence between libertarians and those we might call latent libertarians, that is, those who value individual liberty but don't yet see the market as part of its natural home.

I won't say much here about the strictly economic functions of competition — its role, for example, in driving down prices and driving up the quality of goods and services. Competition among employers is also important for maximizing workers' bargaining clout. This is why earlier American libertarians, like Benjamin R. Tucker and his cohorts, objected to all government limits on competition, including banking restrictions. State-fostered monopoly is the enemy of workers' freedom and prosperity.

Besides these aspects, Nobel laureate F.A. Hayek added to our appreciation of competition when he elaborated its role in the expansion of knowledge. In "Competition as a Discovery Procedure," Hayek wrote,

> Competition is important only because and insofar as its outcomes are unpredictable and on the whole different from those that anyone would have been able to consciously strive for. ...

> Which goods are scarce, however, or which things are goods, or how scarce or valuable they are, is precisely one of the conditions that competition should discover: in each case it is the preliminary outcomes of the market process that inform individuals where it is worthwhile to search.

Thus the competitive process — wherein anyone is free to offer goods and services to potential buyers who in turn are free to decline and look elsewhere — discloses information we would not otherwise obtain. That process is indispensable to human welfare because crucial knowledge about people's preferences, talents, and resources is widely dispersed and thus lies beyond anyone's direct access in its entirety. Moreover, important information is forged only through encounters with unanticipated market alternatives. Hayek was understandably frustrated by theories of competition "in which all essential conditions are assumed to be known — a state that theory curiously designates as perfect competition, even though the opportunity for the activity we call competition no longer exists."

While people of varying ideological persuasions might readily concede these benefits, there nonetheless remains what I think of as an aesthetic objection to free-wheeling rivalry among sellers in the market. Because competition entails winners and losers, in some people's eyes it appears less humane than its supposed opposite: cooperation. But competition and cooperation are not as different as they may appear. Observe: I enter a bazaar with a multitude of vendors. I spot two who are selling shoes. I would like a new pair of shoes and can buy from only one of the vendors. The two, then, are competing — but competing to do what? They're competing to cooperate with me of course.

Competition, then, is the natural offspring of cooperation and freedom. Divorcing freedom from cooperation would mean mandatory cooperation. I don't know about you, but I don't like the sound of that.

It is also odd that some folks who are wary of monopoly don't welcome competition as the only alternative. It is odder still that some who dislike private monopoly are accepting of government monopoly, such as single-payer healthcare or, more generally, state socialism. I see no reason to think that government monopoly would be better than private monopoly. History certainly gives us no reason to think so.

At any rate, we need not choose between forms of monopoly because we can have competition if we want it. All we need to do is keep the government out of all peaceful activity. Monopoly is not a market phenomenon, but rather the product of government privilege, which, like all government activity, is rooted in force. And we all know who has a comparative advantage in procuring favors from the government. Hint: it's not typical working people or the poor.

I raise these issues hoping that advocates of free markets may engage in fruitful conversation with those who long for liberty but have an aversion to competitive markets. Such a conversation has a precedent in America's past. The libertarians associated with the old market-anarchist *Liberty* magazine (1881–1908) actively engaged other opponents of the reigning statism on these matters. For example, in 1888 one W.T. Horn asked in the pages of the magazine "whether is competition or co-operation the truest expression of that mutual trust and fraternal good-will which alone can replace present forms of authority, usages and customs as the social bond of union?" He continued,

> The answer seems obvious enough. Competition, if it means anything at all, means war, and, so far from tending to enhance the growth of mutual confidence, must generate division and hostility among men. If egoistic liberty demands competition as its necessary corollary, every man becomes a social Ishmael. The state of veiled warfare thus implied where

underhand cunning takes the place of open force is doubtless not without its attractions to many minds, but to propose mutual confidence as its regulative principle has all the appearance of making a declaration of war in terms of peace. No, surely credit and mutual confidence, with everything thereby implied, rightly belong to an order of things where unity and good-fellowship characterize all human relations, and would flourish best where co-operation finds its complete expression, — viz., in Communism.

To which editor Benjamin R. Tucker responded,

The supposition that competition means war rests upon old notions and false phrases that have been long current, but are rapidly passing into the limbo of exploded fallacies. Competition means war only when it is in some way restricted, either in scope or intensity, — that is, when it is not perfectly free competition; for then its benefits are won by one class at the expense of another, instead of by all at the expense of nature's forces. When universal and unrestricted, competition means the most perfect peace and the truest co-operation; for then it becomes simply a test of forces resulting in their most advantageous utilization. ... Where freedom prevails, competition and co-operation are identical.

Could anyone seriously think that two vendors at a bazaar are engaging in warfare? Two shops on the street? Two companies? On the contrary, in a freed market devoid of privilege their rivalry would serve consumers and sharpen their own skills. At worst, one vendor may learn he is not cut out for the work, leading him into another occupation for which he has a comparative advantage. Thus we see the efficiency and discovery roles of cooperation-via-competition in action.

Future of Freedom Foundation, November 23, 2012

Chapter 18.
Bastiat on the Socialization of Wealth

> That ... veil which is spread before the eyes of the ordinary man, which even the attentive observer does not always succeed in casting aside, prevents us from seeing the most marvelous of all social phenomena: real wealth constantly passing from the domain of private property into the communal domain.

Wealth marvelously passing from the private to the communal domain? It sounds like a socialist's redistributionist fantasy!

But wait — Frédéric Bastiat, the great laissez-faire radical of 19th-century France, wrote those words in his book *Economic Harmonies*, chapter 8, provocatively titled "Private Property and Common Wealth."

He repeats the point throughout his fascinating chapter:

> And so, as I have already said many times and shall doubtless say many times more (for it is the greatest, the most admirable, and perhaps the most misunderstood of all the social harmonies, since it encompasses all the others), it is characteristic of progress (and, indeed, this is what we mean by progress) to transform onerous utility into gratuitous utility; to decrease value without decreasing utility; and to enable all men, for fewer pains or at smaller cost, to obtain the same satisfactions. Thus, the total number of things owned in *common* is constantly increased; and their enjoyment, distributed more uniformly to all, gradually eliminates inequalities resulting from differences in the amount of property owned.

Here's what Bastiat had in mind. In a competitive marketplace with advancing technology, as the effort required to produce and hence acquire things diminishes, the price of gaining utility falls. For example, if the average worker had to work two hours, 40 minutes, to buy a chicken in 1900, but only 14 minutes as the 21st century approached (actual statistics), Bastiat would say the chicken "is obtained for *less expenditure of human effort; less service* is performed as it passes from hand to hand; it has *less* [exchange] *value*; in a word, it has become *gratis*, [though] not completely." In other words, most of the utility that had to be paid for with painful effort in 1900 was *free* by 2000.

Thus progress through the market order consists in ever more people satisfying more of their wants at less and less effort. Bastiat calls this a move from private property to common wealth because he roots property in effort and greater wealth is now available to all with less effort.

What makes this possible? Technological innovation. As Bastiat puts it, "Production has in large measure been *turned over to Nature*":

> The goal of all men, in all their activities, is to reduce the amount of effort in relation to the end desired and, in order to accomplish this end, to incorporate in their labor a constantly increasing proportion of the forces of Nature. ... They invent tools or machines, they enlist the chemical and mechanical forces of the elements, they divide their labors, and they unite their efforts. How to do more with less, is the eternal question asked in all times, in all places, in all situations, in all things. ...
>
> The gratuitous co-operation of Nature has been progressively added to our own efforts. ...
>
> *A greater amount of gratuitous utility implies a partial realization of common ownership.* [Emphasis added.]

But technology only makes this "marvelous social phenomenon" possible. What makes it actually happen? Competition, of course. If one producer attempted to charge the older, higher price — if he tried to capture the returns to what Bastiat called "the contribution made by Nature" — he would be inviting competitors to undersell him (unless government privileges, such as licensing or intellectual property blocked competition). Rivals would be able to undersell because a lower price would still recover the costs of the human effort involved in production. Competitive entrepreneurship drives prices down toward costs. As Nobel laureate F.A. Hayek put it, "The empirical observation that prices do tend to correspond to costs was the beginning of our science." (On the relationship between cost and price, see "Value, Cost, Marginal Utility, and Böhm-Bawerk" in this volume.)

Bastiat, like his predecessor Adam Smith, acknowledged that this process of passing wealth from the private to the communal domain is driven by self-interest: "What other stimulant would urge them forward with the same degree of energy?" Today it is largely unappreciated that the market order — private property, competitive entrepreneurship, free pricing, profit/loss — aligns private and public interest as no other institutional setting possibly could. (For a pre-Austrian, Bastiat got an amazing number of things right, but he got one thing badly wrong when he rejected the idea that trade requires a double inequality of subjective value. See "The Importance of Subjectivism in Economics" in this volume.)

To be sure, Bastiat did not want his praise of the expanding communal realm to be mistaken for communism. ("I anticipate it, and I am resigned to it.") Unlike the communist, he favored the socialization of the fruits of *nature*, not of human effort:

> By the communal domain is meant those things that we enjoy in common, by the design of Providence, without the need of any effort to apply them to our use. They can therefore give rise to no service, no transaction, no property. Property is based on our right to render services to ourselves or to render them to others for a remuneration. What the communist proposes to make common to all is not the gratuitous gifts of God, but human effort, or service.

So communism and the communal domain have nothing in common but a word root. Bastiat suggested that more people might favor free markets if they understood the distinction he was making.

> If the legitimacy of private property has appeared doubtful and inexplicable, even to those who were not communists, it seemed so because they felt that it concentrated in the hands of some, to the exclusion of others, the gifts of God originally belonging to all. We believe that we have completely dispelled this doubt by proving that what was, by decree of Providence, common to all, remains common in the course of all human transactions, since the domain of private property can never extend beyond the limits of value, beyond the rights laboriously acquired through services rendered.

> And, when it is expressed in these terms, who can deny the right to private property?

While Bastiat appeared sanguine about what was going on around him, he understood that the reigning political-economic system indeed enabled the illegitimate privatization of what in a free market would have gone into the communal realm. "Of course, I know that in practice the ideal principle of property is far from having full sway," he wrote. "Against it are conflicting factors: there are services that are not voluntary, whose remuneration is not arrived at by free bargaining; there are services whose equivalence is impaired by force or fraud; in a word, plunder exists." Bastiat, who coined the phrase "legal plunder," of course had the state in mind as the chief culprit.

Why is Bastiat's distinctive framing of the case for the free market worthwhile? Because there is, I believe, an untapped potential constituency for radical libertarian ideas among people who have an aversion to free markets only because they mistakenly believe free market means corporatism and illegitimate gains. Before these people can be persuaded by libertarian arguments, we must get their attention, and the best way to do that is to present the *free market* as a process that embodies social cooperation and, à la Bastiat, the "socialization" of wealth.

Future of Freedom Foundation, March 22, 2013

Chapter 19.
Monopoly and Aggression

The concepts *monopoly* and *aggression* are intimately related, like *lock* and *key*, or *mother* and *son*. You cannot fully understand the first without understanding the second.

Most of us are taught to think of a monopoly as simply any lone seller of a good or service, but this definition is fraught with problems, as Austrian economists have long pointed out. It overlooks, for example, the factor of *potential* competition. If a lone seller knows that someone could challenge his "monopoly" by entering the market, that will tend to influence the seller's pricing and service policies. Is he then really a monopolist even if, for the time being, he's alone in the market?

In deciding who is a monopolist, we also face the problem of defining the relevant market. The Federal Trade Commission once charged the top few ready-to-eat breakfast cereal companies with monopolizing "the market." But *what* market? The FTC meant the market for ready-to-eat breakfast cereals. But that's not all that people eat or could eat for breakfast. If you define the relevant market to include bacon and eggs; oatmeal; yogurt; English muffins and butter; bagels, lox, and cream cheese; breakfast burritos; and anything else people may find appealing in the morning, a "monopoly" in ready-to-eat cereals looks rather different. Even a single cereal seller (assuming no government privilege) could not price his product without taking into account what his rivals selling other foods and consumers were doing. He could not even be sure who his rivals were until they arose in response to his consumer-alienating actions.

The conventional notion of monopoly has also been subjected to the reductio ad absurdum. In deciding who is a monopolist, where do we stop? Only one shop can occupy the northeast corner of Elm and Main in Anytown. A particular consumer could decide it's too costly in time or effort to cross the street and buy at the rival shop on the northwest corner. Does that make the first shop a monopoly?

I have exclusive domain over my own labor services and tools (laptop, etc.). The same is true for each reader. Does that make us all monopolists? If so, how useful is the concept? (Much of what I've learned over many years about monopoly and antitrust I learned from economist Dominick T. Armentano. See *Antitrust and Monopoly: Anatomy of a Policy Failure*.)

Economist Ludwig von Mises, I should acknowledge, believed that *in theory* there could be "instances of monopoly prices [harmful to consumers] which would appear also on a market not hampered and sabotaged by the interference of the various national governments and by conspiracies between groups of governments." However, he added, these "are of minor importance. They concern some raw materials the deposits of which are few and geographically concentrated, and local limited-space monopolies."

In *Man, Economy, and State*, however, economist Murray Rothbard critiqued the concept *monopoly price* as useless in a free-market context because identifying it would require knowledge of a product's *competitive price*, which itself simply cannot be identified. All we can observe is the price that emerges from buying and selling on the market.

Adam Smith's approach to monopoly makes more sense than the mainstream view. To Smith, monopoly denoted a privilege, a legal barrier to competition, such as a license or a franchise — in other words, a grant from the state. Anyone who attempted to compete with the monopolist would run afoul of the law and be suppressed by force because that's how the state assures its decrees are faithfully carried out. When someone whose actions are consonant with natural rights is suppressed by force, *that* is aggression.

Hence my claim that the concepts *monopoly* and *aggression* are intimately related. *Quod erat demonstrandum.*

Monopoly-building interventions take forms other than outright franchises and licenses. Tariffs and other restrictions on foreign-made consumer goods impose monopolistic, or at least oligopolistic, burdens on consumers by preventing or hampering competition from producers outside the country and thereby raising prices. If the restricted goods are producers' goods, they burden domestic manufacturers as well as consumers.

Intellectual-property laws — patents, copyrights, and the like — have a similar effect by hampering competition through prohibitions on the use of knowledge and formats that people possess mentally. The creation of an artificial property right through patents is practically indistinguishable from a franchise or license. Its harm to consumers is the same. Civilization is a process of imitation, innovative "mutation," and selection in the broad social marketplace.

Nineteenth-century French liberal economist Frédéric Bastiat appears to have understood this, though he was not always clear. In his unfinished magnum opus, *Economic Harmonies*, Bastiat said some interesting things that bear on this issue.

Bastiat praised the competitive market process — where the state abstains from plunder on behalf of any special interests — precisely because it transfers "real wealth constantly … from the domain of private property into the communal domain." (I detail his argument in "Bastiat on the Socialization of Wealth" in this volume.) What he meant was that, when economizing, profit-seeking producers substitute the *free services of nature* (water, gravity, electricity, wind, etc.) for onerous human labor, competition drives down prices to reflect the lower production costs. When consumers obtain the same or greater utility at a lower price, they enjoy — *free of charge* — some of the utility they previously had to pay for ultimately with their labor. Innovation-with-competition delivers the fruits of nature's services gratis, and the whole community benefits.

This is why Bastiat said that the market transfers wealth from the realm of private property to the "communal realm." Producers who formerly reaped returns on human services that provided utility to consumers now instead employ nature's services from which *they can reap no return at all.* As a result, we all get increasing amounts of free stuff.

But free competition is crucial. Bastiat used the example of a producer, John, who invented a new process "whereby he can complete his task with half the labor it previously took, everything included, even the cost of making the implement used to harness the forces of Nature." In that case, Bastiat wrote, "as long as he keeps his secret, there will be no change" in his product's price.

(For Bastiat, prices are formed, not according to the amount of labor that goes into goods, but by the toil and trouble, subjectively conceived, that consumers are saved by engaging in exchanges of services rather than by producing goods for themselves. He calls the English economists' axiom that value comes from labor "treacherous.")

Why will there be no change in price, or what Bastiat called "value"? "Because," he replies, "the service is the same. The person furnishing [the good] performs the same service before as after the invention." So long as John can keep his secret, other things equal, the terms of exchange will remain unchanged.

The important question is: *how long can John keep his secret?* Bastiat went on to say that the old price will fall "when Peter, [a consumer and producer of another good to be offered in exchange], can say to John: 'You ask me for two hours of my labor in exchange for one of yours; but *I am familiar with your process*, and if you place such a high price on your service, I shall do it for myself.'" [Emphasis added.]

Bastiat is clearly happy about this. I interpret this to mean that he did not approve of patents, which would prevent Peter from exploiting his knowledge of John's invention in order to save himself (and other people) money.

In fact, Bastiat followed up that passage with this: "Now this day comes inevitably. When a new process is invented, *it does not remain a secret for long.*" [Emphasis added.]

The resulting fall in price "represents value [but not utility] eliminated, ... private property made public, utility previously onerous, now gratuitous."

What I want to emphasize is this: in *Economic Harmonies*, which Bastiat wrote late in life and despite what he may have said elsewhere (and in distinguishing between patents and copyright, he was by no means unambiguous), he appeared not to regret that an inventor was unable reap returns by forcibly thwarting imitators. In a letter, he wrote, "I must admit that I attach immense and extremely beneficial importance to imitation." (Hat tip: Bastiat scholar David Hart.) He expressed no concern that imitation would discourage innovation.

So-called intellectual property is the dominant engine of monopoly in modern economies. Fortunately, cheap technology makes enforcement increasingly difficult, and we may look forward to the day when IP disappears entirely. That underscores my point: to rid society of monopoly we must rid society of aggression.

Future of Freedom Foundation, December 19, 2014

Chapter 20.
Rights Violations Aren't the Only Bads

More than a few libertarians appear to hold the view that only rights violations are wrong, bad, and deserving of moral condemnation. If an act does not entail the initiation of force, so goes this attitude, we can have nothing critical to say about it.

On its face this is strange. If you observed an adult being rude to his elderly mother, it is surely reasonable to be appalled, even though the offender did not use force. And, being appalled, you may be justified under the circumstances in responding, such as by cancelling a social engagement or telling others of his obnoxious behavior. One can reasonably say that this person's mother is owed better treatment, without the word *owed* implying legal, that is, coercive, enforceability. (Words can have different senses, of course.) Therefore, the rude son may be judged negatively.

This example may be uncontroversial, but observe the attitude in another context. I have argued that "intellectual property" (IP) can't really be property (as can land, cars, and socks) and that it is, rather, a government grant of monopoly power over expressions of ideas, which perforce limits other people in the use of *their* property, while creating scarcities where there would have been none.

The article brought vigorous critical responses, one of which informed me that if I don't believe that expressions of ideas can be owned, I would have no right to object if someone were to plagiarize or adulterate my own written work.

Before diving in, I'd like to draw attention to the strange habit IP proponents have of bringing up plagiarism (or adulteration) as soon as the legitimacy of copyright is challenged. This is strange because so-called copyright infringement per se differs in a crucial respect from plagiarism. The publishing industry doesn't strenuously lobby the government for fortified copyright laws because it is worried I will publish *Atlas Shrugged* with *my* name on the cover. (Who'd buy it?) On the contrary, it worries that I (or someone else) will publish the novel with *Ayn Rand's name* on the cover. Copyright and plagiarism must be considered apart from each other.

Be that as it may, the premise of my critic's claim — that I cannot logically object to plagiarism or adulteration because I don't believe expressions of ideas can be owned — must be that the only *legitimate* ground for objection would be that these activities are property violations. So if they are *not* property violations, there is no basis to complain.

With all due respect, this is ridiculous. One who rejects the legitimacy of intellectual property can still have perfectly good moral grounds for objecting to the plagiarist's or adulterator's misconduct. Libertarians ought to think long and hard before buying the idea that rights violations are the only species of wrongful conduct.

If someone attaches his name to something I wrote, the plagiarist's declaration that he is not a thief (because ownership of expressions of ideas cannot be legitimately asserted) is hardly germane. I would not accuse him of being a thief. Rather, I'd accuse him of being a fake — of pretending to have accomplished something he in fact did not accomplish. Likewise, the adulterator is not a thief, but a fraud who misrepresents what he sells. Both are to be held in contempt for they have violated the maxim that we should treat each person (as Kant put it) "never merely as a means to an end, but always at the same time as an end." Their assertions that they are not thieves are as relevant as a burglar's assertion that he is not a murderer.

Slight digression: Metaphor pervades all language. When one says that a copyright infringer "stole" from an author or publisher, one cannot mean this literally (no pun intended), for what was actually stolen? We can easily imagine an "infringement" that entails no physical violation whatsoever. IP has the impossible premise that an author or publisher owns a Platonic form of a work, which is embodied in, yet transcends, every physical instantiation of that work, even those owned by other people. In other words, you can buy a book, but you cannot buy *the* book. The anti-IP response is that abstractions cannot be owned.

The upshot is that a rejecter of IP may consistently take offense at the plagiarism or adulteration of his work and expose the fakes and scoundrels. "The same mechanisms that make copying easy make plagiarism very difficult," Karl Fogel writes in "The Surprising History of Copyright and the Promise of a Post-Copyright World."

I should add that customers may justly claim they are victims of fraud. On what grounds? On the same grounds that any fraud victim has: the buyers were tricked into entering transactions on terms other than those they would have agreed to. The remedy might come through a class-action suit, the award being a refund plus costs. (Context is crucial. Someone who buys a $10 Rolex on the streets of Manhattan probably cannot credibly claim that he thought he was buying a genuine Rolex.)

What I'm arguing for is a common-sense category of *noninvasive moral offenses*, wrongful acts that do not involve force. Since force plays no part, the remedies must not entail force (state-backed or otherwise) either. But forced-backed remedies are not the only — or even the best — remedies available.

Nonviolent responses, including boycotts, shunning, and gossip, can be highly effective.

Libertarians ought to beware of embracing such a narrow view of morality that only forceful invasions of persons and property are deserving of moral outrage and response. Think of all the cruel ways people can treat others without lifting a hand. Are we to remain silent in the face of such abuse?

The erroneous belief that only conduct for which a coercive response is appropriate may be condemned leads too easily to the corollary error that if some conduct is deserving of condemnation, it must somehow be a rights violation. The initiation of force is not the only bad thing in the world.

Future of Freedom Foundation, January 17, 2014

Chapter 21.
Patent Nonsense

Staunch advocates of private property might be expected to support "intellectual property rights" — patents and copyrights — but these days that expectation is more than likely to be wrong. IP has come in for a thrashing from libertarians, among others, in the last few years, and it may be all over but the funeral.

The issue can be viewed from three vantage points: moral, economic, and political. The pro-IP lobby tends to conflate the first two, moving back and forth between assertions about justice and economic incentives. Their case is something of a moving target, so let's break it down.

The moral claim is that an inventor has an exclusive, enforceable right to his useful, novel application of an idea, while an author or composer has such a right to his original work or expression. IP specialists insist that what is owned is not an idea per se, but it's hard to make sense of that assertion since an application or expression of an idea is itself an idea. IP really is about the ownership of ideas, and therein lies the problem.

Why should an inventor or author have an exclusive right, whether in perpetuity or for a finite period? Ayn Rand, the late novelist-philosopher who vigorously defended intellectual property, replied, "Patents and copyrights are the legal implementation of the base of all property rights: a man's right to the product of his mind. Every type of productive work involves a combination of mental and physical effort." Patent and copyright laws "protect the mind's contribution in its purest form." In this view, all property is ultimately intellectual property. As 19th-century free-market anarchist Lysander Spooner wrote, an individual's "right of property, in ideas, is intrinsically the same as, and stands on identically the same grounds with his right of property in material things ... no distinction of principle, exists between the two cases." (Not all 19th- and early 20th-century libertarians agreed — a notable counterexample being the individualist anarchist Benjamin Tucker, who thought patents were a pillar of plutocracy.)

But contrary to Rand and Spooner, there is a distinction between physical objects and ideas that is crucial to the property question. Two or more people cannot use the same pair of socks at the same time and in the same respect, but they can use the same idea — or if not the same idea, ideas with the same content. That tangible objects are scarce and finite accounts for the emergence of property rights in civilization. Considering the nature of human beings and the physical world they inhabit, if individuals are to flourish in society they need rules regarding thine and mine. But "ideal objects" are not bound by the same restrictions. Ideas can be multiplied infinitely and almost costlessly; they can be used nonrivalrously.

If I articulate an idea in front of other people, each now has his own "copy." Yet I retain mine. However the others use their copies, it is hard to see how they have committed an injustice.

Contrary to Rand, ideas, while inherent in purposeful human action, have no role in establishing ownership. If I own the inputs of productive effort, that suffices to establish that I own the output. If I build a model airplane out of wood and glue, I own it not because of any idea in my head, but because I owned the wood, the glue, and myself. On the other hand, if Howard Roark's evil twin trespasses on your land and, using your materials, builds the most original house ever imagined, he would not be the rightful owner. You would be, and — bad law notwithstanding — you would have the objective moral right to use the design.

In practical terms, when one acquires a copyright or a patent, what one really acquires is the power to ask the government to stop other people from doing harmless things with their own property. IP is thus inconsistent with the right to property.

An IP advocate might challenge the proposition that two or more people can use the "same" idea at the same time by noting that the originator's economic return from exploiting the idea will likely be smaller if unauthorized imitators are free to enter the market. That is true, but this confuses property with economic value. In traditional property-rights theory, one owns objects, not economic values. If someone's otherwise unobjectionable activities lower the market value of my property, my rights have not been violated.

This objection exposes what is at stake in IP: monopoly power granted by the state. In fact, patents originated as royal grants of privilege, while copyright originated in the power to censor. This in itself doesn't prove these practices clash with liberty, but their pedigrees are indeed tainted.

Property rights arose to grapple with natural scarcity; "intellectual property" rights were invented to create scarcity where it does not naturally exist.

Don't patents encourage innovation and therefore bestow incalculable benefits on all us? This crosses the boundary from justice to utilitarian considerations. The concern here is not with rewards to the innovator but with the good of society. What does the IP opponent say?

First, as libertarian legal theorist Stephan Kinsella points out, the implied cost-benefit analysis is a sham. Defenders tout IP's hypothesized benefits while presuming the costs are virtually zero. Ignored are the costs in innovation never ventured for fear of legal reprisal, in resources consumed during litigation, in talent diverted to protecting IP rather than producing useful goods, and so on.

"Anyone who argues that patents yield a net gain is obliged to estimate the total cost (including suppressed innovation) as well as the value of any innovation thereby stimulated. But IP proponents never provide these estimates," writes Kinsella, an IP lawyer himself. "They say we have more innovation at a low price. Yet virtually every empirical study I've seen on this matter is either inconclusive or finds a net cost and/or a suppression of innovation."

Second, IP proponents are guilty of doing a priori history. Real history undermines the utilitarian case for patents and copyright. In their book, *Against Intellectual Monopoly*, pro-market economists Michele Boldrin and David K. Levine show that IP impedes innovation. For example, James Watt's steam engine improved very little while his patents were in effect — he was too busy suing anyone he could for patent infringement. Only once the patents expired in 1800 did improvements in the steam engine accelerate.

The IP defender might counter that without patents there might not have been a steam engine at all. Boldrin and Levine's historical analysis shows this to be implausible. People invented things long before patents. Innovators have understood the advantages of being first to market even without the prospect of monopoly privilege. (Shakespeare created without copyright, as did Charles Dickens in the U.S. market.) The first company to put wheels on luggage, Travelpro, had no patent, and the idea was soon copied. But the company is still a player in the industry.

Perhaps wheeled luggage is a bad example because it is so simple. What about products that require more substantial research and development — software, perhaps? Of course, we are in the midst of a booming open-source software industry in which complex programs are given away and open to modification and commercial exploitation. (See the Linux operating system, for example.) Are the programmers altruists who have renounced worldly goods for the purity of their craft? Hardly. Their free programs establish their reputations, which in turn yield handsome returns for consulting and other services. There are more business models than the one that depends on state-bestowed monopoly.

No less a personage than Bill Gates has acknowledged what IP would have meant at the dawn of the PC age: "If people had understood how patents would be granted when most of today's ideas were invented, and had taken out patents, the industry would be at a complete standstill today."

Boldrin and Levine devote an entire chapter to the toughest nut, pharmaceuticals, which we supposedly would have to do without but for the protection of intellectual property. The high fixed cost of research, development, and testing, and the low marginal cost of production are said to preclude any significant innovation without the monopoly protection afforded by patents. Who would sink so much money into a product only to face copycat competitors with no development costs? Here IP is thought to be literally a matter of life and death.

Things are not what they seem. Write Boldrin and Levine:

> Historically, intellectual monopoly in pharmaceuticals has varied enormously over time and space. The summary story: the modern pharmaceutical industry developed faster in those countries where patents were fewer and weaker. … If patents were a necessary requirement for pharmaceutical innovation, as claimed by their supporters, the large historical and cross-country variations in the patent protection of medical products should have had a dramatic impact on national pharmaceutical industries. In particular, at least between 1850 and 1980, most drugs and medical products should have been invented and produced in the United States and the United Kingdom, and very little if anything produced in continental Europe. Further, countries such as Italy, Switzerland, and, to a lesser extent, Germany, should have been the poor, sick laggards of the pharmaceutical industry until recently. Instead, the opposite was true for longer than a century.

There is clear value in being first to market with a product, especially a drug. Moreover, copying successes is not the low-cost piece of cake it's assumed to be. For one thing, the imitator has to wait to see which product is worth copying, but all that time the originator will be reaping market-monopoly returns and securing his reputation for innovation and trustworthiness.

We mustn't overlook the wasteful costs of the current system, in particular the incentive to tweak existing drugs whose patent terms are nearing expiration in order to extend the monopoly. What other drugs might have been invented in that socially wasted time?

Underlying the IP defense is the faulty assumption that imitation produces little value when in fact it is critical to competitive markets and progress, most of which comes through incremental improvements to existing ideas rather than big dramatic breakthroughs. Copying combined with product differentiation equals rising living standards. Had imitation been forbidden earlier in human history, stagnation would have been mankind's lot. Attempts in that direction today concentrate economic power and increase the cost of living for the rest of us.

The IP regime helps entrenched interests prevent the competition made possible by the high-tech revolution. In the industrial age, producer goods were expensive and rigid, while workers were interchangeable. Think of Henry Ford's assembly line. Today in information-based industries, the reverse is true. The cost of producer goods — computers and software — is falling while the cost of human capital — know-how — is rising. In Ford's day, there was little danger that a worker would quit and open a rival automaker. But today the chief assets of many firms aren't on a factory floor but in the minds of the staff. The danger of competition from breakaway firms is omnipresent.

"In this environment," social theorist Kevin A. Carson writes,

> the only thing standing between the old information and media dinosaurs and their total collapse is their so-called intellectual property rights — at least to the extent they're still enforceable. Ownership of intellectual property becomes the new basis for the power of institutional hierarchies and the primary buttress for corporate boundaries. ... Without intellectual property, in any industry where the basic production equipment is widely affordable, and bottom-up networking renders management obsolete, it is likely that self-managed, cooperative production will replace the old managerial hierarchies.

Carson says the development of low-cost small-scale CNC — computer numerical control — machine tools promises to bring similar changes to more traditional manufacturing: "production as such has become far less capital-intensive over the past three decades, with the old mass-production core outsourcing increasing shares of total production to flexible manufacturing networks and job-shops."

The powers that be won't give up without a fight, which is why imposition of a strict IP regime is the centerpiece of every bilateral and multilateral "free trade" agreement with the developing world. Yet despite their best efforts, cheaper technology and the increasing unenforceability of IP may be ushering in a full-fledged economic revolution marked by smaller, flatter, even nonhierarchical worker-owned firms in a newly decentralized competitive marketplace. In other words, the postcapitalist world could look like a genuinely free market.

The American Conservative, January 18, 2012

Chapter 22.
Entrepreneurship and
Social Cooperation

We may laud the market order as an indispensable arena for large-scale social cooperation, but let's not forget that people cannot cooperate with one another if they don't know that the potential for mutually beneficial exchanges exists.

In the real world ignorance is pervasive, and we mustn't fall prey to the mainstream economists' unreal assumption that full knowledge about means, ends, and preferences is "just there" at the disposal of market participants or, presumably, an economic planner. We know this is not the case in real life. First, knowledge is dispersed throughout society, not concentrated in some repository. Second, much relevant knowledge is in the nature of knowing *how*, not knowing *that*; that is, it's tacit, unarticulated, and even inarticulable. Third, much relevant knowledge is *discovered serendipitously* in the course of acting, extinguishing ignorance that a person wasn't even aware he suffered. (This kind of ignorance is distinguished from rational ignorance, where one *chooses* to remain in the dark about some matter until one decides the benefits of the information exceed the cost of obtaining it.)

If all that economics notices is already *known* means, ends, and preferences, it misses the defining creative and entrepreneurial character of human action. Think about how you make real decisions, and you'll see the point.

F.A. Hayek, beginning in the 1930s, called economics to account on this matter. What's the point of thinking about an economy in equilibrium, with its assumption of complete knowledge about resources and preferences, Hayek asked, if no explanation is given of *how* an economy in theory could ever evolve to such a state. After all, we never have complete knowledge about resources and preferences. If economics as a discipline is to have any relevance for the real world, it must address the question of how a society rife with ignorance and incomplete knowledge can progress. Otherwise, economics is justly mocked in the joke about the economist who, stranded with nothing but canned food, "assumes a can opener."

Here's how Hayek indicted mainstream economics in his path-breaking essay "Economics and Knowledge" (1937):

The problem which we pretend to solve is how the spontaneous interaction of a number of people, each possessing only bits of knowledge, brings about a state of affairs in which prices correspond to costs, etc., and which could be brought about by deliberate direction only by somebody who possessed the combined knowledge of all those individuals. Experience shows us that something of this sort does happen, since the empirical observation that prices do tend to correspond to costs was the beginning of our science. But in our analysis, instead of showing what bits of information the different persons must possess in order to bring about that result, we fall in effect back on the assumption that everybody knows everything and so evade any real solution of the problem.

Hayek of course went on to develop this critique in great detail, showing that sound economic theory void of unrealistic assumptions — the Austrian theory of Carl Menger and Ludwig von Mises — can explain the process by which markets tend to equilibrate. (Of course, they can never reach equilibrium, because change is unceasing.) It's an explanation rooted in purposeful individual action and interaction (cooperation), that is, exchange in the market. In an imperfect world, prices contain potential clues (if interpreted correctly) to hither-to overlooked opportunities for coordination and exchanges that would leave people better off.

But how, exactly, does this come about? Enter the entrepreneur, whom Mises made central to our understanding of the market's operation. To fully appreciate the role of entrepreneurship, we turn to Israel Kirzner, one of Mises's doctoral students. It was Kirzner who elaborated on what the entrepreneur does to help individuals better realize their objectives; that is, to facilitate cooperation that would not have taken place otherwise for lack of the requisite knowledge. "Kirzner's contribution to market process theory provides the missing link to the neoclassical theory," Peter Boettke notes in his book *Living Economics*. (See my review in this volume.)

In chapter 6 of *Competition and Entrepreneurship*, Kirzner writes,

Now for an exchange transaction to be completed it is not sufficient merely that the conditions for exchange which prospectively will be mutually beneficial be present; it is necessary also that each participate *be aware* of his opportunity to gain through the exchange. ...

Where the conditions for exchange in fact exist but are not exploited owing to ignorance there now exists scope for profitable entrepreneurship. If A would be prepared to offer as much as twenty oranges for a quantity of B's apples, and B would be prepared to accept, in exchange for his apples, any number of oranges greater than ten, then (as long as A and B are each unaware of the opportunity presented by the attitude of the other) entrepreneurial profit can be secured by buying B's apples at a price (in oranges) greater than ten and then reselling them to A for a price less than twenty.

In effect, the entrepreneur enables A and B to cooperate in a way that otherwise would have eluded them — which is to say they would have been disappointed to learn that they missed out on an opportunity to exchange apples and oranges. The entrepreneur thus facilitates cooperation by being alert to potential price discrepancies, which are the inevitable result of our ignorance and error.

To simplify, we could say that he buys low and sells high when no one else notices that such arbitrage is possible. By so doing, he brings buyers and sellers together — while profiting from the price difference. Of course, in a competitive environment he simultaneously conveys knowledge about that difference, setting in motion a process that makes the "pure entrepreneurial profit" disappear. By exploiting the profit opportunity, he assures that it will be short-lived. But people are better off because of his alertness. That's what markets enable.

We now see that the battle cry "People before profits!" is based on a misunderstanding. In a *freed* market, profit is a sign of new social cooperation. Thus, a better battle cry would be "Exploit price discrepancies, not people!"

Future of Freedom Foundation, March 8, 2013

Chapter 23.
Mind Your Metaphors

Metaphor consists in giving a thing a name that belongs to something else. — Aristotle, *Poetics*

Language is metaphorical through and through. — Thomas Szasz, *Insanity: The Idea and Its Consequences*

In a lecture delivered at the London School of Economics in March 1933, F.A. Hayek, a 33-year-old economist recently appointed to the faculty (and a future Nobel laureate), lamented that the "oldest and most general result of the theory of social phenomena has never been given a title which would secure it an adequate and permanent place in our thinking."

Which part of the theory of social phenomena did Hayek have in mind? He explained in "The Trend in Economic Thinking," later published in the journal *Economica*:

> From the time of Hume and Adam Smith, the effect of every attempt to understand economic phenomena — that is to say, of every theoretical analysis — has been to show that, in large part, *the coordination of individual efforts in society is not the product of deliberate planning*, but has been brought about, and in many cases could only have been brought about, by means which nobody wanted or understood, and which in isolation might be regarded as some of the most objectionable features of the system. It showed that changes implied, and made necessary, by changes in our wishes, or in the available means, were brought about without anybody realising their necessity. In short, it showed that an immensely complicated mechanism existed, worked and solved problems, frequently by means which proved to be the only possible means by which the result could be accomplished, but which could not possibly be the result of deliberate regulation because nobody understood them. Even now, when we begin to understand their working, we discover again and again that necessary functions are discharged by *spontaneous institutions*. If we tried to run the system by deliberate regulation, we should have to invent such institutions, and yet at first we did not even understand them when we saw them. [Emphasis added.]

Today, thanks to Hayek, we call this phenomenon that had no title in 1933 "spontaneous order." For me, what's so fascinating about this lecture (for my awareness of which a hat tip is due to economist Daniel B. Klein and his book *Knowledge and Coordination: A Liberal Interpretation*) is what Hayek went on to say:

> The limitations of language make it almost impossible to state it without using misleading metaphorical words. The only intelligible form of explanation for what I am trying to state would be to say — as we say in German — that there is sense [*Sinn*] in the phenomena; that they perform a necessary function. But as soon as we take such phrases in a literal sense, they become untrue. It is an animistic, anthropomorphic interpretation of phenomena, the main characteristic of which is that they are not willed by any mind. And as soon as we recognise this, we tend to fall into an opposite error, which is, however, very similar in kind: we deny the existence of what these terms are intended to describe.

Talk about navigating between Scylla and Charybdis! On the one hand we have little choice but to talk about the complex-yet-*undesigned* social order as if it were a purposeful and problem-solving agent. But if we take the required metaphors literally, the phenomena won't really be understood. Indeed, if people believe that social order was designed, they might think it can be improved through a *redesign* — and we know where that leads. On the other hand, if we avoid metaphorical language, we will have a harder time explaining the coordination that only the market makes possible.

Hayek continued,

> It is, of course, supremely easy to ridicule Adam Smith's famous "invisible hand" — which leads man "to promote an end which was no part of his intention." But it is an error not very different from this anthropomorphism to assume that the existing economic system serves a definite function only in so far as its institutions have been deliberately willed by individuals. This is probably the *last* remnant of that primitive attitude which made us invest with a human mind everything that moved and changed in a way adapted to perpetuate itself or its kind. In the natural sciences, we have gradually ceased to do so and have learned that the interaction of different tendencies may produce what we call an order, without any mind of our own kind regulating it. But we still refuse to recognise that the spontaneous interplay of the actions of individuals may produce something which is not the deliberate object of their actions but an organism in which every part performs a necessary function for the continuance of the whole, without any human mind having devised it. In the words of an eminent Austrian economist Ludwig von Mises, we refuse to recognise that society is an organism and not an organisation and that, in a sense, we are part of a "higher" organised system which, without our knowledge, and long before we tried to understand it, solved problems the existence of which we did not even recognise, but which we should have had to solve in much the same way if we had tried to run it deliberately. [Emphasis added.]

Economic discussion is full of metaphors, some helpful, and some, in my view, detrimental to understanding. Hayek used two in these passages: *mechanism* and *organism*. The market is not literally a mechanism, and society is not literally an organism, but those terms can help us understand what goes on in markets and societies. We need metaphors to understand and to teach, but we must not treat them as if they were literal truths.

My least favorite metaphor in economics (Hayek preferred *catallactics*) concerns rationing and allocation. Defenders of the market will say, "The market rations (allocates) by price, which is superior to rationing (or allocating) by government." Many people — including some economists — may not fully realize this is a metaphor. The word "ration" implies a rational plan to distribute goods. But the market is the antithesis of this. It's where millions of people exchange goods (property) and services with one another in countless discrete transactions. As a result, resources and goods change hands, but no distribution or rationing takes place. (Thus, government cannot *re*distribute wealth.) I would banish the word *ration* from the economic conversation. It's a wild elephant of a metaphor and may take you where you don't want to go.

In fact, markets don't ration goods or solve problems because markets don't *do* anything. People do things. Hayek stressed this in *The Fatal Conceit* (1988):

> The extended order [society] … is formed into a concordant structure by its members' observance of similar rules of conduct in the pursuit of different individual purposes. The result of such diverse efforts under similar rules will indeed show a few characteristics resembling those of an individual organism possessing a brain or mind, or what such an organism deliberately arranges, but it is misleading to treat such a "society" animistically, or to personify it by ascribing to it a will, an intention, or a design.

Economist and Nobel laureate James M. Buchanan made the same point in "What Should Economists Do?" (1963):

> The market or market organization is not a means toward the accomplishment of anything. It is, instead, the institutional embodiment of the voluntary exchange processes that are entered into by individuals in their several capacities. … The network of relationships that emerges or evolves out of this trading process, the institutional framework, is called "the market." It is a setting, an arena, in which we, as economists, as theorists (as onlookers), observe men attempting to accomplish their own purposes, whatever those may be.

In my experience, the thinker who wrote most eloquently about the metaphor was Thomas Szasz, the psychiatrist who challenged the deepest premises (and practices) of psychiatry by showing they were built on a metaphor that was later literalized. Szasz spent his professional life trying to teach people — including medical students — the difference between literal illness (cancer, for example) and metaphorical illness (homesickness, for example). He acknowledged that he didn't have much success. "Medical students are educated persons," he wrote in *Insanity: The Idea and Its Consequences* (1987). "But most of them do not know what a metaphor is."

The same year as Hayek's lecture, author C.S. Lewis published *The Pilgrim's Regress*, in which he wrote, "We must use metaphors. The feelings and the imagination need that support. The great thing … is to keep the intellect free from them: to remember that they are metaphors."

To which Szasz replied: "Obviously, doing so cannot be easy, or else wise men would not have felt it necessary — in every age and every language — to keep reminding us of the duty of this remembrance."

Future of Freedom Foundation, February 15, 2013

Chapter 24.
Austrian Exploitation Theory

Eugen von Böhm-Bawerk (1851–1914), the second-generation giant of the Austrian school of economics, famously refuted the theory, most commonly associated with Marx, that the employer-employee relationship is intrinsically exploitative. Less well known is that Böhm-Bawerk had an exploitation theory of his own, which he expressed in his 1889 masterpiece, *Positive Theory of Interest*, volume two of his three-part *Capital and Interest*.

To recap Böhm-Bawerk's refutation, found in *History and Critique of Interest Theories* (volume one of *Capital and Interest*, 1884): Marx (and pre-Marxian thinkers) believed workers are routinely exploited by being paid less than what their products fetch in the market. That's because, as the *Stanford Encyclopedia of Philosophy* notes, for Marx labor is priced "in terms of the amount of socially necessary labour power required to produce it," that is, the products necessary just to keep the worker alive. (Marx derived this from the labor theory of value he inherited from Adam Smith and David Ricardo.) Yet a worker may produce *more* than that bare amount in a day. In that case the "surplus value" goes to the employer, or capitalist. Capitalists get away with this because they control the means of production. Workers, having been deprived of those means, have no choice but to offer themselves as laborers and take whatever they can get. The alternative is starvation. Thus they are ripe for exploitation.

In focusing on the exploitation question, Böhm-Bawerk took the legitimacy of the "distribution" of the means of production for granted, and of course he rejected the labor theory of value, or of price formation. (I can't discuss here the legitimate objection that historically governments arranged for the few, its ruling-class sponsors, to control the means of the production at the expense of the many, forcing them onto the labor market. To the extent that is true, the wage system is exploitative, but the culprit is the state and its sponsors, not the market.)

Böhm-Bawerk responded to the exploitation theorists that the difference between what a worker is paid and the market price of his product can be explained without resort to an exploitation theory. One component of the employer's profit is interest on the money he advances workers as wages while the product is being readied for sale. Making and marketing products take time. Typically, Böhm-Bawerk said, workers cannot afford to wait until the product is sold before they are paid. They want a check every week. But how can they be paid before their products have been sold? Their employers pay them out of money accumulated previously. Thus wages are in effect a loan, which like all loans is repaid with interest. This is so because of the phenomenon known as time preference: we value present goods more highly than future goods, meaning the value of present goods is discounted from their future value. Other things equal, X dollars available in the future are worth less than X dollars available today. Or to look at it from the other direction, if you want to use my X dollars today, requiring me to abstain from using them, I'll want to be paid more than X dollars when the loan comes due. The interest payment is my reward for abstention.

As Böhm-Bawerk wrote, "We have traced all kinds and methods of acquiring interest to one identical source — the increasing value of future goods as they ripen into present goods."

If Böhm-Bawerk is right, and wages are in effect a loan to be "repaid" when the product sells, then we shouldn't be surprised if the revenue from the sale is greater than wages paid (and other input costs). No exploitation need have occurred. ("Profit" has other components as well, including the entrepreneur's wages and pure profit from arbitrage, that is, from actualizing the hitherto overlooked potential value of undervalued resources.)

Böhm-Bawerk was writing pure theory as if he were saying, "In a free market here is what would happen." He was not implying that the theory would describe a particular time and place where the market was less than free. "[T]he essence of an institution is one thing, and the circumstances which may accidentally accompany it in its practical working out are another," he wrote.

In fact, Böhm-Bawerk noted, exploitation can occur when competition among employers for labor is suppressed, raising the employer's rate of interest to a level higher than it would have been under free competition and thus lowering wages. That, he said, was usury.

"It is undeniable," he wrote, "that, in this exchange of present commodities against future, the circumstances are of such a nature as to threaten the poor with exploitation of monopolists."

Böhm-Bawerk was merely applying the more general exploitation theory held by free-market thinkers at least back to Adam Smith: monopolies and oligopolies (suppressed competition) harm consumers and workers through higher prices and lower wages. For Smith monopoly was the result of government privilege. This largely has been the view of later Austrians, also. (Mises allowed for the theoretical possibility of a rare resource monopoly without government privilege.) However, Böhm-Bawerk did not explicitly attribute monopolistic exploitation to the state in this discussion.

"Every now and then," he wrote,

something will suspend the capitalists' competition, and then those unfortunates, whom fate has thrown on a local market ruled by monopoly, are delivered over to the discretion of the adversary. … [H]ence the low wages forcibly exploited from the workers — sometimes the workers of individual factories, sometimes of individual branches of production, sometimes — though happily not often, and only under peculiarly unfavourable circumstances — of whole nations. [Emphasis added.]

Böhm-Bawerk didn't say what that "something" might be. Maybe he meant private collusion; maybe he meant government protection from competition. He gives only this clue: "like every other human institution, interest is exposed to the danger of exaggeration, degeneration, abuse; and, perhaps, to a greater extent than most institutions." (Alas, thanks to government-corporate collusion, what he thought was rare has actually been the rule in so-called "capitalist" countries.)

He cautioned that

what we might stigmatise as "usury" does not consist in the obtaining of a gain out of the loan, or out of the buying of labour, but in the immoderate extent of that gain. … Some gain or profit on capital there would be if there were no compulsion on the poor, and no monopolising of property. … It is only the height of this gain where, in particular cases, it reaches an excess, that is open to criticism, and, of course, the very unequal conditions of wealth in our modern communities bring us unpleasantly near the danger of exploitation and of usurious rates of interest.

Böhm-Bawerk took pains to emphasize that he was not condemning interest per se: "But what is the conclusion from all this? Surely that, owing to accessory circumstances, interest may be associated with a usurious exploitation and with bad social conditions; not that, in its innermost essence, it is rotten."

Yet he asks, "What if these abuses are so inseparably connected with interest that they cannot be eradicated, or cannot be quite eradicated?" His response:

Even then it is by no means certain that the institution should be abolished. … Arrangements absolutely free from drawback are never allotted to us in human affairs. …

Instead of the absolute good, which is beyond reach, we must choose what, on the whole, is the relative best, where the balance, between attainable advantage and the drawbacks that must be taken into the bargain, is the most favourable possible for us.

In the end he didn't believe abuse was inseparably connected to interest: "There is no inherent blot in the essential nature of interest. Those, then, who demand its abolition may base their demand on certain considerations of expediency, but not, as the Socialists do at present, on the assertion that this kind of income is essentially unjustifiable."

Unanswered questions remain about Böhm-Bawerk's position, but we do know that the thinker who refuted Marx's exploitation theory had one of his own.

Future of Freedom Foundation, September 14, 2012

Chapter 25.
Can Mutually Beneficial Exchanges Be Exploitative?

When two people not under duress enter into an exchange for goods or labor services, both must be expecting to benefit or the exchange would not occur. In any such exchange there necessarily exists a double inequality of value. Each trader gives up something to obtain what he or she prefers. Moreover, we have at least *prima facie* grounds for pronouncing the exchange legitimate since no compulsion is apparent.

This principle of sound economics (and moral theory) is unexceptionable. Indeed, we couldn't make sense of buying and selling were this not the case. Going further, if such were not the case, we could not even say we had witnessed a *sale* (in the praxeological sense); it is something else, perhaps a game or a ritual. This is a matter of logic. The nature of a particular action is determined by the actors' intentions and understanding. What might look to an outsider like an exchange of money for goods or labor services may in fact be a move in a game in which the "money" isn't money at all but merely pieces of metal. This point was well recognized by, among others, three important Austrians (only the first two of which were economists): Ludwig von Mises, F.A. Hayek, and Ludwig Wittgenstein.

We must take care, however, in applying the free-exchange principle. Knowing that parties enter into an exchange freely (that is, without duress) may be a necessary condition for our pronouncing it legitimate, but it is not a sufficient condition.

For example, you enter a post office and buy a first-class stamp for 55 cents. May we conclude that you prefer the services the stamp will buy to whatever else you might have spent the 55 cents on? If you were not ordered into the post office at gunpoint, I should think so.

Is the transaction therefore legitimate? I should think not — not entirely. Why not? Because your alternatives were artificially constricted by a system supported by violence.

The post office of course is a protected government monopoly. No one may compete with the state in the delivery of first-class mail. (Lysander Spooner and others tried and were stopped.)

Apparently it isn't enough to know that parties to a transaction entered it without duress. There are other criteria that a transaction must satisfy for it to be pronounced entirely legitimate.

Someone might object that transactions with the post office are not really free because someone who wants to mail a first-class letter has no choice but the post office. True enough. Still, no one is forced to send a first-class letter. In that sense, no one is forced to do business with the U.S. Postal Service. One chooses to deal with the post office because *under the (unjust) circumstances* one *prefers* that option to its alternatives (which may only include not sending the letter at all). Thus one can still be said to be better off because of the transaction.

Extending this analysis to private companies with monopolistic government privileges should incite no controversy. If the U.S. government outlawed competition with Federal Express for overnight delivery, the situation would be essentially the same as with the post office. No one would be forced to do business with FedEx. Likewise, if the government erected explicit or implicit barriers to entry in an industry. Transactions with the protected oligopolistic firms might still be mutually beneficial.

Exchanges therefore with a coercive monopoly can be mutually beneficial, though we should be reluctant to call them legitimate. Any coercive monopolist will set its price low enough to produce the desired revenue. No sane monopolist would set a price so high that it would exceed consumers' subjective estimate of the utility of the product. What would be the point? But that means every sale entails a buyer who believes he or she is better off engaging in the transaction despite the lack of alternative sellers.

Thus even with a monopoly, subjective marginal utility plays a role in governing price. As Kevin Carson notes in "Rejoinder to Gregory" (Center for a Stateless Society), "Monopoly pricing targets the price to the highest amount the consumer is able to pay and still get enough utility to make the exchange worthwhile."

And yet we libertarians don't want to declare the exchanges fully legitimate, do we? The seller is a coercive monopoly or protected firm after all. (This does not necessarily mean the seller is morally culpable for the situation, though he or she may be.)

The great thing about competitive markets is not that marginal utility sets prices, but that rivalry (or potential rivalry) among sellers drives prices *below* the level that approximates many people's marginal utility. This produces a consumer surplus. (How far below is governed by producers' subjective opportunity costs, including workers' preference for leisure.) We all have bought things at a price below that which we were prepared to pay. Ralph Hood put it when discussing the falling price of electronic calculators: "Technology allowed the price to drop. Competition made it drop" ("No

Bad Thing at All," *The Freeman*). In a manner of speaking, competition *socializes* consumer surplus.

On the other hand, in the absence of competition a coercive monopolist is able to charge more than in a free market, capturing some of the surplus that would have gone to consumers. That's a form of exploitation via government privilege. (Eugen Böhm-Bawerk saw the possibility of similar exploitation of workers by employers sheltered from competition.)

The counterintuitive conclusion, as Carson puts it, is this: "A person can be better off from an exchange, and still be exploited."

We should keep this in mind the next time we're tempted to defend a state of affairs in the corporate state or, say, sweatshops in an authoritarian third-world country. Before we say, "The exchange was voluntary and therefore both mutually beneficial and legitimate," we should make sure the larger context satisfies libertarian standards of legitimacy by asking this empirical question: did government privilege play a significant role in creating the circumstances in which the exchange takes place?

Foundation for Economic Education, June 27, 2012

Chapter 26.
Value, Cost, Marginal Utility, and Böhm-Bawerk

Does cost of production determine price or does price determine cost of production? In the world of economic caricatures, the classical economists (Smith, Ricardo, et al.) took the former position, the Austrians the latter. Specifically, the Austrian view supposedly is that demand driven by marginal utility determines the price of consumer goods, which is then imputed backward to the factors of production.

But like all caricatures, the picture is an imperfect reflection of reality. Regarding the classicals, it will suffice to quote David Ricardo: "Corn is not high because a rent is paid [but] a rent is paid because corn is high." So whatever else he might have written on the subject, he was aware (at least with respect to land) that factors ultimately get their value from final consumer goods. We value the means because we value the end, not vice versa.

And then there is this quotation: "A thing cannot have value, if it is not a useful article. If it is not useful, then the labor it contains is also useless, does not count as labor and hence does not create value."

Karl Marx wrote that in *Capital*, volume one. I found the quote in a footnote in Austrian economist Eugen von Böhm-Bawerk's writings refuting Marx's exploitation theory. It should put to rest the claim that according to Marxian economics, a mud pie requiring one hour's labor should have the same market price as a cherry pie requiring the same amount of labor. Somebody has to find the darn thing useful first.

The question is: what forces govern value and price on the market (assuming a market freed of government-bestowed monopoly and other privilege)?

Böhm-Bawerk (1851–1914), one of the pioneers of Austrian economics, Ludwig von Mises's teacher, and an unrivaled authority on the theory of subjective marginal utility, had an answer that has received surprisingly little attention since he first offered it. I draw on his 1892 paper "Value, Cost, and Marginal Utility." (One economist who has given this matter a great deal of attention is George Reisman. Reisman received his Ph.D. under Ludwig von Mises and is the author of *Capitalism: A Treatise on Economics*, which, among other objectives, attempts the seemingly impossible task of integrating Misesian and Ricardian economics.)

We learn from Böhm-Bawerk that it is misleading to say that marginal utility always or usually governs the price and value of consumer goods directly, and in turn governs the prices of the factors used to produce those goods. "One is in fact correct, when one says that costs govern value," Böhm-Bawerk wrote.

That got my attention.

He elaborated in response to criticism that the marginal-utility school rejected the law of costs:

> We too recognize the necessity of "supplementing" the universal law of marginal utility by means of special provisions that relate to the value of goods reproducible at will and that the substance of these is precisely the *law of costs*. And we have accomplished this "supplementing" in full detail, both for the field of subjective value and for that of objective value and prices. [Emphasis added.]

But he quickly pointed out that this is not the end of the story:

> The law of costs is no fulcrum on the basis of which the rest of the explanation can be supported, without it itself needing a support. Rather, it stands in the middle of the course of explanation: it explains certain phenomena, but must itself be first further explained on the basis of certain other, more general phenomena. In order to provide the explanation with this necessary conclusion, we marginal-value theorists make an addition. Be it noted, not an addition which would run counter to or detract from the validity of the law of costs, but one which supports it and makes it intelligible. Namely, we supplement the theory of the value of products with a theory of the value of the means of production, or cost goods, whereby we reach the conclusion that this value itself is *ultimately once again grounded in marginal utility*. As far as we are concerned, therefore, costs apply not as an ultimate cause, but only as an intermediate cause of the value of products — though a very important and widespread one. [Emphasis added.]

So by a roundabout route, Böhm-Bawerk ends up where he started: at subjective marginal utility. Cost of production governs price. Marginal utility governs costs. How so?

An example will be helpful. Imagine the earbuds that came with your beloved iPod (in the days before it was embedded in a phone) have broken. Now an iPod with no earbuds is useless (for private listening). Therefore, other things equal, you would be willing to pay almost as much for replacement buds as you would for a new iPod. In other words, if the price of replacement earbuds were governed by the marginal utility of the iPod, that price would have to be only as far below the price of a new iPod as necessary to attract you. So if a new iPod costs $300, those replacement buds might cost, say, $200. (Obviously, if it was much more, you might as well buy a new iPod.)

But earbuds cost well under $10. How can that be? Here's the Böhm-Bawerkian explanation: in a competitive market for earbuds (even our government-hampered one), anyone who tried to charge, say, $200 for (basic) buds would invite competitors who would charge less. The competitive process would drive the price further and further below the price that the marginal utility of iPods would set.

But how low could the price go? To answer that, imagine that you wanted to go into earbud manufacturing. You would need to buy materials such as wire and plastic, and you would need to hire labor. To bid those factors away from their current uses, you would only need to outbid the manufactures of the *marginal* products made from those factors, that is, of alternative products least valued by consumers.

Thus the *marginal utility* of the *marginal products* governs the prices of those materials. And under competition, those prices — those costs of production — provide the lower limit toward which the price of above-marginal (supra-marginal) products will tend.

Böhm-Bawerk put it clearly:

> The value of all production-related goods together is determined by the utility of the "last," most easily dispensable product which is brought forth from the common production source, or, as we call it, by the marginal utility of the "marginal product." This provides the measure both for the value of the common cost good as well as, via this last, the value of all other products produced by means of same.

In the market, everything is interrelated with everything else. It's the original World Wide Web.

Reisman emphasizes that Böhm-Bawerk's theory in no way violates the theory of marginal utility: "Classical economics mistakenly held cost of production to be the ultimate explanation of the value and price of goods, which it is not, being in fact, as Böhm-Bawerk shows, merely *the vehicle for the transmission of marginal utility* from the value of marginal products to that of supra-marginal products." [Emphasis added.]

Friedrich von Wieser, the other second-generation giant of Austrian economics, agreed: "Between cost and utility there is no fundamental opposition. Utility remains the sole source of value, and the law of cost is the most usual form of the general law of value" (*Natural Value*, 1889).

We've been talking about price, but what about value? Just as cost of production governs price, so it governs value. This might seem un-Austrian, but remember the law of diminishing marginal utility: as the supply of a homogeneous good increases, other things equal, the value of any given unit falls and vice versa. Here's Böhm-Bawerk:

> The less the material and labor that the production of a jacket costs, the more jackets, of course, can one produce with the means of production available. Thus the more completely can the need for clothing be satisfied. And thus, other things being equal, the lower will be the marginal utility of a jacket. The technical conditions of production are, therefore, to be sure a cause of the value of goods lying further back, a "more ultimate" cause, than marginal utility.

Thus marginal value varies with supply, which is governed by the cost of materials and labor, which is governed by the marginal utility of the marginal product of those factors. (I realize I've left out the disutility of labor, or the value of leisure, another subjective element.)

Austrian economics never fails to fascinate.

Foundation for Economic, January 14, 2011

Chapter 27.
Capitalism, Corporatism,
and the Freed Market

When a front-running presidential contender, Mitt Romney in 2012, tells the country that thanks to incumbent President Barack Obama, "we are only inches away from ceasing to be a free market economy," one is left scratching one's head. How refreshing it is, then, to hear a prominent establishment economist — a Nobel laureate yet — tell it straight:

> The managerial state has assumed responsibility for looking after everything from the incomes of the middle class to the profitability of large corporations to industrial advancement. This system ... is ... an economic order that harks back to Bismarck in the late nineteenth century and Mussolini in the twentieth: corporatism.

In "Blaming Capitalism for Corporatism," Columbia University Professor Edmund S. Phelps, who won the 2006 Nobel Prize in economics, and his coauthor, Saifedean Ammous, assistant professor of economics at the Lebanese American University, held that the U.S. economy ceased to be a free market some time ago, yet the free market was blamed for the economic crisis of 2008. (An interesting question is whether the American economy was ever really free.)

Phelps and Ammous condemned corporatism unequivocally:

> In various ways, corporatism chokes off the dynamism that makes for engaging work, faster economic growth, and greater opportunity and inclusiveness. It maintains lethargic, wasteful, unproductive, and well-connected firms at the expense of dynamic newcomers and outsiders, and favors declared goals such as industrialization, economic development, and national greatness over individuals' economic freedom and responsibility. Today, airlines, auto manufacturers, agricultural companies, media, investment banks, hedge funds, and much more has [sic] at some point been deemed too important to weather the free market on its own, receiving a helping hand from government in the name of the "public good."

It's great that their list includes the corporate state's declared goals. Too many people are willing to accept government-set goals (such as energy independence) so long as the "private sector" is induced to achieve them. Regardless of how the goals are achieved, if government sets them, that's corporatism, not the free market.

The cost of corporatism is high, and Phelps and Ammous provide a partial list:

> dysfunctional corporations that survive despite their gross inability to serve their customers; sclerotic economies with slow output growth, a dearth of engaging work, scant opportunities for young people; governments bankrupted by their efforts to palliate these problems; and increasing concentration of wealth in the hands of those connected enough to be on the right side of the corporatist deal.

Again, kudos to them for noting the increasing concentration of wealth. The corporate state, after all, is a form of exploitation, the victims of which are workers and consumers, who would have been better off (absolutely and comparatively) without anticompetitive privileges for the well-connected and without government-induced recessions.

The authors are optimistic that time will work against the corporate state. Young people coming of age in the internet's decentralized and wide-open market of ideas and merchandise can't be expected to show enthusiasm for a system that protects entrenched corporations from the forces of competition. Moreover "the legitimacy of corporatism is eroding along with the fiscal health of governments that have relied on it. If politicians cannot repeal corporatism, it will bury itself in debt and default."

My main beef with Phelps and Ammous's essay is their use of capitalism to name the economic system that corporatism corrupted. Like many others, they believe that word "used to mean" the free market. To be sure, it was used that way starting in the mid-20th century. But there was an older usage (of *capitalist* specifically), coined by free-market liberals like Thomas Hodgskin who predated Marx, associating it with government privileges for the capital-owning class. That undertone has never left.

It's tempting to dismiss this as mere semantics. Yet we are trying to communicate, aren't we? Libertarian theorist Roderick Long, however, shows that more than semantics is involved. For Long, *capitalism* is what Ayn Rand called an anti-concept, a term that confuses rather than enlightens. One kind of anti-concept is the package deal, (in his words) "referring to any term whose meaning conceals an implicit presupposition that certain things go together that in actuality do not."

As a thought experiment Long asks us to consider his coinage of *zaxlebax*, which he defines as "a metallic sphere, like the Washington Monument." Obviously this is incoherent. Nevertheless, says Long:

Some linguistic subgroup might start using the term "zaxlebax" as though it just meant "metallic sphere," or as though it just meant "something of the same kind as the Washington Monument." And that's fine. But my definition incorporates both, and thus conceals the false assumption that the Washington Monument is a metallic sphere; any attempt to use the term "zaxlebax," meaning what I mean by it, involves the user in this false assumption.

Long sees capitalism in its common usage as similar:

By "capitalism" most people mean neither the free market *simpliciter* nor the prevailing neomercantilist system *simpliciter*. Rather, what most people mean by "capitalism" is this free-market system that currently prevails in the western world. In short, the term "capitalism" as generally used conceals an assumption that the prevailing system is a free market. And since the prevailing system is in fact one of government favoritism toward business, the ordinary use of the term carries with it the assumption that the free market is government favoritism toward business.

Similarly for socialism, Long writes. He thinks most people mean nothing more specific than "the opposite of capitalism":

And that, I suggest, is the function of these terms: to blur the distinction between the free market and neomercantilism. Such confusion prevails because it works to the advantage of the statist establishment: those who want to defend the free market can more easily be seduced into defending neomercantilism, and those who want to combat neomercantilism can more easily be seduced into combating the free market.

"Either way," Long concludes, "The state remains secure."

Foundation for Economic, January 14, 2011

Chapter 28.
Is Capitalism Something Good?

The question concerning the relationship (if any) between the free market and capitalism can be addressed at many levels. Let's start with history. The word capitalist was indeed first used disparagingly by opponents of "capitalism." But it is important to realize that among those opponents were *advocates of property rights and free markets*, such as Thomas Hodgskin and later Benjamin Tucker. Why?

The reason is this: In the periods regarded as classic capitalist eras, government intervention on behalf of capital was commonplace. Moreover, it was *integral* not incidental. In both England and the United States government intervened — on behalf of a privileged landed and then mercantile class — with land grants, subsidies, patents, and commercial regulations. In America this was true to various degrees at all levels of government, both before and after the Civil War.

Thus *capitalism* did not mean the free market, or laissez faire, back then. It's not that the system fell short of an ideal. To the people on the ground, and to historians looking back, this was the system that was intended. Thus pro-business interventionism has a far better claim to the term *capitalism* than any unrealized free-market system.

The mercantilist particulars of this era have been available to advocates of free markets for years. For example, Jonathan R.T. Hughes's *The Governmental Habit Redux* and Arthur A. Ekirch Jr.'s *The Decline of American Liberalism*, as well as Albert Jay Nock's earlier *Our Enemy The State*, have been in the libertarian canon for decades.

I will focus on the post-Civil War 19th century because the abomination known as chattel slavery in the first half of the century makes it too easy to undermine the claim that this was the free market's halcyon days. (In a *free* market, people can't own people.) Post-Civil War capitalism, however, is often seen as the heyday of free-market society. This is odd, to say the least. Libertarians embrace Randolph Bourne's maxim, "War is the health of the state." It so happens there was a war in the United States just past the midpoint of the century, so we should expect that it had the effects on the political economy that war always has: centralization, consolidation, and close government-business partnerships. That is exactly what happened.

A few quotations from Ekirch make this clear.

On all sides, in the North as well as in the South, the new nationalism that succeeded the Civil War marked a *further retreat* from liberalism. ... North and South the alliance of government and business had been much strengthened by the Civil War and its aftermath. Although business interests occasionally espoused a philosophy of laissez faire, basically they relied upon the favors and subsidies of the government. Especially in the North, Whiggery became the order of the day. [Emphasis added.]

Ekirch quoted Merle Curti, an earlier historian: "A supreme national government, controlled by Republicans friendly to industry and finance, could insure favors to corporations, protective tariffs, a centralized banking system, the redemption of government securities, and subsidies to railroads."

Ekirch again:

- "The nationalistic ideas of Alexander Hamilton and Henry Clay had been revived."
- "Beginning with the economic legislation of the war years, the Republican party gave the business interests of the North the protection and encouragement they desired."
- "Instead of the limited state desired by Jeffersonian believers in an agrarian society, the post-Civil War era was characterized by the passage of a stream of tariffs, taxes, and subsidies unprecedented in their volume and scope."
- "Also vital to big business was patent law, with its provisions granting exclusive rights to an inventor for seventeen years; this enabled companies to buy up and hoard patents, using such control to maintain a monopoly."

The era was a far cry from the free market.

At the semantic level, *capitalism* is an unfortunate word when applied to the free market. It suggests a privileged status for capital over other factors of production, which is not the case in a freed market. A capitalist is not a believer in capitalism but rather an owner of capital. One can be a socialist capitalist, that is, one who owns capital while favoring a system called socialism. All this was pointed out in *The Freeman* many years ago by historian Clarence Carson in "Capitalism: Yes and No," where he wrote:

In sum, capitalism gained its currency from Marx and others as a blunderbuss word, misnames what it claims to identify, and carries with it connotations which unfit it for precise use in discourse. Even so, there has been a considerable effort to reclaim the word for discourse by some of those who are convinced of the superiority of privately owned capital in the production, distribution, and exchange of goods. It is a dubious undertaking. For one thing, Marx loaded the word [as we've seen, it had been loaded by real free-market advocates], and when all that he put into it has been removed, only the shell remains. For another, linguistically, it does not stand for private property, free enterprise, and the free market.

It is false labeling to make it appear to do so. Capitalism means either a system in which capital holds sway, which is largely what Marx apparently meant, or an ideology to justify such a system.

Carson went on to point out the irony that "in view of Marx and socialist doctrine generally, capitalism is most rampant in Communist countries. It is there that the most extreme measures are taken to accumulate capital."

Finally, at the rhetorical level, we should appreciate how powerful the word *capitalism* is in its capacity to miscommunicate. Since free-market advocates are trying to persuade, this should be troubling. In "Caribbean Communism versus Capitalism," the left-leaning journalist Stephen Kinzer compared socialist Cuba to what he described as its "capitalist" Caribbean neighbors. Who? Haiti, Guatemala, the Dominican Republic, Honduras, among others! For Kinzer a capitalist country apparently is simply one that has not declared Marxism its official ideology or one that has de jure private ownership of the means of production no matter how much of a plutocracy it is. On the other side of the spectrum we find business commentators Lawrence Kudlow, Ben Stein, and others regularly condemning policies such as Barack Obama's for "undermining our capitalist system." That implies we have a capitalist system today.

If *capitalism* designates what we have today, we should flee from it as we flee for the exits when we hear a fire alarm. I'll take the free market.

Foundation for Economic Education, April 16, 2010

Chapter 29.
No Laissez Faire There

Friends of the free market tend to see the Gilded Age, roughly 1870–1890, as the closest thing in history to a laissez-faire economy. In *some* respects that is true — but it's not saying much because the bar is so low. I'd rather we didn't mark on a curve. The period could be closest to laissez faire without being terribly close. (In important respects, including the legal status of blacks, women, and others, the period compares rather poorly with our time.)

It would be surprising if the Gilded Age had been marked by genuinely free markets for the simple reason that it followed a major war. War, Randolph Bourne wrote, is the health of the state. He meant this in a spiritual sense. In war people who were previously busy with their own individual and community lives suddenly develop a new-found awe for the state and the nation it claims to embody. State-worship doesn't go away with the war's end. Rather a permanent change occurs in the people's psyche. Robert Higgs's analysis in *Crisis and Leviathan* adds a material dimension to Bourne's theme. Not only does government gain new prestige in war, it also gains new powers, few of which are relinquished when the war ends.

Thus we would expect that the economy following the American Civil War to be profoundly shaped by the war. For one thing, individuals made fortunes by selling goods and services to the government and by handling its debt. Influential business figures cultivated close relationships with leading politicians and bureaucrats — if they didn't have them already. Government needed to buy all sorts of things and to borrow money. Who was it going to call? War is lucrative even without letter-of-the-law corruption.

The administration of Abraham Lincoln finally gave America the Alexander Hamilton-Henry Clay program: a national bank, railroad subsidies and land grants, high tariffs, excise taxes, and other interventions. It was a rent-seeker's delight. As Richard Kaufman wrote in *The War Profiteers*,

> The most important of the nineteenth-century American capitalists acquired their first great fortunes during the war. J.P. Morgan, Philip Armour, Clement Studebaker, John Wanamaker, Cornelius Vanderbilt, and the du Ponts had all been government contractors. Andrew Carnegie got rich speculating in bridge and rail construction while assistant to the Assistant Secretary of War in charge of military transport.

This wouldn't seem to present ideal conditions for the postwar emergence of a free market. Too many people had a taste of power, privilege, and fortune, not to mention the inside track with federal and state officials and they were unlikely to give up those benefits voluntarily. The eradication of evil — chattel slavery — came with a good deal of pro-business economic intervention (corporatism). The result was the forced, conscious creation of a *national* economy according to a politically worked-out blueprint rather than spontaneous market evolution. (Benjamin Tucker's identification of four state sources of monopoly — patents, tariffs, money, and land — is relevant here.)

The Gilded Age of course has been criticized by opponents of the free market — corporatism and the free market have been sloppily and even intentionally conflated — but what's often unappreciated is that writers *sympathetic* to the free market have disparaged the Gilded Age as broadly illiberal and contrary to the spirit of free enterprise. Where many libertarians see laissez faire, these writers saw corruption and privilege distorting commerce. I'll cite two examples here: Arthur A. Ekirch Jr. and George C. Roche III.

Ekirch was a distinguished professional historian and academic whose book *The Decline of American Liberalism* still merits close attention. (*Liberal* for Ekirch meant free markets, decentralized power, and individual liberty.) Ekirch observed that "later, in the postwar period, it would be forgotten that many of the national problems associated with the rise of big business and monopoly had their origins in this earlier era of expansion and consolidation during the Civil War." He quoted the 1876 liberal Democratic president candidate, Samuel Tilden, who said:

> The demoralization of war — a spirit of gambling adventure, engendered by false systems of public finance; a grasping centralism, absorbing all functions from the local authorities, and assuming to control the industries of individuals by largesses to favored classes from the public treasury of moneys wrung from the body of the people by taxation — were then, as now, characteristics of the period. ... The classes who desire pecuniary profit from existing governmental abuses have become numerous and powerful beyond any example in our country. ... For the first time in our national history such classes have become powerful enough to aspire to be in America the ruling classes, as they have been and are in the corrupt societies of the Old World.

Just a bit more from Ekirch:

> Beginning with the economic legislation of the war years, the Republican party gave the business interests of the North the protection and encouragement they desired. ...

Instead of the limited state desired by Jeffersonian believers in an agrarian society, the post-Civil War era was characterized by the passage of a stream of tariffs, taxes, and subsidies unprecedented in their volume and scope. ...

Also vital to big business was patent law, with its provisions granting exclusive rights to an inventor for seventeen years; this enabled companies to buy up and hoard patents, using such control to maintain a monopoly.

Roche, who was the president of Hillsdale College for many years, the author of *Frederic Bastiat: A Man Alone*, and a staff member of the pro-free-market Foundation for Economic Education, in 1974 published *The Bewildered Society*, which contains a scathing portrayal of the Gilded Age. Here are a few choice quotations:

The businessmen of the nineteenth century *are* to be blamed for courting government to gain special privilege. ... The late nineteenth century was an era conspicuously dominated by the assumption that government could be used to achieve various special interest projects, whether it was building a railroad or the development of an "infant industry." ...

Corruption soon followed the new American acceptance of highly centralized political power as a problem-solving device. The process quite clearly began with the American Civil War. ... It is true that a time of tremendous building did occur in industry, communication, and transportation across our American continent following the Civil War. But it is also true that the era brought with it the spoilsmen in politics and the exploiters in economic life who were quite willing to work hand in glove in taking the American people for a ride. Boss Tweed and Jim Fisk were all too symbolic of their era. ...

Never before in American life had the temptation for corruption been so great. Following the Civil War, politicians found themselves dealing in land grants, tariffs, mail contracts, subsidies, mining claims, pensions. The power of taxation gave them power to protect or destroy individual businesses. ...

The corporation is now and has always been derived entirely from power granted by the state, power directly dependent upon continued enforcement of laws providing it with its special privileges and immunity. ...

The interpretation of American history which views the latest nineteenth-century businessman as a free enterpriser, while describing government activity as an attempt to restrain *laissez-faire*, is simply not borne out by the facts.

You get the idea. Similar views were expressed six decades earlier by laissez-faire advocate William Graham Sumner, a pioneering sociologist at Yale University.

It would behoove free-market advocates not to view this period of corporatist privilege with nostalgia — doing so undermines their cause. This doesn't mean that government-business control over economic activity was total. There were spaces for genuine competitive market activity and entrepreneurship, which is why the period saw dramatic economic growth and rising living standards. It's also why big business helped usher in the Progressive-era regulatory "reforms," as documented by Gabriel Kolko in *The Triumph of Conservatism*.

Foundation for Economic Education, May 6, 2011

Chapter 30.
Forgotten Critic of Corporatism

In 1888, at the height of the Gilded Age, a rather prominent American said some startling things. First he observed:

> Our cities are the abiding places of wealth and luxury; our manufactories yield fortunes never dreamed of by the fathers of the Republic; our business men are madly striving in the race for riches, and immense aggregations of capital outrun the imagination in the magnitude of their undertakings.

But this did not mean all was well with America. The speaker went on:

> We view with pride and satisfaction this bright picture of our country's growth and prosperity, while only a closer scrutiny develops a somber shading. Upon more careful inspection we find the wealth and luxury of our cities mingled with poverty and wretchedness and unremunerative toil.

Has this man forgotten, as many people do, that in market-based societies the growth of wealth, while inevitably uneven, is over time steady and general? That's not relevant to what he has in mind: he wishes to assign blame for the poverty he observed:

> We discover that the fortunes realized by our manufacturers are no longer solely the reward of sturdy industry and enlightened foresight, but that they result from the discriminating favor of the Government and are largely built upon undue exactions from the masses of our people. The gulf between employers and the employed is constantly widening, and classes are rapidly forming, one comprising the very rich and powerful, while in another are found the toiling poor.

> As we view the achievements of aggregated capital, we discover the existence of trusts, combinations, and monopolies, while the citizen is struggling far in the rear or is trampled to death beneath an iron heel. Corporations, which should be the carefully restrained creatures of the law and the servants of the people, are fast becoming the people's masters.

Rewards unrelated to effort! Undue exactions from the masses! Widening gulf between employers and employed! Rapidly forming classes! Rich and powerful versus the toiling poor!

Where have we heard this before?

But this man has more to say:

> Under the ... laws ... the Government permits many millions more to be added to the cost of the living of our people and to be taken from our consumers, which unreasonably swell the profits of a small but powerful minority. ...

> The Government, under pretext of an exercise of its taxing power, enters gratuitously into partnership with these favorites, to their advantage and to the injury of a vast majority of our people.

> This is not equality before the law.

And he's not finished. The speaker calls for reform, which he expects would have the support "of all who believe that the contented competence and comfort of many accord better with the spirit of our institutions than colossal fortunes unfairly gathered in the hands of a few."

Who is this man? Progressive politician William Jennings Bryan? Socialist Party presidential candidate and union leader Eugene V. Debs?

It is neither of them.

Casting a wider net, perhaps it is the anarchist and "free-market socialist" writer and editor Benjamin Tucker?

Again, no.

It is Grover Cleveland, the 22nd and 24th president of the United States. The occasion was his December 1888 State of the Union address, delivered a month after losing his reelection bid in the electoral college (but not in the popular vote) to Benjamin Harrison. (There is high irony here considering that Cleveland had a long and close relationship with the House of Morgan, the center of American corporate statism.)

The source of corporate privilege that raised Cleveland's ire was the tariff, one of Tucker's despised "four monopolies." (Back in the day, it was said, "The tariff is the mother of trusts.") As Cleveland put it,

> It can not be denied that the selfish and private interests which are so persistently heard when efforts are made to deal in a just and comprehensive manner with our tariff laws are related to, if they are not responsible for, the sentiment largely prevailing among the people that the General Government is the fountain of individual and private aid.

Then, astoundingly, he added:

Communism is a hateful thing and a menace to peace and organized government; but the *communism of combined wealth and capital*, the outgrowth of overweening cupidity and selfishness, which insidiously undermines the justice and integrity of free institutions, is not less dangerous than the communism of oppressed poverty and toil, which, exasperated by injustice and discontent, attacks with wild disorder the citadel of rule. [Emphasis added.]

Note what Cleveland is saying: The impetus for communism is not the masses' or intellectuals' envy of wealth earned through achievement in the market, but rather honest people's frustration at being exploited through the collusion of capital and state, which Cleveland also labels a form of "communism." In another place he refers to the "communism of pelf."

Thus, judging by Cleveland's address, America in the Gilded Age was no era of laissez faire characterized by rugged entrepreneurship. Rather, it was a neomercantilist *corporate state*, where government — as only government can — empowered privileged business interests to make fortunes at the expense of regular working and consuming Americans. Cleveland, in this speech at least, echoed the pro-market "anti-capitalist" critique voiced by contemporaries Lysander Spooner, Benjamin Tucker, and their compatriots for whom justice for worker-consumers was the very basis of their seminal libertarian movement.

Foundation for Economic Education, May 4, 2012

Chapter 31.
Class Struggle Rightly Conceived

Karl Marx is famous for drawing attention to the idea of class struggle. Yet remarkably in 1852, as historian David Hart recounts, Marx wrote, "As far as I am concerned, the credit for having discovered the existence and the conflict of classes in modern society does not belong to me. Bourgeois historians presented the historical development of this class struggle, and the economists showed its economic anatomy long before I did."

By bourgeois historians Marx meant laissez-faire liberals such as Charles Comte, Charles Dunoyer, and other early 19th-century French writers, who were also economists. According to Hart, "Marx plundered what he could from their work to assist him in this project, or … apparently misread them in his haste to move onto more important matters."

In light of Marx's words it's worth exploring the historical development of this class struggle as seen from the perspective of the classical liberals. At first this analysis of class may seem paradoxical. Free-market advocates have long emphasized that trade brings increasingly elaborate forms of social cooperation through the division of labor and free exchange. As the 20th-century economist Ludwig von Mises pointed out, the realization that specialization and trade allow unlimited mutual benefits induces people to put aside their differences and to cooperate in the productive process. How could the classical liberals of the early 19th century have been interested in class struggle?

Comte and Dunoyer, along with Augustin Thierry, whose publication, *Le Censeur Européen*, was a hotbed of radical free-market thought, were influenced by the important, but underappreciated, French free-market economist J.B. Say, whom economist and historian Murray Rothbard lauded as "brilliantly innovative and the superior of Adam Smith." The seeds of early classical-liberal class theory can be found in the second and subsequent editions of Say's *Treatise on Political Economy* (first published in 1803), which reflected his response to Napoleon's military spending and intervention in the French economy. For Say the government's power to tax the fruits of labor and to distribute largess and jobs is the source of class division and exploitation. As he wrote in another work, "The huge rewards and the advantages which are generally attached to public employment greatly excite ambition and cupidity. They create a violent struggle between those who possess positions and those who want them." Of course someone has to provide the largess.

Comte and Dunoyer took that seed and nurtured it into a full-blown class analysis. At issue was exactly who comprises the classes. Say's view that services provided in the marketplace are immaterial goods and that the entrepreneur, like the laborer, is a *producer* made an impression on Comte and Dunoyer. Hart writes, "A consequence of Say's view is that there were many productive contributors to the new industrialism, including factory owners, entrepreneurs, engineers and other technologists as well as those in the knowledge industry such as teachers, scientists and other 'savants' or intellectuals."

Getting the members of the classes straight is important if we are to accurately distinguish the exploiters from the exploited. Marx thought only members of the proletariat were creators of value, with owners of capital belonging to the exploiting class (and the state as its "executive committee"). He placed owners of producer goods, the means of production, among the exploiters because of his labor theory of value (inherited from Adam Smith and David Ricardo): since the value of goods was equivalent to the socially necessary labor required to produce them, the profit and interest collected by "capitalists" must be extracted from the workers' just rewards — hence their exploitation. (N.B.: For Marx this was true whether or not an owner of producer goods received favors from the government.) But if Marx's labor theory of value falls and if exchange is fully voluntary and void of state privilege, then no exploitation occurs. (Marx's exploitation theory was later systematically refuted by the Austrian economist Eugen von Böhm-Bawerk, who showed that some of what we call profit is in fact *interest* arising from employers' *advancing* wages to workers before their products sold.)

So the theorists whom Marx credited with teaching him class analysis placed in the productive class *all* who create value (in the eyes of consumers ultimately) through the transformation of resources and voluntary exchange. The capitalist (meaning in this context the owner of producer goods who is unconnected to the state) belongs in the industrious class along with workers. Marx didn't learn this part of the lesson.

Who are the exploiters? All who live off of the industrious class. Besides common torts, there is only one way to do that: state privilege financed at some point by taxation. The conclusions drawn from this by Comte and Dunoyer (and Thierry) is that there existed an "expanded class of 'industrials' (which included manual labourers and the above-mentioned entrepreneurs and savants) who struggled against others who wished to hinder their activity or live unproductively off it," Hart writes.

> The theorists of industrialism concluded from their theory of production
> that it was the state and the privileged classes allied to or making up the

state … which were essentially nonproductive. They also believed that throughout history there had been conflict between these two antagonistic classes which could only be brought to an end with the *radical separation* of peaceful and productive civil society from the inefficiencies and privileges of the state and its favourites. [Emphasis added.]

In this view political-economic history is the record of conflict between producers, no matter their station, and the parasitic and predatory political class, both inside and outside of government. Or to use terms of a later British subscriber to this view, John Bright, it was a clash between "tax-payers" and "tax-eaters."

Comte's and Dunoyer's work advanced Say's analysis in important respects, Hart notes.

Where Say regarded economics and politics as separate disciplines, with the latter having little effect on the former, the liberal class analysts saw that Say's own work had more radical implications. The science of political economy was "value laden" as we might say and implied quite specific policies on property, government intervention in the economy and individual liberty, something Say did not appreciate but which Dunoyer and Comte incorporated into their work.

As both Hart and historian Ralph Raico pointed out, Comte and Dunoyer also absorbed much from another great liberal, Benjamin Constant, who had penned important essays showing that an era of commerce had replaced the era of war and that the modern notion of liberty — centering on personal freedom and private property — is poles apart from the ancient notion of liberty — which exclusively meant participation in politics. As Hart puts it, "Dunoyer was interested in [Constant's] sentence '[t]he unique end of modern nations is peace (repos), and with peace comes comfort (aisance), and the source of comfort is industry,' which nicely summed up his own thoughts on the true aim of social organisation."

Liberal class analysis is also to be found in the writings of the Manchester peace and free-trade activists Bright and Richard Cobden and of Herbert Spencer, as Raico pointed out. He quoted Bright on the struggle against the Corn Laws (grain import tariffs): "I doubt that it can have any other character [than that of] … a war of classes. I believe this to be a movement of the commercial and industrial classes against the Lords and the great proprietors of the soil."

Raico emphasized that the Manchester school understood that war and big-power politics were key elements of the political class's quest for more unearned wealth. Nothing was better at quieting a population tired of taxes than a foreign threat. Similar ideas were present among other liberal thinkers, including Thomas Paine, John Taylor of Caroline, Albert Jay Nock, and Mises. I can't resist quoting Paine, from *The Rights of Man*:

War is the common harvest of all those who participate in the division and expenditure of public money, in all countries. It is the art of conquering at home; the object of it is an increase of revenue; and as revenue cannot be increased without taxes, a pretence must be made for expenditure. In reviewing the history of the English Government, its wars and its taxes, a bystander, not blinded by prejudice nor warped by interest, would declare that *taxes were not raised to carry on wars, but that wars were raised to carry on taxes.* [Emphasis added.]

In summary, the taxing power necessarily produces two classes: those who create wealth and those who take and/or receive it. The producers of wealth naturally want to keep it and use it for their own purposes. Those who wish to expropriate it look for clever ways to get it without unduly upsetting its creators. One way is to teach people that *they are* the state and that paying ever-more in taxes benefits themselves. The public schools have been particularly useful in that mission.

As long as the government is in the wealth-transfer business, class conflict will persist. Class in this sense is an important tool of political analysis. It's time that advocates of individual liberty and free markets reclaimed it from the Marxists.

Foundation for Economic Education, July 13, 2007

Chapter 32.
Seeing Like a Ruling Class

In the beginning ruling classes had a problem. It will be familiar to those acquainted with the Austrian critique of central economic planning: rulers could not know what they needed to know to do the job they wanted to do. Societies, even seemingly primitive ones, are complex networks held together by unarticulated — and largely inarticulable — know-how. That presents a formidable obstacle to centralized rule, which requires minimum resistance from the ruled if it is to endure.

Rulers, however, were not without recourse. If they couldn't *know* the society they aspired to rule, they could (try to) *shape* it into something they *could* know. To use the term James C. Scott uses in his book *Seeing Like a State*, they could strive to make society "legible" in order to make it controllable.

Scott came to understand this point when studying "why the state has always seemed to be the enemy of 'people who move around.'" He discovered that

> nomads and pastoralists (such as Berbers and Bedouins), hunter-gatherers, Gypsies, vagrants, homeless people, itinerants, runaway slaves, and serfs have always been a thorn in the side of states. Efforts to permanently settle these mobile peoples (sedentarization) seemed to be a perennial state project — perennial, in part, because it so seldom succeeded.

He adds:

> The more I examined these efforts at sedentarization, the more I came to see them as a state's attempt to make a society legible, to arrange the population in ways that simplified the classic state functions of taxation, conscription, and prevention of rebellion. ... I began to see legibility as a central problem in statecraft.

The problem facing rulers ran deep:

> The premodern state was, in many crucial respects, partially blind; it knew precious little about its subjects, their wealth, their landholdings and yields, their location, their very identity. It lacked anything like a detailed "map" of its terrain and its people. It lacked, for the most part, a measure,

116

a metric, that would allow it to "translate" what it knew into a common standard necessary for a synoptic view.

Apprehending this problem was like shining a light on phenomena hitherto obscured by shadow.

> Suddenly, processes as disparate as the creation of permanent last names, the standardization of weights and measures, the establishment of cadastral surveys and population registers, the invention of freehold tenure, the standardization of language and legal discourse, the design of cities, and the organization of transportation seemed comprehensible as attempts at legibility and simplification.

He compares such devices aimed at legibility and simplification, which he calls "high modernism," to scientific forestry, in which resource management is strictly determined by the need for revenue. His list will raise eyebrows among classical-liberal devotees of spontaneous social processes. Are we to believe that last names, freehold tenure, and standardization of weights, measures, language, and legal discourse were foisted on societies by rulers for their own convenience?

The story isn't quite so simple, but it is close. Scott acknowledges that the growth of commerce had a hand in the promotion of some of these devices. But his historical evidence shows that things we have tended to regard as the spontaneous products of liberal progress were in fact contrivances to benefit rulers. This is not to say these institutions are bad in themselves or that none of them would have evolved spontaneously. That seems unlikely. But it is reasonable to think they would have evolved *differently* in important respects had they not been driven primarily by a quest for social control. The contrasting processes — spontaneous order versus what F.A. Hayek called "constructivist rationalism" — would seem to guarantee this. It is unfortunate that those institutions were born in association with tyranny, prompting resistance from average people who felt imposed on by their rulers.

Let's pause to appreciate the depth of the rulers' problem. What we learn from Scott is similar to what we learn from Elinor Ostrom, the Nobel laureate who studied the innovative ways that people communally manage common-pool resources without government assistance. Left to their own devices, people jointly find ingenious methods of overcoming obstacles to the efficient management of land and other resources. This category of solutions demonstrates that the simple one-person/one-parcel model is not the only *private* alternative to state ownership of resources. Moreover the number of potential solutions is effectively limitless. Thus how a given community will grapple with a given situation is inherently unpredictable. People really are the creative, entrepreneurial beings acting in an open-ended world that Israel Kirzner, inspired by Ludwig von Mises, describes.

117

That's what made the rulers' job so tough as nation-states were formed, driving them to measures intended to simplify the societies they wished to control and, yes, also to establish national markets. Scott writes:

> Local practices of measurement and landholding were "illegible" to the state in their raw form. They exhibited a diversity and intricacy that reflected a great variety of purely local, not state, interests. That is to say, they could not be assimilated into an administrative grid without being either transformed or reduced to a convenient, if partly fictional, shorthand. ... Backed by state power through records, courts, and ultimately coercion, these state fictions transformed the reality they presumed to observe, although never so thoroughly as to precisely fit the grid. ... In place of a welter of incommensurable small communities, familiar to their inhabitants but mystifying to outsiders, there would rise a single national society perfectly legible from the center.

The great classical liberal Benjamin Constant (1767–1830), whom Scott quotes, understood this well:

> The conquerors of our days, peoples or princes, want their empire to possess a unified surface over which the superb eye of power can wander without encountering any inequality which hurts or limits its view. The same code of law, the same measures, the same rules, and if we could gradually get there, the same language; that is what is proclaimed as the perfection of the social organization. ... The great slogan of the day is uniformity.

Nowhere is the process more clear than in the case of land tenure. Indigenously evolved customary rights over land made taxation based on income and holdings nigh impossible. It was difficult (if possible at all) to know who owned what. Based on his research, Scott hypothesizes a village in which families have a complex of rights and responsibilities regarding cropland, grazing land, trees, and fallen fruit and tree limbs, with customs addressing all manner of situations, including what is to be done during shortages and famines. The customs, however, are not static. They "are better understood as a living, negotiated tissue of practices which are continually being adapted to new ecological and social circumstances — including, of course, power relations." (Scott has no wish to romanticize such arrangements: "They are usually riven with inequalities based on gender, status, and lineage.")

What's a ruler who wants to impose taxes on his realm to do? While the people within communities understand their customs, outsiders do not.

> The mind fairly boggles at the clauses, sub-clauses, and sub-sub-clauses that would be required to reduce these practices to a set of regulations that an administrator might understand, never mind enforce. ... [E]ven

if the practices could be codified, the resulting code would necessarily sacrifice much of their plasticity and subtle adaptability. The circumstances that might provoke a new adaptation are too numerous to foresee, let alone specify, in a regulatory code. That code would in effect freeze a living process.

And what of the *next* village, and the village after that?

Obviously, the ruling class cannot tolerate this "cacophony of local property regulations." An alternative needed to be found — and it was. "Indeed," Scott writes, "the very concept of the modern state presupposes a vastly simplified and uniform property regime that is legible and hence manipulable from the center."

The answer was "individual freehold tenure." Scott writes: "Modern freehold tenure is tenure that is mediated through the state and therefore readily decipherable only to those who have sufficient training and a grasp of the state statutes."

> [T]he complex tenure arrangements of customary practice are reduced to freehold, transferrable title. In an agrarian setting, the administrative landscape is blanketed with a uniform grid of homogeneous land, each parcel of which has a legal person as owner and hence taxpayer. How much easier it then becomes to assess such property and its owner on the basis of its acreage, its soil class, the crops it normally bears, and its assumed yield than to untangle the thicket of common property and mixed forms of tenure.

The device for accomplishing this was the cadastral map. "The cadastral map and property register are to the taxation of land as the maps and tables of the scientific forester were to the fiscal exploitation of the forest," Scott writes. "Just as the scientific forester needed an inventory of trees to realize the commercial potential of the forest, so the fiscal reformer needed a detailed inventory of landownership to realize the maximum, sustainable revenue yield."

For the map to be of use, the facts on the ground had to be made to conform to it. In other words, the lives of the inhabitants were to be disrupted to satisfy the ruler's appetite for revenue.

> The mode of production in such communities was simply incompatible with the assumption of individual freehold tenure implicit in a cadastral map. ... The state's case against communal forms of land tenure, however, was based on the correct observation that it was fiscally illegible and hence fiscally less productive. ... [T]he historical resolution has generally been for the state to impose a property system in line with its fiscal grid.

119

This is not to say all went as planned. Scott points out that people in the communities often continued to use their land as before, ignoring the scheme their rulers attempted to impose. But the rulers were undeterred. They proceeded *as though* their models reflected what was essential about reality — much as macroeconomists do today. Of course their tax decrees had unintended consequences. For example, the 18th-century French tax on doors and windows, which were used as proxies for determining the size of houses, encouraged the construction of homes with few doors and windows.

The people's ability to work around their rulers, however, was limited. Social life was disrupted, resources were extracted, and communities were prevented from further spontaneous development. How the world would have looked in the absence of ruling classes, one can only speculate.

Foundation for Economic Education, March 30, 2012

Chapter 33.
Financial Regulation
and the "Money Power"

In one of his essays criticizing inflationary free-silver proposals in the late 19th century, the great laissez-faire champion William Graham Sumner, a founder of sociology, wrote:

> We hear fierce denunciations of what is called the "money power." It is spoken of as mighty, demoniacal, dangerous, and schemes are proposed for mastering it which are futile and ridiculous, if it is what it is said to be. Every one of these schemes only opens chances for money-jobbers and financial wreckers to operate upon brokerages and differences while making legitimate finance hazardous and expensive, thereby adding to the cost of commercial operations. The parasites on the industrial system flourish whenever the system is complicated. Confusion, disorder, irregularity, uncertainty are the conditions of their growth. The surest means to kill them is to make the currency absolutely simple and absolutely sound. Is it not childish for simple, honest people to set up a currency system which is full of subtleties and mysteries, and then to suppose that they, and not the men of craft and guile, will get the profits of it?

It seems to me that this point is entirely applicable to the perennial debate over financial regulation. In the end, it will best serve the insiders, the "money power."

Let's begin by noting that there has been no shortage of financial regulation over the last 40 years. The much-faulted era of deregulation is a laughable myth. If anything can be said to have failed, it is the regulatory state. (Of course, much else also failed, including the Federal Reserve System and in the case of the Great Recession of 2008, housing policy.) The idea that we suffer from a shortage of regulation is wrong. Therefore, the idea that we need more regulation to prevent another debacle is worse than wrong.

Some advocates of regulation may agree that we don't need more regulation but rather better regulation. I agree. We do need *better* regulation. But what does that mean? Once we understand the nature of markets and bureaucracies, there's only one reasonable conclusion: better regulation means regulation by market forces. Free markets are not unregulated markets. Instead, they are severely regulated by competition and the threat of losses and bankruptcy. Anything the government does to weaken those forces simultaneously weakens the otherwise unforgiving discipline imposed on business firms (and their counterparties) — to the detriment of workers and consumers. Public well-being suffers.

Admittedly, this is a hard sell. Explaining how markets work when they are free of the government's easy money, favoritism, implicit guarantees, and other perverse incentives takes time and the listener's concentration. Denouncing markets, railing against greed (which of course never taints politicians), and calling for more government power make for good sound bites. In the internet and remote-controlled cable-TV era, patience is a scarce commodity. So advocates of liberty have barriers to overcome.

Of course government interference with free exchange (misleadingly called "regulation") is portrayed as necessary for the public good. A key to understanding why it is not is to grasp the inability of bureaucrats to know what they would need to know to do the job they promise to do. Markets — particularly financial markets — are too complex for government officials (or anyone else) to manage. No matter how much power they are given, they will not be able to see the future, spot "excessive risk," or anticipate how things might go wrong. But they can be counted on unwittingly to interfere with innovation that would yield public benefits. Any move toward central direction courts disaster. Decentralization and the discipline of competition are our only hope for economic security.

If government management of financial activity does not serve the public, whom does it serve? This is where Sumner's quote comes in. He understood that government regulation creates a complicated web of rules and procedures, and powerful bureaucracies, which in turn create rich opportunities for manipulation, advantage-seeking, and outright corruption. And who will be in the best position to game the system? The "money-jobbers and financial wreckers"; that is, the insiders, the "money power." They will be closest to the regulators. They alone will have the information and incentive needed to turn the vague and complex rules — which they will no doubt help to write — to their benefit. How many times must this happen before we learn?

As Sumner said, "The parasites on the industrial system flourish whenever the system is complicated. Confusion, disorder, irregularity, uncertainty are the conditions of their growth."

So, he asks, "Is it not childish for simple, honest people to set up a ... system which is full of subtleties and mysteries, and then to suppose that they, and not the men of craft and guile, will get the profits of it?"

The "money power" ought to be suspect in a corporatist economy such as ours, with its central bank, cartelizing regulations, and "too big to fail" guarantees. Sumner was onto something when he said the "surest means to kill [the money power] is to make the currency absolutely simple and absolutely sound." But we should go further: subject the financial system to the brisk winds of open competition, profit and loss, and bankruptcy.

We won't get that from government regulatory "reform." Rather, the money power will win again.

Foundation for Economic Education, September 28, 2012

Chapter 34.
How the Rich Rule

ERNEST HEMINGWAY: I am getting to know the rich.

MARY COLUM: I think you'll find the only difference between the rich and other people is that the rich have more money.

Irish literary critic Mary Colum was mistaken. Greater net worth is not the only way the rich differ from the rest of us — at least not in a corporatist economy. More important is influence and access to power, the ability to subordinate regular people to larger-than-human-scale organizations, political and corporate, beyond their control.

To be sure, money can buy that access, but only in certain institutional settings. In a society where state and economy were separate (assuming that's even conceptually possible), or better yet in a stateless society, wealth would not pose the sort of threat it poses in our corporatist (as opposed to a decentralized free-market) system.

Adam Smith famously wrote in *The Wealth of Nations* that "people of the same trade seldom meet together, even for merriment and diversion, but the conversation ends in a conspiracy against the public, or in some contrivance to raise prices." Much less famously, he continued: "It is impossible indeed to prevent such meetings, by any law which either could be executed, or would be consistent with liberty or justice. But though the law cannot hinder people of the same trade from sometimes assembling together, it ought to do nothing to facilitate such assemblies; much less to render them necessary."

The fact is, in the corporate state government indeed facilitates "conspiracies" against the public that could not otherwise take place. What's more, because of this facilitation, it is reasonable to think the disparity in incomes that naturally arises by virtue of differences among human beings is dramatically exaggerated. We can identify several sources of this unnatural wealth accumulation.

A primary source is America's financial system, which since 1914 has revolved around the government-sponsored central banking cartel, the Federal Reserve. To understand this, it must first be noted that in an advanced market economy with a well-developed division of labor, the capital market becomes the "locus for entrepreneurial decision-making," as

Walter E. Grinder and John Hagel III, writing within the perspective of the Austrian school of economics, put it in their 1977 paper, "Toward a Theory of State Capitalism: Ultimate Decision-Making and Class Structure" (*The Journal of Libertarian Studies*).

Grinder and Hagel, emphasizing the crucial role of entrepreneurship in discovering and disseminating knowledge and coordinating diverse production and consumption plans, write: "The evolution of market economies ... suggests that entrepreneurial activity may become increasingly concentrated within the capital market as the functional specialization of the economy becomes more pronounced."

That sounds ominous, but as long as the market is free of government interference, this "concentration" poses no threat. "None of this analysis should be construed as postulating an insidious process of monopolization of decision-making within the non-state market system," they write.

> Market factors [that is, free and open competition] preclude the possibility that entrepreneurial decision-making could ever be monopolized by financial institutions. ... The decision-making within the capital market operates within the severe constraints imposed by the competitive market process and these constraints ensure that the decision-making process contributes to the optimum allocation of economic resources within the system.

All bets are off, however, when government intervenes. Then the central role of the banking system in an advanced economy is not only magnified but transformed through its "insulation ... from the countervailing competitive pressures inherent in a free market." Only government can erect barriers to competitive entry and provide other advantages to special interests that are unattainable in the marketplace.

The original theory of class formulated by early 19th-century French classical liberal economists is relevant here. It was these laissez faire radicals who pointed out that two more or less rigid classes arise as soon as the state starts distributing the fruits of labor through taxation: taxpayers and tax-consumers. Rent-seeking is born.

It takes little imagination to see that wealthier individuals — many of whom, in Anglo-American history, first got that way through the enclosure of commons, land grants, and mercantilist subsidies — will have an advantage over others in maintaining control of the state apparatus. (Economic theorist Kevin A. Carson calls the continuing benefit of this initial advantage "the subsidy of history.") And indeed they have.

"It seems reasonable to assume that individuals [in the tax-consuming class] sharing objective interests will tend toward an emerging and at least hazy common 'class consciousness,'" Grinder and Hagel write. (Karl Marx acknowledged his debt to the French economists for his own, crucially different, class analysis.)

Unsurprisingly, in a money-based market economy the financial industry, with the central role already mentioned, will be of special interest to rulers and their associates in the "private" sector. "Historically, state intervention in the banking system has been one of the earliest forms of intervention in the market system," Grinder and Hagel write. They emphasize how this intervention plays a key role in changing a population's tacit ideology:

> In the U.S., this intervention initially involved sporadic measures, both at the federal and state level, which generated inflationary distortion in the money supply and cyclical disruptions of economic activity. The disruptions which accompanied the business cycle were a major factor in the transformation of the dominant ideology in the U.S. from a general adherence to laissez-faire doctrines to an ideology of political capitalism which viewed the state as a necessary instrument for the rationalization and stabilization of an inherently unstable economic order.

In short, financial intervention on behalf of well-heeled, well-connected groups begets recessions, depressions, and long-term unemployment, which in turn beget vulnerable working and middle classes which, ignorant of economics, are willing to accept more powerful government, which begets more intervention on behalf of the wealthy, and so on — a vicious circle indeed.

Fiat money, central banking, and deficit spending foster and reinforce plutocracy in a variety of ways. Government debt offers opportunities for speculation by insiders and gives rise to an industry founded on profitable trafficking in Treasury securities. That industry will have a profit interest in bigger government and chronic deficit spending.

Government debt makes inflation of the money supply an attractive policy for the state and its central bank — not to mention major parts of the financial system. In the United States, the Treasury borrows money by selling interest-bearing bonds. When the Federal Reserve System wants to expand the money supply to, say, juice the economy, it buys those bonds from banks and security dealers with money created out of thin air. Now the Fed is the bondholder, but by law it must remit most of the interest to the Treasury, thus giving the government a virtually interest-free loan. With its interest costs reduced in this way, the government is in a position to borrow and spend still more money — on militarism and war, for example — and the process can begin again. (These days the Fed has a new role as central allocator of credit to specific firms and industries, as well.)

Meanwhile the banking system has the newly created money, and therein lies another way in which the well-off gain advantage at the expense of the rest of us. Money inflation under the right conditions produces price inflation, as banks pyramid loans on top of fiat reserves. (This can be offset, as it largely is today, if the Fed pays banks to keep the new money in their interest-bearing Fed accounts rather than lending it out.)

But the Austrian school of economics has long stressed two overlooked aspects of inflation. First, the new money enters the economy at specific points, rather than being distributed evenly through the textbook "helicopter effect." Second, money is non-neutral.

Since Fed-created money reaches particular privileged interests before it filters through the economy, early recipients — banks, securities dealers, government contractors — have the benefit of increased purchasing power before prices rise. Most wage earners and people on fixed incomes, on the other hand, see higher prices before they receive higher nominal incomes or Social Security benefits. Pensioners without cost-of-living adjustments are out of luck.

The non-neutrality of money means that price inflation does not evenly raise the "general price level," leaving the real economy unchanged. Rather, inflation changes *relative prices* in response to the spending by the earlier recipients, skewing production toward those privileged beneficiaries. Considering how essential prices in a free market are to coordinating production and consumption, inflation clearly makes the economic system less efficient at serving the mass of consumers. Thus inflation, economist Murray Rothbard wrote, "changes the distribution of income and wealth."

Price inflation, of course, is notorious for favoring debtors over creditors because loans are repaid in money with less purchasing power. This at first benefits lower income people as well as other debtors, at least until credit card interest rates rise. But big businesses are also big borrowers — especially in this day of highly leveraged activities — so they too benefit in this way from inflation. Though banks as creditors lose out in this respect, big banks more than make up for it by selling government securities at a premium and by pyramiding loans on top of security dealers' deposits.

When people realize their purchasing power is falling because of the implicit inflation tax, they will want to undertake strategies to preserve their wealth. Who's in a better position to hire consultants to guide them through esoteric strategies, the wealthy or people of modest means?

The result is "financialization," in which financial markets and bankers play an ever larger role in people's lives. For example, the Fed's inflationary low-interest-rate policy makes the traditional savings account useless for preserving and increasing one's wealth. Where once a person of modest means could put his or her money into a liquid account at a local bank at about 5 percent interest compounded, today that account earns about 1 percent if not less while the consumer price index rises at about 2 percent. Savers thus are forced into less liquid certificates of deposit or less familiar money market mutual funds (which arose because in the inflationary 1970s government capped interest on savings accounts). Fed policy thus increases business for the financial industry.

Inflation is also the culprit in the business cycle, which is not a natural feature of the market economy. Fed policy aimed at lowering interest rates, a policy especially favored by capital-intensive businesses remote from the consumer-goods level, distorts the time structure of production. In a free market, low interest rates signal an increase in savings, that is, a shift from present to future consumption, and high rates do the reverse. Behold the coordinative function of the price system: deferred consumption lowers interest rates, making interest-rate-sensitive early stages of production — such as research and development, and extractive industries — more economical. Resources and labor may appropriately shift from consumer goods to producer goods.

But what if interest rates fall not because consumers' time preferences have changed but because the Fed created credit? Investors will be misled into thinking resources are newly available for early-stage and other interest-rate-sensitive production, so they will divert resources and labor to those sectors. But consumers still want to consume now. Since resources can't be put to both purposes, the situation can't last. Bust follows boom. Think of all those unemployed construction workers and "idle resources" that had been drawn to the housing industry in the early 2000s.

While some rich people may be hurt by the recession, they are far better positioned to hedge and recover than workers who are laid off from their jobs. Moreover, even after the recovery, the knowledge that the threat of recession looms can make the workforce more docile. The business cycle thus undermines workers' bargaining power, enabling bosses to keep more of the fruits of increased productivity.

Bottom line: inflation and the business cycle channel wealth from poorer to richer.

The financial system isn't the only way that the rich benefit at the expense of everyone else. The corporate elite have better access to the regulatory agencies and rule writers than the rest of us. (University of Chicago economist George Stigler dubbed this "regulatory capture.") Wealth also gives the elite a clearer path to politicians and candidates for office, who will be amenable to policies that make wealthy contributors happy, such as subsidies, bailouts, and other measures that socialize costs and privatize extra-market profits. Campaign finance "reform" doesn't change this, and even tax-funded campaigns would only drive the quid-pro-quo process underground.

Finally, a significant source of upward wealth distribution is intellectual property. By treating ideas and information as though they were objects to be owned, IP law encloses the intellectual commons and deprives the public of benefits that a competitive market would naturally socialize.

The conventional understanding of rich and poor, capitalism and socialism, is profoundly misleading. A corporatist, mixed economy institutionalizes financial privilege in ways that are overlooked in everyday political discourse — in part because of the ideological deformations created by the system itself. As Austrian-school macroeconomist Steven Horwitz put it, one need not be a Marxist to see that the state is indeed the executive committee of the ruling class.

The American Conservative, December 5, 2012

Chapter 35.
Libertarian Left

Ron Paul's 2008 presidential campaign introduced many people to the word "libertarian." Since Paul is a Republican, and Republicans, like libertarians, use the rhetoric of free markets and private enterprise, people naturally assume that libertarians are some kind of quirky offshoot of the American right wing. To be sure, some libertarian positions fit uneasily with mainstream conservatism — complete drug decriminalization, legal same-sex marriage, and the critique of the national-security state alienate many on the right from libertarianism.

But the dominant strain of libertarianism still seems at home on that side of the political spectrum. Paeans to property rights and free enterprise — the mainstream libertarian conviction that the American capitalist system, despite government intervention, fundamentally embodies those values — appear to justify that conclusion.

But then one runs across passages like this:

> Capitalism, arising as a new class society directly from the old class society of the Middle Ages, was founded on an act of robbery as massive as the earlier feudal conquest of the land. It has been sustained to the present by continual state intervention to protect its system of privilege without which its survival is unimaginable.

And this:

> [Building worker solidarity] means formal organisation, including unionization — but I'm not talking about the prevailing model of "business unions" ... but *real* unions, the old-fashioned kind, committed to the working *class* and not just union members, and interested in worker autonomy, not government patronage.

These passages — the first by independent scholar Kevin Carson, the second by Auburn University philosophy professor Roderick Long — read as though they come not from libertarians but from radical leftists, even Marxists. That conclusion would be only half wrong: these words were written by pro-free-market left-libertarians. (The preferred term for their — our — economic ideal is "freed market," coined by William Gillis.)

These authors — and a growing group of colleagues — see themselves as both libertarians and leftists. They are standard libertarians in that they believe in the moral legitimacy of private ownership and free exchange and oppose all government interference in personal and economic affairs — a groundless, pernicious dichotomy. Yet they are leftists in that they share traditional left-wing concerns, about exploitation and inequality, for example, that are largely ignored, if not dismissed, by other libertarians. Left-libertarians favor worker solidarity vis-à-vis bosses, support poor people's squatting on government or abandoned property, and prefer that corporate privileges be repealed *before* the regulatory restrictions on how those privileges may be exercised. They see Walmart as a symbol of corporate favoritism — supported by highway subsidies and eminent domain — view the fictive personhood of the limited-liability corporation with suspicion, and doubt that Third World sweatshops would be the "best alternative" in the absence of government manipulation.

Left-libertarians tend to eschew electoral politics, having little confidence in strategies that work through the government. They prefer to develop alternative institutions and methods of working around the state. The Alliance of the Libertarian Left encourages the formation of local activist and mutual-aid organizations, while its website promotes kindred groups and posts articles elaborating its philosophy. The new Center for a Stateless Society (C4SS) encourages left-libertarians to bring their analysis of current events to the general public through op-eds.

These laissez-faire left-libertarians are not to be confused with other varieties of left-wing libertarians, such as Noam Chomsky or Hillel Steiner, who each in his own way objects to individualist appropriation of unowned natural resources and the wealth inequality that freed markets can produce. The left-libertarians under consideration here have been called "market-oriented left-libertarians" or "market anarchists," though not everyone in this camp is an anarchist.

There are historical grounds for placing pro-market libertarianism on the left. In the first half of the 19th century, the laissez-faire liberal economist Frédéric Bastiat sat on the left side of the French National Assembly with other radical opponents of the *ancien régime*, including a variety of socialists. The right side was reserved for reactionary defenders of absolute monarchy and plutocracy. For a long time "left" signified radical, even revolutionary, opposition to political authority, fired by hope and optimism, while "right" signified sympathy for a status quo of privilege or a return to an authoritarian order. These terms applied even in the United States well into the 20th century and only began to change during the New Deal, which prompted regrettable alliances of convenience that carried over into the Cold War era and beyond.

At the risk of oversimplifying, there are two wellsprings of modern pro-market left-libertarianism: the theory of political economy formulated by Murray N. Rothbard and the philosophy known as "Mutualism" associated

131

with the pro-market anarchist Pierre-Joseph Proudhon — who sat with Bastiat on the left side of the assembly while arguing with him incessantly about economic theory — and the American individualist anarchist Benjamin R. Tucker.

Rothbard (1926–1995) was the leading theorist of radical Lockean libertarianism combined with Austrian economics, which demonstrates that free markets produce widespread prosperity, social cooperation, and economic coordination without monopoly, depression, or inflation — evils whose roots are to be found in government intervention. Rothbard, who called himself an "anarcho-capitalist," first saw himself as a man of the "Old Right," the loose collection of opponents of the New Deal and American Empire epitomized by Sen. Robert Taft, journalist John T. Flynn, and more radically, Albert Jay Nock. Yet Rothbard understood libertarianism's left-wing roots.

In his 1965 classic and sweeping essay "Left and Right: The Prospects for Liberty," Rothbard identified "liberalism" — what is today called libertarianism — with the left as "the party of hope, of radicalism, of liberty, of the Industrial Revolution, of progress, of humanity." The other great ideology to emerge after the French revolution "was conservatism, the party of reaction, the party that longed to restore the hierarchy, statism, theocracy, serfdom, and class exploitation of the Old Order."

When the New Left arose in the 1960s to oppose the Vietnam War, the military-industrial complex, and bureaucratic centralization, Rothbard easily made common cause with it. "The Left has changed greatly, and it is incumbent upon everyone interested in ideology to understand the change. … The change marks a striking and splendid infusion of libertarianism into the ranks of the Left," he wrote in "Liberty and the New Left." His left-radicalism was clear in his interest in decentralization and participatory democracy, pro-peasant land reform in the feudal Third World, "black power," and worker "homesteading" of American corporations whose profits came mainly from government contracts.

But with the fading of the New Left, Rothbard deemphasized these positions and moved strategically toward right-wing paleoconservatism. His left-libertarian colleague, the former Goldwater speechwriter Karl Hess (1923–1994), kept the torch burning. In *Dear America* Hess wrote, "On the far right, law and order means the law of the ruler and the order that serves the interest of that ruler, usually the orderliness of drone workers, submissive students, elders either totally cowed into loyalty or totally indoctrinated and trained into that loyalty," while the left "has been the side of politics and economics that opposes the concentration of power and wealth and, instead, advocates and works toward the distribution of power into the maximum number of hands."

Benjamin Tucker (1854–1939) was the editor of *Liberty*, the leading publication of American individualist anarchism. As a Mutualist, Tucker rigorously embraced free markets and voluntary exchange void of all government privilege and regulation. Indeed, he called himself a "consistent Manchester man," a reference to the economic philosophy of the English free-traders Richard Cobden and John Bright. Tucker disdained defenders of the American status quo who, while favoring free competition among workers for jobs, supported capitalist suppression of competition among employers through government's "four monopolies": land, the tariff, patents, and money.

"What causes the inequitable distribution of wealth?" Tucker asked in 1892.

> It is not competition, but monopoly, that deprives labor of its product. … Destroy the banking monopoly, establish freedom in finance, and down will go interest on money through the beneficent influence of competition. Capital will be set free, business will flourish, new enterprises will start, labor will be in demand, and gradually the wages of labor will rise to a level with its product.

The Rothbardians and Mutualists have some disagreements over land ownership and theories of value, but their intellectual cross-pollination has brought the groups closer philosophically. What unites them, and distinguishes them from other market libertarians, is their embrace of traditional left-wing concerns, including the consequences of plutocratic corporate power for workers and other vulnerable groups. But left-libertarians differ from other leftists in identifying the culprit as the historical partnership between government and business — whether called the corporate state, state capitalism, or just plain capitalism — and in seeing the solution in radical laissez faire, the total separation of economy and state.

Thus behind the political-economic philosophy is a view of history that separates left-libertarians from both ordinary leftists and ordinary libertarians. The common varieties of both philosophies agree that essentially free markets reigned in England from the time of the Industrial Revolution, though they evaluate the outcome very differently. But left-libertarians are revisionists, insisting that the era of near laissez faire is a myth. Rather than a radical freeing of economic affairs, England saw the ruling elite rig the social system on behalf of propertied class interests. (Class analysis originated with French free-market economists predating Marx.)

Through enclosure, peasants were dispossessed of land they and their kin had worked for generations and were forcibly turned into rent-paying tenants or wage-earners in the new factories with their rights to organize and even to move restricted by laws of settlement, poor laws, combination laws, and more. In the American colonies and early republic, the system was similarly rigged through land grants and speculation (for and by railroads, for example), voting restrictions, tariffs, patents, and control of money and banking.

In other words, the twilight of feudalism and the dawn of capitalism did not find everyone poised at the starting line as equals — far from it. As the pro-market sociologist Franz Oppenheimer, who developed the conquest theory of the state, wrote in his book *The State*, it was not superior talent, ambition, thrift, or even luck that separated the property-holding minority from the propertyless proletarian majority — but legal plunder, to borrow Bastiat's famous phrase.

Here is something Marx got right. Indeed, Kevin Carson seconds Marx's "eloquent passage": "these new freedmen became sellers of themselves only after they had been robbed of all their own means of production, and of all the guarantees afforded by the old feudal arrangements. And the history of this, their expropriation, is written in the annals of mankind in letters of blood and fire."

This system of privilege and exploitation has had long-distorting effects that continue to afflict most people to this day, while benefiting the ruling elite; Carson calls it "the subsidy of history." This is not to deny that living standards have generally risen in market-oriented mixed economies but rather to point out that living standards for average workers would be even higher — not to mention less debt-based — and wealth disparities less pronounced in a freed market.

The "free-market anti-capitalism" of left-libertarianism is no contradiction, nor is it a recent development. It permeated Tucker's *Liberty*, and the identification of worker exploitation harked back at least to Thomas Hodgskin (1787–1869), a free-market radical who was one of the first to apply the term "capitalist" disparagingly to the beneficiaries of government favors bestowed on capital at the expense of labor. In the 19th and early 20th centuries, "socialism" did not exclusively mean collective or government ownership of the means or production but was an umbrella term for anyone who believed labor was cheated out of its natural product under historical capitalism.

Tucker sometimes called himself a socialist, but he denounced Marx as the representative of "the principle of authority which we live to combat." He thought Proudhon the superior theorist and the real champion of freedom. "Marx would nationalize the productive and distributive forces; Proudhon would individualize and associate them."

The term *capitalism* certainly suggests that capital is to be privileged over labor. As left-libertarian author Gary Chartier of La Sierra University writes,

> [I]t makes sense for [left-libertarians] to name what they oppose "capitalism." Doing so … ensures that advocates of freedom aren't

confused with people who use market rhetoric to prop up an unjust *status quo*, and expresses solidarity between defenders of freed markets and workers — as well as ordinary people around the world who use "capitalism" as a short-hand label for the world-system that constrains their freedom and stunts their lives.

In contrast to nonleft-libertarians, who seem uninterested in, if not hostile to, labor concerns per se, left-libertarians naturally sympathize with workers' efforts to improve their conditions. (Bastiat, like Tucker, supported worker associations.) However, there is little affinity for government-certified bureaucratic unions, which represent little more than a corporatist suppression of the pre-New Deal spontaneous and self-directed labor/mutual-aid movement, with its "unauthorized" sympathy strikes and boycotts. Before the New Deal Wagner Act, big business leaders like GE's Gerard Swope had long supported labor legislation for this reason.

Moreover, left-libertarians tend to harbor a bias against wage employment and the often authoritarian corporate hierarchy to which it is subject. Workers today are handicapped by an array of regulations, taxes, intellectual-property laws, and business subsidies that on net impede entry to potential alternative employers and self-employment. As well, periodic economic crises set off by government borrowing and Federal Reserve management of money and banking threaten workers with unemployment, putting them further at the mercy of bosses.

Competition-inhibiting cartelization diminishes workers' bargaining power, enabling employers to deprive them of a portion of the income they would receive in a freed and fully competitive economy, where employers would have to compete for workers — rather than vice versa — and self-employment free of licensing requirements would offer an escape from wage employment altogether. Of course, self-employment has its risks and wouldn't be for everyone, but it would be more attractive to more people if government did not make the cost of living, and hence the cost of decent subsistence, artificially high in myriad ways — from building codes and land-use restrictions to product standards, highway subsidies, and government-managed medicine.

In a freed market left-libertarians expect to see less wage employment and more worker-owned enterprises, co-ops, partnerships, and single proprietorships. The low-cost desktop revolution, internet, and inexpensive machine tools make this more feasible than ever. There would be no socialization of costs through transportation subsidies to favor nationwide over regional and local commerce. A spirit of independence can be expected to prompt a move toward these alternatives for the simple reason that employment to some extent entails subjecting oneself to someone else's arbitrary will and the chance of abrupt dismissal. Because of the competition from self-employment, what wage employment remained would most likely take place in less-hierarchical, more-humane firms that, lacking political favors, could not socialize diseconomies of scale as large corporations do today.

Left-libertarians, drawing on the work of New Left historians, also dissent from the conservative and standard libertarian view that the economic regulations of the Progressive Era and New Deal were imposed by social democrats on an unwilling freedom-loving business community. On the contrary, as Gabriel Kolko and others have shown, the corporate elite — the House of Morgan, for example — turned to government intervention when it realized in the waning 19th century that competition was too unruly to guarantee market share.

Thus left-libertarians see post-Civil War America not as a golden era of laissez faire but rather as a largely corrupt business-ruled outgrowth of the war, which featured the usual military contracting and speculation in government-securities. As in all wars, government gained power and well-connected businessmen gained taxpayer-financed fortunes and hence unfair advantage in the allegedly free market of the Gilded Age. "War is the health of the state," leftist intellectual Randolph Bourne wrote. Civil war too.

These conflicting historical views are well illustrated in the writings of the pro-capitalist novelist Ayn Rand (1905–1982) and Roy A. Childs Jr. (1949–1992), a libertarian writer-editor with definite leftist leanings. In the 1960s Rand wrote an essay with the self-explanatory title "America's Persecuted Minority: Big Business," which Childs answered with "Big Business and the Rise of American Statism." "To a large degree it has been and remains big businessmen who are the fountainheads of American statism," Childs wrote.

One way to view the separation of left-libertarians from other market libertarians is this: the others look at the American economy and see an essentially free market coated with a thin layer of Progressive and New Deal intervention that needs only to be scraped away to restore liberty. Left-libertarians see an economy that is corporatist to its core, although with limited competitive free enterprise. The programs constituting the welfare state are regarded as secondary and ameliorative, that is, intended to avert potentially dangerous social discontent by succoring — and controlling — the people harmed by the system.

Left-libertarians clash with regular libertarians most frequently when the latter display what Carson calls "vulgar libertarianism" and what Roderick Long calls "Right-conflationism." This consists of judging American business activity in today's statist environment as though it were taking place in the freed market. Thus while nonleft-libertarians theoretically recognize that big business enjoys monopolistic privileges, they also defend corporations when they come under attack from the left on grounds that if they were not serving consumers, the competitive market would punish them. "Vulgar libertarian apologists for capitalism use the term 'free market' in an equivocal sense," Carson writes, "[T]hey seem to have trouble remembering, from one moment to the next, whether they're defending actually existing capitalism or free market principles."

Signs of Right-conflationism can be seen in the common mainstream libertarian defensiveness at leftist criticism of income inequality, America's corporate structure, high oil prices, or the healthcare system. If there's no free market, why be defensive? You can usually make a nonleft-libertarian mad by comparing Western Europe favorably with the United States. To this, Carson writes, "If you call yourself a libertarian, don't try to kid anybody that the American system is less statist than the German one just because more of the welfare queens wear three-piece suits. ... If we're choosing between equal levels of statism, of course I'll take the one that weighs less heavily on my own neck."

True to their heritage, left-libertarians champion historically oppressed groups: the poor, women, people of color, gays, and immigrants, documented or not. Left-libertarians see the poor not as lazy opportunists but rather as victims of the state's myriad barriers to self-help, mutual aid, and decent education. Left-libertarians of course oppose government oppression of women and minorities, but they wish to combat nonviolent forms of social oppression such as racism and sexism as well. Since these are not carried out by force, the measures used to oppose them also may not entail force or the state. Thus, sex and racial discrimination are to be fought through boycotts, publicity, and demonstrations, not violence or antidiscrimination laws. For left-libertarians, southern lunch-counter racism was better battled through peaceful sit-ins than with legislation in Washington, which merely ratified what direct action had been accomplishing without help from the white elite.

Why do left-libertarians *qua* libertarians care about nonviolent, nonstate oppression? Because libertarianism is premised on the dignity and self-ownership of the individual, which sexism and racism deny. Thus all forms of collectivist hierarchy undermine the libertarian attitude and hence the prospects for a free society.

In a word, left-libertarians favor equality. Not material equality — that can't be had without oppression and the stifling of initiative. Not mere equality under the law — for the law might be oppressive. And not just equal freedom — for an equal amount of a little freedom is intolerable. They favor what Roderick Long, drawing on John Locke, calls equality in authority: "Lockean equality involves not merely equality *before* legislators, judges, and police, but, far more crucially, equality *with* legislators, judges, and police."

Finally, like most ordinary libertarians, left-libertarians adamantly oppose war and the American empire. They embrace an essentially economic analysis of imperialism: privileged firms seek access to resources, foreign markets for surplus goods, and ways to impose intellectual-property laws on emerging industrial societies to keep foreign manufacturers from driving down prices through competition. (This is not to say there aren't additional, political factors behind the drive for empire.)

These days left-libertarians feel vindicated. American foreign policy has embroiled the country in endless overt and covert wars, with their high cost in blood and treasure, in the resource-rich Middle East and Central Asia — with torture, indefinite detention, and surveillance among other assaults on domestic civil liberties thrown in for good measure. Meanwhile, the historical Washington-Wall Street alliance — in which recklessness with other people's money, fostered by guarantees, bailouts, and Federal Reserve liquidity masquerades as deregulation — has brought yet another financial crisis with its heavy toll for average Americans, additional job insecurity, and magnified Wall Street influence.

Such nefariousness can only hasten the day when people discover the left-libertarian alternative. Is that expectation realistic? Perhaps. Many Americans sense that something is deeply wrong with their country. They feel their lives are controlled by large government and corporate bureaucracies that consume their wealth and treat them like subjects. Yet (one hopes) they have little taste for European-style social democracy, much less full-blown state socialism. Left-libertarianism may be what they're looking for. As the Mutualist Carson writes,

> Because of our fondness for free markets, mutualists sometimes fall afoul of those who have an aesthetic affinity for collectivism, or those for whom "petty bourgeois" is a swear word. But it is our petty bourgeois tendencies that put us in the mainstream of the American populist/radical tradition, and make us relevant to the needs of average working Americans.

Carson believes ordinary citizens are coming to "distrust the bureaucratic organizations that control their communities and working lives, and want more control over the decisions that affect them. They are open to the possibility of decentralist, bottom-up alternatives to the present system." Let's hope he's right.

The American Conservative, February 3, 2011

Chapter 36.
Nock Revisited

Some books and essays require regular rereading. In the course of our busy lives, we can allow their subtle wisdom to fade into the landscape and lose their initial effect. A work of this kind is easy to spot: it is fresh and sparkling on every subsequent reading; each encounter with it feels like the first.

For me, Albert Jay Nock's masterly essay "On Doing the Right Thing" is one of those works. (Written in 1924, it is reprinted in the Nock collection *The State of the Union: Essays in Social Criticism*, edited by Charles H. Hamilton and published by Liberty Fund.) Nock (1870–1945) was an exquisite essayist, individualist, and libertarian, whose book *Our Enemy, the State* (1935) is just what one needs to change from a youthful enthusiast of freedom to a mature advocate of the free society.

Nock's essay is a reminder that the advocates of the paternalistic state, whether "left" or "right," have it backward: good conduct isn't a *precondition* of freedom; it is a *consequence* of freedom. He contrasted the "region of conduct" regulated by force, that is, by government, with the region regulated by the individual's sense of doing the Right Thing.

Nock wrote,

> The point is that *any* enlargement [of the first region], good or bad, reduces the scope of individual responsibility, and thus retards and cripples the education which can be a product of nothing but the free exercise of moral judgment. Like the discipline of the army, again, any such enlargement, good or bad, depraves this education into a mere routine of mechanical assent. The profound instinct against being "done for our own good" … is wholly sound. Men are aware of the need of this moral experience as a condition of growth, and they are aware, too, that anything tending to ease it off from them, even for their own good, is to be profoundly distrusted. *The practical reason for freedom, then, is that freedom seems to be the only condition under which any kind of substantial moral fibre can be developed.* [Emphasis added.]

In other words … no, there *are* no other, that is, better, words.

Across the political spectrum, social engineers think they need to deprive us of freedom in order to make us moral or in some way better. (See former New York City Mayor Michael Bloomberg's plan to outlaw some sugared drinks larger than 16 ounces in eateries and ballparks.) So they use the law to keep us from discriminating, gambling, eating allegedly fattening foods, taking drugs, smoking in restaurants, abstaining from helping others, leaving our seatbelts unbuckled, you name it.

Nock saw through this long ago:

> Freedom, for example, as they keep insisting, undoubtedly means freedom to drink oneself to death. The anarchist [that's what Nock called himself] grants this at once; but at the same time he points out that it also means freedom to say with the gravedigger in *Les Misérables*, "I have studied, I have graduated; I never drink." It unquestionably means freedom to go on without any code of morals at all; but it also means freedom to rationalise, construct and adhere to a code of one's own. The anarchist presses the point invariably overlooked, that freedom to do the one without correlative freedom to do the other is impossible; and that just here comes in the moral education which legalism and authoritarianism, with their denial of freedom, can never furnish.

Of course, some people will choose badly. Nock wasn't naïve. But rather than wallowing in that fact, he "turns to contemplate those men and women who act responsibly decent, decent by a strong, fine, self-sprung consciousness of the Right Thing, and ... declares [his] conviction that the future lies with them."

The Nockian understands that it is not the threat of state action that keeps most people decent. He "does not believe that any considerable proportion of human beings will promptly turn into rogues and adventuresses, sots and strumpets, as soon as they find themselves free to do so; but quite the contrary."

Here he echoed Thomas Paine in *The Rights of Man*:

> Great part of that order which reigns among mankind is not the effect of government. It has its origin in the principles of society and the natural constitution of man. It existed prior to government, and would exist if the formality of government was abolished. The mutual dependence and reciprocal interest which man has upon man, and all the parts of civilised community upon each other, create that great chain of connection which holds it together. The landholder, the farmer, the manufacturer, the merchant, the tradesman, and every occupation, prospers by the aid which each receives from the other, and from the whole. Common interest regulates their concerns, and forms their law; and the laws which common usage ordains, have a greater influence than the laws of government. In fine, society performs for itself almost everything which is ascribed to government.

Nock concluded that the purpose of his advocating freedom was nothing less than "that men may become as good and decent, as elevated and noble, as they might be and really wish to be."

The lesson of Nock's essay is that champions of the freedom philosophy need never be silenced by the charge that freedom makes vice possible — for without freedom, there can be no virtue.

Foundation for Economic Education, June 1, 2012

Chapter 37.
For Equality; Against Privilege

The freedom philosophy can be boiled down to two phrases: for equality and against privilege.

Intuitively, this should sound uncontroversial. In the Declaration of Independence, Thomas Jefferson's elegant statement of the freedom philosophy proclaims: "We hold these truths to be self-evident, that all men are created equal." But since then the idea of equality has acquired many meanings that either work against the freedom philosophy or give it weak support. So how can it be a pillar of liberty?

As Auburn University philosopher Roderick T. Long wrote in *The Freeman* ("Liberty: The Other Equality"), notions such as equality under the law and equality of freedom fall short as libertarian ideals. After all, we could be equal under unlibertarian law (everyone gets drafted) or we could all have an equally small area of freedom (everyone may do whatever he wants between noon and three on alternate Wednesdays). That would be equality of a sort but not liberty.

The objections to economic equality are well known. Since in the free market unequal incomes are to be expected as a result of variations in intelligence, talent, ambition, energy, health, luck, perception of consumer preferences, and so on, economic equality could be attempted (but not achieved) only through monstrous and continuing aggression by government officers. Something approaching equal poverty might be achieved (the political elite would no doubt be more equal than others), but equality at a decent level of prosperity is beyond the state's ability, as Cuba and North Korea illustrate.

This would seem to leave little content for Jefferson's ringing phrase. But Long shows that this is not the case. There is a significant sense of equality that gets short shrift in political philosophy, most likely because it is the libertarian sense. We do our cause an injustice by neglecting it.

The best-known formulation of this sense is from John Locke, Jefferson's inspiration for the Declaration. Long quoted Locke's description of a state of equality

> as one wherein all the power and jurisdiction is reciprocal, no one having
> more than another, there being nothing more evident than that creature
> of the same species and rank, promiscuously born to all the same

advantages of nature, and the use of the same faculties, should *also be equal one amongst another, without subordination or subjection.* [Emphasis added.]

In short, by the equality of men Locke and Jefferson meant not that all men are or ought to be equal in material advantages, but that all men (today it would be all persons, regardless of gender) are equal in authority. To subject an unconsenting person to one's own will is to treat that person as one's subordinate — illegitimately so, if we are all naturally equal.

Locke reinforced his thought thus:

> [B]eing all equal and independent, no one ought to harm another in his life, health, liberty or possessions. ... And, being furnished with like faculties, sharing all in one community of nature, there cannot be supposed any such subordination among us that may authorise us to destroy one another, as if we were made for one another's uses, as the inferior ranks of creatures are for ours.

Long went on to say that this Lockean equality (it can also be found in earlier writers, such as the Levellers, a group of English laissez-faire radicals) provides a powerful underpinning for the freedom philosophy:

The upshot of libertarian equality — equality in authority — is that government can possess no rights that its subjects lack — unless they freely surrender such rights by, in Locke's terms, "deputation, commission, and free consent." Long elaborated:

> Since I have no right over anyone else's person or property, I cannot delegate to government a right over anyone else's person or property. ... Libertarian equality ... involves not merely equality before those who administer the law, but equality with them. Government must be restrained within the moral bounds applicable to private citizens. If I may not take your property without your consent, neither may the state.

Frederic Bastiat made the same argument in his great work *The Law.*

Opposition to *privilege* is simply the corollary of libertarian equality. If all are equal in authority, then no one may live at the expense of others without their consent. The word privilege is often used equivocally, but it has its roots in the idea of legal favoritism. It is composed of *privus*, meaning single, and *lex* or *lege*, meaning law. Thus a privilege is a government act that (forcibly) bestows favors on one person or the few.

Historically, government's primary function has been to exploit the industrious — anyone who works and trades in the market — for the sake of the political class, which prefers collecting subsidies to earning wages or profits. (This original class analysis was formulated by the laissez-faire theorists Charles Comte and Charles Dunoyer, students of the economist J.B. Say, in the first half of the 19th century.) The privileges take the form of tariffs, licenses, monopolies, land grants, patents, copyrights, and other subsidies. These enable favored interests to increase their incomes beyond what the market would provide either by forcibly extracting wealth from producers or by barring them from competitively serving consumers. This privilege-based system can exist even in market-oriented economies, which is why they are often called mixed economies. The privilege part of the mix is a rank injustice against all honest industrious people and a violation of the principle of equal authority.

Champions of liberty have a constant challenge in finding fresh and compelling ways to teach their philosophy to people with different perspectives. I have a hunch there is an audience looking for a philosophy that embraces equality of authority and opposes privilege.

Foundation for Economic Education, May 11, 2012

Chapter 38.
Government Is Force

Some pundits really don't understand why libertarians dislike government and therefore want it to do little if anything at all. Unable to grasp the reason, the pundits assign bad motives to those who disparage government: they don't like poor people or workers or the sick or education.

But what's so hard to understand? Government is significantly different from anything else in society. It is the only institution that can legally threaten and initiate violence; that is, under color of law its officers may use physical force, up to and including lethal force — not in defense of innocent life but against individuals who have neither threatened nor aggressed against anyone else. "Government is not reason. It is not eloquence. Government is force; like fire, it is a dangerous servant — and a fearful master." (This quotation is often attributed, without evidence, to George Washington.)

That's not a controversial description of the state. Even people enthusiastic about government would agree it is accurate.

Given this unique feature, then, why isn't everyone wary of the state? Whether or not one thinks it's necessary, it's dangerous by its very nature, and we ought to assume it will remain so no matter how many paper checks and balances and bills of rights are thought to constrain it.

Yet if you talk about government this way, *you* will be eyed warily and even marginalized. This is not confined to just one side of the conventional political spectrum. Progressives and conservatives each have their pet areas where they enthusiastically wish to see the force of government unleashed. Each then regards anyone else's wariness as a defect. So progressives, who reputedly (but don't really) care about privacy, have no problem, for example, with intrusion into that most personal of matters: medical care. Here they trust power and dismiss rational fears of arbitrary bureaucratic control over health and life. On the other hand, conservatives, who (at least used to) pay lipservice freedom and free enterprise, are eager to trust power when the objective is policing the world, hounding unauthorized immigrants, and persecuting manufacturers, merchants, and consumers of disapproved substances.

We are all raised to believe that using force (except in self-defense) is wrong. We're taught not to hit other people or take their things. This applies to our associations as well. Yet as we grow up, we are expected to believe that one institution — government — gets to operate by different rules.

Sure, if you push hard enough, you will hear pseudo-explanations for this exception. Someone will inevitably invoke tacit consent. You know: you choose to live here, and those are the rules — love it or leave it. But the assertion that we all somehow at some point tacitly agreed to be subject to violence while behaving peacefully is ludicrous. Moreover, as Charles "Rad Geek" Johnson asks, in "Can Anybody Ever Consent to the State?": is consent possible when withholding consent is deemed impossible. How would one demonstrate one's refusal to consent. Anyone who says a refuser would have to leave the country has indulged in question begging.

Push harder, and someone will invoke democracy, but again that gets us nowhere. In my lifetime the only elections held have been to determine *who* would run the government, not what its powers, if any, would be. (Yes, candidates sometimes promise to reduce government power, but campaign promises usually aren't worth much, and when changes occur, they are typically marginal.) The fiction of democratic representation is more intended to limit dissent than to describe reality. Let's get real: The average congressional district has more than 700,000 residents. How could one person truly represent a group so large and diverse? Taxation *with* representation has yet to be realized.

Most people would agree that the sign of an individual's maturity and rationality, not to mention social skills, is his or her understanding that the cooperation of others must be obtained exclusively through persuasion. If you want something from someone you make an offer or an argument. You don't demand, bully, or terrorize. And yet we tolerate an institution that demands, bullies, and terrorizes as a matter of course across a large and growing range of matters. It doesn't demand merely that we not harm others or take their belongings. It bullies us into turning over our money for all kinds of purposes. It demands that we comply with its (ever-changing) rules about what we consume, how we manage our medical care, and in what manner we trade with others — and whom those others may be. And it increasingly terrorizes us in its brutal crusade against self-medication and recreation drug-taking.

It matters not for my purpose here whether the government's officers think they are looking out for our welfare, indulging their taste for power, or doing the bidding of well-connected and well-heeled interests. The result is the same: we are routinely hassled in our efforts to live, to cooperate, and to mutually benefit one another. *We* are the economy they presume to manage.

Apologists for power will claim that without expansive government, the weak will be vulnerable to the strong, the masses to the rich. But that appeal falls apart when one reviews the history of government and realizes that, appearances aside, power ultimately sides with the strong and the rich and well-connected against the rest. Indeed, power — what Frédéric Bastiat called "legal plunder" — is the source of their strength and a good deal of wealth.

Economic and social theory furnish ample reason for wariness about the state, but we mustn't let moral theory take a back seat. Government, even when it appears to do good, diminishes our freedom and humanity. How revoltingly ironic that people who claim to champion goodwill and cooperation regard violence as a legitimate means to their ends.

Foundation for Economic Education, September 16, 2011

Chapter 39.
Government as Consumer

Destutt de Tracy was a French economist whom Thomas Jefferson did his utmost to bring to the attention of America. The first part of Tracy's *A Treatise on Political Economy* (1817), the translation of which Jefferson arranged, is a primer in economics that will satisfy any aficionado of Austrian economics. It builds up a theory of exchange and commercial society beginning with a notion of value rooted in subjective utility and using the praxeological method rooted in the very structure of human action.

Tracy's book also discussed the nature and economic effect of government. And how refreshingly lucid is his treatment! It makes most modern descriptions of government look childish by comparison.

Today mainstream observers regard government as a source of investment in society. Across the political spectrum, overlooking differences in detail, one finds agreement that government spending, at least at some level, creates value.

Tracy did not see it that way. Like other liberal free-market economists of early 19th-century France, Tracy saw the state essentially as a predator, a destroyer of value, and the source of class conflict. (Which is not to say, alas, that he thought government should be abolished.)

"In every society the government is the greatest of consumers," he wrote. This puts him at odds with most of what is believed about government now. Government spending, he insisted, does not create wealth.

Nor does it stimulate others to create wealth, a belief that is dominant today — and not just among self-conscious Keynesians. Prosperity cannot be achieved through consumption, he held, and he didn't buy the "multiplier" effect that Keynes promoted. Tracy wrote:

> Those who persuade themselves that consumptions can be a cause of direct riches, maintain that the levies made by government, on the fortunes of individuals, powerfully stimulate industry; that its expenses are very useful, by augmenting consumption; that they animate circulation; and that all this is very favourable to the public prosperity. To see clearly the vice of these sophisms, we must always follow the same track, and commence by well establishing the facts.

He then proceeded to refute Keynes — a mere 119 years before publication of *The General Theory of Employment, Investment, and Money*:

The expenditure [government] makes does not return into its hands with an increase of value. It does not support itself on the profits it makes. I conclude, then, that its consumption is very real and definitive; that nothing remains from the labour which it pays; and that the riches which it employs, and which were existing, are consumed and destroyed when it has availed itself of them.

In other words, real investment in a free market, which is driven by entrepreneurs' attempts to satisfy consumers who — crucially — are free to say no, produces value, as indicated by the resulting profit. Thus we know that the output is esteemed more highly than the untransformed inputs. Government spending is not of that nature.

But what about government spending on infrastructure, those "shovel-ready projects" so beloved by the champions of government "stimulus"? Tracy cleverly pulls the rug out from under the argument by seeming at first to approve of such spending. Unlike the waste of other government spending, he says, "It is quite otherwise with funds employed in public labours of a general utility, such as bridges, ports, roads, canals, and useful establishments and monuments. These expenses are always favourably regarded, when not excessive. They contribute in effect very powerfully to public prosperity."

And yet, "they cannot be regarded as directly productive, in the hands of government, since they do not return to it with profit and do not create for it a revenue which represents the interest of the funds they have absorbed."

Besides, Tracy wrote, even government projects aiming at valued outcomes crowd out private efforts that would have been more efficient: "We must conclude that individuals could have done the same things, on the same conditions, if they had been permitted to retain the disposal of the sums taken from them for this same use; and it is even probable that they would have employed them with more intelligence and economy."

Even spending on science, government appropriations for which are supported across the mainstream political spectrum, would be better left to private entrepreneurs:

Finally, we may say the same things of what the government expends, on different encouragements of the sciences and arts. These sums are always small enough and their utility is most frequently very questionable. For it is very certain that in general the most powerful encouragement that can be given to industry of every kind, is to let it alone, and not to meddle with it. The human mind would advance very rapidly if only not restrained; and it would be led, by the force of things to do always what is most essential on every occurrence. To direct it artificially on one side rather than on another, is commonly to lead it astray instead of guiding it.

Then Tracy went in for the kill:

> From all this I conclude, that the whole of the public expenses ought to be ranged in the class of expenses justly called sterile and unproductive, and consequently that whatever is paid to the state, either under the title of a tax or even of a loan, is a result of productive labour previously executed, which ought to be considered as entirely consumed and annihilated the day it enters the national treasury. Once more I repeat it, this is not saying that this sacrifice is not necessary, and even indispensable. ... But [every citizen] should know that it is a sacrifice he makes; that what he gives is immediately lost, to the public riches, as to his own; in a word, that it is an expense and not an investment.

The upshot? For Tracy it is that government should be kept small and inexpensive. Note the jab he gives to "the greatest politicians":

> Finally, no one should be so blind as to believe that expenses of any kind are a direct cause of the augmentation of fortune; and that every person should know well that for political societies, as well as for commercial ones, an expensive regimen is ruinous, and that the best is the most economical. On the whole, this is one of those truths which the good sense of the people had perceived for a long time before it was clear to the greatest politicians.

Foundation for Economic Education, June 29, 2010

Chapter 40.
Libertarianism = Anti-Racism

Some years ago, Sen. Rand Paul's comments regarding the federal ban on racial discrimination in public accommodations (Civil Rights Act of 1964, Title II) brought the libertarian position on civil rights to public attention. (This is odd because Paul has insisted that he is "not a libertarian.")

It was not an entirely comfortable experience for libertarians. For obvious reasons libertarians are committed to freedom of association, which of course includes the freedom *not* to associate, and the right of property owners to set the rules on their property. Yet libertarians don't want to be mistaken for racists, who have been known to (inconsistently) invoke property rights in defense of racial discrimination. (I say "inconsistently" because historically they did not object to laws requiring segregation, just as Jim Crow laws.)

Evelyn Beatrice Hall could say, summarizing Voltaire's views, "I disapprove of what you say, but I will defend to the death your right to say it," but no libertarian I know relishes saying, "I disapprove of your bigotry, but I will defend to the death your right to live by it."

Yet that *is* the libertarian position, and we should not shrink from it. Defending the freedom of the virtuous is easy. The test is in defending it for the vicious. What I want to show here, however, is that this is not the *entire* libertarian position. There's more, and we do the philosophy — not to mention the cause of freedom — an injustice if we leave out the rest.

Let's start with a question of some controversy. Should a libertarian even care about racism? (By *racism* here I focus on racism per se even if it is nonviolent. Moreover, I accept for the argument's sake the dubious proposition that races even exist.) I am not asking if people who are libertarians should care about racism, but rather: are there specifically *libertarian grounds* to care about it?

Some say no, arguing that since liberty is threatened only by the initiation of physical force (and fraud), nonviolent racist conduct — repugnant as it is — is not a *libertarian* concern. (This is not to say libertarians wouldn't have other reasons to object.)

But I and others disagree with that claim. I think there are good *libertarian* grounds to abhor racism — and not only that, but also to publicly object to it and even to take peaceful but vigorous *nonstate and nonviolent* actions to stop it.

What could be a libertarian reason to oppose nonviolent racism? Charles Johnson has spelled it out in his article "Libertarianism through Thick and Thin." Libertarianism is a commitment to the nonaggression principle or obligation. That principle rests on some justification. Thus it is conceivable that a principle of nonviolent action, such as racism, though not involving the initiation of force and contradicting libertarianism per se, could nevertheless contradict the justification for one's libertarianism.

For example, a libertarian who holds his or her philosophy out of a conviction that all men and women are (and should be) equal in authority and thus none may subordinate another against his or her will (the most common justification) — that libertarian would naturally abhor even nonviolent forms of subordination. Racism could be just such a form (though not the only one), since existentially it entails at least an obligatory humiliating deference by members of one racial group to members of the dominant racial group. (The obligatory deference need not always be enforced by physical coercion.)

Seeing fellow human beings locked into a servile role — even if that role is not explicitly maintained by force — properly, *reflexively* summons in libertarians an urge to object. (I'm reminded of what H.L. Mencken said when asked what he thought of slavery: "I don't like slavery because I don't like slaves.")

Another, related libertarian reason to oppose nonviolent racism is that it all too easily metamorphoses from subtle intimidation into outright violence. Even in a culture where racial "places" have long been established by custom and require no coercive enforcement, members of a rising generation of the subordinate group will sooner or later defiantly reject their assigned places and demand equality of authority. What happens then? It takes little imagination to envision members of the dominant group — even if they have professed a "thin" libertarianism to that point — turning to physical force to protect their "way of life."

It should go without saying that a libertarian protest of nonviolent racist conduct must not itself be violent. Thus a libertarian campaign against racism in public accommodations would take the form of boycotts, sit-ins, and the like, rather than assaults and destruction of property. And it follows that state action would also be beyond the pale, since government is force. Hence the libertarian objection to government bans on segregation in privately owned places.

It would be a mistake, however, to think that ruling out government action would severely limit the scope of protest. Lunch counters throughout the American South were being desegregated years before passage of the 1964 Act. How so? Through sit-ins, boycotts, and other kinds of nonviolent, nongovernmental confrontational social action.

Yes, people got worthwhile things done without government help. Amazing, isn't it?

Two more points in closing. First, libertarians lose credibility when they pretend to deny the obvious social distinction between a privately owned public place — such as a restaurant — and a privately owned private place — such as a home. We see this too often. A libertarian will challenge a progressive thus: "If you really believe there should be laws against whites-only restaurants, to be consistent you should also demand laws against whites-only house parties."

That's a lousy argument.

When I walk past a restaurant, I have this thought in the back of my mind: "I can go in there." I have no such thought when I walk past a home. It's a matter of expectations reasonably derived from the owner's chosen function of the place. Homes and restaurants are alike in some important respects — they're privately owned — but they're also different in some important respects. Why deny that?

Of course, it does not follow from this distinction that government should set the rules for the restaurant. The libertarian needs to challenge *incorrect inferences* from the distinction — not the distinction itself.

Finally, no doubt someone will have raised an eyebrow at my inclusion of sit-ins in the list of appropriate nonviolent forms of protest against racist conduct. Isn't a sit-in at a private lunch counter a trespass?

It is — and the students who staged the sit-ins in the South did not resist when they were removed by the police. (Sometimes they were beaten by thugs who themselves were not subjected to police action.) The students never forced their way into any establishment. They simply entered, sat well-behaved at the counter, and waited to be served. When told they would not be served, they said through their actions, "You can remove me, but I will not help you." (Actually, blacks could shop at Woolworth's and similar stores; they just couldn't sit at the lunch counters. National boycotts hurt the stores' bottom lines.)

I could buttress this defense of sit-ins by pointing out that those stores were not operating in a free and competitive market. An entrepreneur who tried to open an integrated lunch counter across the street from Woolworth's would likely have been thwarted by zoning, licensing, and building-inspection officers. He would have had a hard time buying supplies and equipment because the local White Citizens' Council (the "respectable" white-collar bigots) would have "suggested" to wholesalers that doing business with the integrationist might be, shall we say, ill-advised. And if the message needed to be underscored, the Ku Klux Klan (with government's implicit sanction and even participation) was always available for late-night calls.

Did the beneficiaries of that oppressive system really have a good trespass case against the sit-in participants?

Foundation for Economic Foundation, May 28, 2010

Chapter 41.
We Can Oppose Bigotry
Without the Politicians

Should the government coercively sanction business owners who, out of apparent religious conviction, refuse to serve particular customers?

While such behavior is repugnant, the refusal to serve someone because of his or her race, ethnicity, or sexual orientation is nevertheless an exercise of self-ownership and freedom of nonassociation. It is both nonviolent and nonviolative of other people's rights. If we are truly to embrace freedom of association, logically we must also embrace freedom of nonassociation. The test of one's commitment to freedom of association, like freedom of speech, is whether one sticks by it even when the content repulses.

But does this mean that *private individuals* may not peacefully sanction businesses that invidiously discriminate against would-be customers?

No! They may, and they should. Boycotts, publicity, ostracism, and other noncoercive measures are also constituents of freedom of association.

So why do many people assume that the only remedy for anything bad — including bads that involve no physical force — is state action, which always entails the threat or use of violence? Are we really so powerless to deal with nonviolent repulsive conduct unless politicians act on our behalf?

Some years ago the Arizona legislature passed — then the governor vetoed — a bill that would have amended the state's Religious Freedom Restoration Act (RFRA), which holds that even a seemingly religiously neutral law may not "substantially burden" the exercise of religion in the absence of a "compelling government interest" and a less-restrictive method of advancing that interest.

The bill was reportedly prompted by a New Mexico Supreme Court ruling in the case of a commercial photographer who, apparently on religious grounds, refused to take pictures at a same-sex civil-commitment ceremony. The court held that the state's RFRA does not apply in cases involving private individuals, that is, cases in which the government is not a party. Thus a private person or business owner accused of violating the prohibition on discrimination against a designated protected group in public accommodations cannot invoke a religious exemption. ("Public accommodations" generally refers to businesses and government offices open to the general public.) Similar cases have arisen elsewhere.

The Arizona bill would have extended the RFRA to any "individual, association, partnership, corporation, church, religious assembly or institution, estate, trust, foundation or other legal entity." This was interpreted as intended to permit anti-gay discrimination in public accommodations — and maybe it was — but the bill made no reference to sexual preference or gender identity. (Arizona law bans discrimination on the basis of race and sex, but not sexual orientation.) As the *New York Times* noted at the time, "A range of critics — who included business leaders and figures in both national political parties — said it was broadly discriminatory and would have permitted all sorts of denials of service, allowing, say, a Muslim taxi driver to refuse to pick up a woman traveling solo."

What's an advocate of individual freedom, peaceful social cooperation, and tolerance to make of all this?

Right off I'd ask how a "compelling state interest" — whatever that may be — could license the government to impose burdens, substantial or otherwise, on anyone's peaceful exercise of religion. The state is an organization of mere mortals who, by one dubious method or another, have been allowed to don the mantle of political legitimacy and to command obedience on pain of imprisonment even of those who never consented to the preposterous arrangement.

Next I'd ask why religion is the only consideration to be taken into account. Shouldn't the state also be restrained from burdening the exercise of secular convictions?

As the economist and social commentator Mario Rizzo of New York University wrote on Facebook,

> The difficulty is that the law singled out an approved reason — religious — why someone could refuse his or her services to another person. The default used to be freedom of association and contract unless there was some very good countervailing reason. Now it seems that the default is you must behave according to "progressive" values or else. No one in Arizona would have been in danger of being deprived of vital services — the environment is competitive and people want to make money. It is totally unlike the old south. But, hey, no one has the interest in subtle distinctions about liberty.

When Rizzo says that "No one in Arizona would have been in danger of being deprived of vital services — the environment is competitive and people want to make money," he's referring to the fact that unless government intervention protects bigoted business interests (as it did in the old South), markets will punish them and reward inclusive establishments.

Now the moment anyone says that government should have no power to prohibit business owners from discriminating in public accommodations, a progressive interlocutor will respond, "So a business should be allowed to refuse service to someone because the person is black or gay?"

To which I would say, No, the business *should not be allowed* to do that. But by "not be allowed," I mean that *the rest of us should nonviolently impose costs on those who offend decency by humiliating persons through the refusal of service.* As noted, this would include boycotts, publicity, and ostracism. The state should not be seen as a remedy, and considering that its essence is violence, it certainly should not punish nonviolent conduct, however objectionable.

State prohibitions drive bigotry into the shadows, making private responses more difficult. Would a Jewish couple want an anti-Semite photographing their wedding? Would a gay couple want a homophobe baking their cake? Moreover, legal prohibitions may cut both ways. Should a black photographer have to work the wedding of a white-supremacist couple? Shouldn't the thought of forced labor make us squirm?

Let intolerance be exposed to the daylight, where it can be shamed and ridiculed.

Private action is not only morally superior to government action; it is also more effective. Direct nonviolent social action had been working several years before Title II was enacted. Beginning in 1960 sit-ins and other Gandhi-style confrontations were desegregating department-store lunch counters throughout the South. No laws had to be passed or repealed. Social pressure — the public shaming of bigots — was working.

Even earlier, during the 1950s, David Beito and Linda Royster Beito report in *Black Maverick: T.R.M. Howard's Fight for Civil Rights and Economic Power*, black entrepreneur T.R.M. Howard led a boycott of national gasoline companies that forced their franchisees to allow blacks to use the restrooms from which they had long been barred.

It is sometimes argued that Title II was an efficient remedy because it affected all businesses in one fell swoop. But the social movement was also efficient: whole groups of offenders would relent at one time after an intense sit-in campaign. There was no need to win over one lunch counter at a time.

Title II, in other words, was unnecessary. But worse, it was detrimental. History's greatest victories for liberty were achieved not through lobbying, legislation, and litigation — not through legal briefs and philosophical treatises — but through the sort of direct "people's" struggle that marked the Middle Ages and beyond. [See also Thaddeus Russell's *A Renegade History of the United States.*] As a mentor of mine says, what is given like a gift can be more easily taken away, while what one secures for oneself by facing down power is less easily lost.

The social campaign for equality that was desegregating the South was transmogrified when it was diverted to Washington. Focus then shifted from the grassroots to a patronizing white political elite in Washington that had scurried to the front of the march and claimed leadership.

We will never know how the original movement would have evolved — what independent mutual-aid institutions would have emerged — had that diversion not occurred.

In other words, libertarians need not shy away from the question, "Do you mean that whites should have been allowed to exclude blacks from their lunch counters?" Libertarians can answer proudly, "No. They should not have been allowed to do that. They should have been stopped — not by the State, which can't be trusted, but by nonviolent social action on behalf of equality."

The libertarian answer to bigotry, in other words, is community organizing.

Future of Freedom Foundation, February 28, 2014

Chapter 42.
What an Honest Conversation
About Race Would Look Like

Ever since George Zimmerman's fatal shooting of Trayvon Martin hit the national headlines in 2012, calls for an "honest conversation about race" have been heard throughout America. (Up until then, apparently, we've had only a conversation about having a conversation about race.) However, one need not believe that the Zimmerman shooting and verdict were about race to think that an honest conversation is long overdue.

First on the agenda should be the many ways that *government policies* — either by intent or by palpable effect — embody racism. Let's call them vehicles for official racism. I have in mind things like the war on certain drug manufacturers, merchants, and consumers; the crusade against "illegal" guns; the minimum wage and related laws regulating labor; and the government schools. All of these by far take their greatest toll on people of color.

Private racism, whether violent or nonviolent, is evil and abhorrent; it is also *unlibertarian*, as I point out in "Libertarianism = Anti-Racism" (in this volume).

But as bad as private racism is, official racism is worse, since it is committed under color of law and leaves its victims all the more vulnerable.

No one with open eyes can possibly believe that a black or Hispanic male walking down the street at night — or even during the day — faces the same hazards presented by the police that a white person does. The criminal justice system — from the police to the courts to the prison complex — is far more entangled in the lives of men of color than those of white men. Blacks and Hispanics were stopped disproportionately under New York City's abominable stop-and-frisk policy. What were the cops looking for? Drugs and guns. Police have been able to stop virtually anyone because the official standard for suspicion is low and subjective — and that gives racist cops plenty of scope to harass (and worse) people they dislike. It's a vehicle for official racism.

The drug laws were originally inspired by racial and ethnic animus against blacks, Mexicans, and Chinese. (See Thomas Szasz's books *Ceremonial Chemistry: The Ritual Persecution of Drugs, Addicts, and Pushers* and *Our Right to Drugs: The Case for a Free Market*.) Since drug *prohibition* is a crime by the standard of natural-law justice, and since it was motivated by racism and is racist in effect, those who passed and those who now enforce those laws are arguably guilty of hate crimes.

Prohibition — and the violent black markets and gang culture it spawns — makes the inner cities barely livable, while chasing legal businesses and jobs away. (Other government regulations contribute to this devastating result.) The cost to young people in terms of their futures is incalculable.

What about the war against "illegal" guns? It's much the same story. As gun historian Clayton E. Cramer writes,

> The historical record provides compelling evidence that racism underlies gun control laws — and not in any subtle way. Throughout much of American history, gun control was openly stated as a method for keeping blacks and Hispanics "in their place," and to quiet the racial fears of whites. ...
>
> It is not surprising that the first North American English colonies, then the states of the new republic, remained in dread fear of armed blacks, for slave revolts against slave owners often degenerated into less selective forms of racial warfare. The perception that free blacks were sympathetic to the plight of their enslaved brothers, and the dangerous example that "a Negro could be free" also caused the slave states to pass laws designed to disarm all blacks, both slave and free. Unlike the gun control laws passed after the Civil War, these antebellum statutes were for blacks alone.

While the drug and gun laws today may not be racial in intent (though they may be), they are such in consequence. Again, they are vehicles for official racism. Whose neighborhood has more to fear from a local militarized police SWAT raid?

The government's schools for decades consigned black children to ramshackle custodial institutions misleadingly called "schools," where the kids' future choices were systematically narrowed to a demeaning few. With white-controlled elitist school boards depriving minority communities of resources (through taxation), it took heroic family and neighborhood action to help kids to overcome these official barriers. Things are little different today. Even though a great deal more tax money is spent on inner-city schools now than previously, the results are not much better.

These handicaps on minority children are reinforced by the minimum wage and related laws, such as the Davis-Bacon Act. By pricing low-skilled, poorly educated workers out of the market, these laws make getting a first job especially hard if not impossible. For many unfortunate victims of the law, their lives are stifled in ways that cannot be reversed without herculean effort.

Tragic coincidence? No. The laws were racially motivated — intended as barriers against black workers aspiring to compete with exclusionist white unions.

And to this list of offensive interventions let us add immigration controls, zoning laws, occupational licensing, and restrictions on street vendors and taxi drivers, all of which impose their heaviest burdens on people of color, who are thwarted at every turn, as my account here indicates. Most tragically, all these government inventions, which serve to create dysfunctional communities, feed the private racists' poisonous narrative.

This hardly exhausts the discussion of official racism. So, yes, let's have that honest conversation about race. And let's begin with the biggest enabler of racism of all: the state.

Future of Freedom Foundation, July 19, 2013

Chapter 43.
There Is No Such Thing
as Economic Freedom, Only Freedom

In 1938 the U.S. Supreme Court ruled that a federal law prohibiting the interstate shipping of filled milk violated neither the commerce clause nor the due-process clause of the Constitution. What is best remembered about that opinion is the famous "Footnote Four," which has influenced American jurisprudence ever since.

Writing for the majority in *United States v. Carolene Products Company,* Justice Harlan F. Stone set out the doctrine that some kinds of freedom are more equal than others. Specifically, certain government acts warrant higher judicial scrutiny than other kinds. Harlan wrote, "There may be narrower scope for operation of the presumption of constitutionality when legislation appears on its face to be within a specific prohibition of the Constitution, such as those of the first ten amendments."

In other words, when the Court decides that a government regulation lies beyond an explicit constitutional prohibition, for example, one found in the Bill of Rights, the court should presume it is constitutional and not subject to the strict scrutiny that regulations lying within some explicit prohibition deserve. The footnote is better understood when we see the text it is attached to:

> The existence of facts supporting the legislative judgment is to be presumed, for regulatory legislation affecting *ordinary commercial transactions* is not to be pronounced unconstitutional unless, in the light of the facts made known or generally assumed, it is of such a character as to preclude the assumption that it rests upon some rational basis within the knowledge and experience of the legislators. [Emphasis added.]

That is, the Court will simply assume members of Congress had a good reason to regulate some aspect of commerce unless it can be shown otherwise. When it comes to economic activity, there is to be no presumption of liberty as there is in other matters.

Hence the bifurcated system of freedoms — noneconomic and economic — we labor under today.

Advocates of freedom know this doctrine is based on an error and invoke the indivisibility of freedom in response to it. But too often they undercut their own case by talking about *economic freedom*.

I realize this phrase may be meant only to emphasize the depreciated aspect of freedom, but as free-market advocates know, intentions don't nullify effects. Whenever one says "economic freedom," one implies that other kinds of freedom exist. That of course does not imply that some freedoms are more equal than others, but it certainly opens the possibility. That can't happen if we insist that freedom is indivisible.

The case for the indivisibility of freedom is not hard to make when one remembers that there are no *economic* ends. There are only ends, namely, the values we pursue in the course of our lives. I recall first hearing Thomas Sowell make this point about 30 years ago. He writes in *Basic Economics*:

> One of the last refuges of someone whose pet project or theory has been exposed as economic nonsense is to say: "Economics is all very well, but there are also non-economic values to consider." Presumably, these are supposed to be higher and nobler concerns that soar above the level of crass materialism.
>
> Of course there are non-economic values. In fact, there are only non-economic values. Economics is not a value in and of itself. It is only a way of weighing one value against another.

There are *only* non-economic values. If that is so, then there is no *economic* freedom. There is only freedom. Full stop.

People act to achieve objectives that they believe will help them to flourish (however they may conceive that). Sometimes they pursue material values; other times they pursue nonmaterial, or "spiritual," values. But the material values serve the same sort of purposes as the nonmaterial ones. They are not pursued for economic reasons.

Now this works very well with the Austrian insight — developed also by the British economist Philip Wicksteed — that the classical economists erred in thinking their discipline applied only to the self-interested pursuit of material wealth. But economics (or praxeology, to use Ludwig von Mises's term for the broader study of human action) analyzes purposeful action in itself. It doesn't matter what the objective is; the logic of action is universal. As Wicksteed put it in his introduction to *The Common Sense of Political Economy*,

> It will easily be shown that the [marginal utility] principle ... is not exclusively applicable to industrial or commercial affairs, but runs as a universal and vital force through the administration of all our resources. It follows that the general principles which regulate our conduct in business are identical with those which regulate our deliberations, our

selections between alternatives, and our decisions, in all other branches of life.

And as Mises wrote in *Epistemological Problems of Economics*,

> Everything that we say about action is independent of the motives that cause it and of the goals toward which it strives in the individual case. It makes no difference ... whether it is directed toward the attainment of materialistic or idealistic ends.

Living a human life consists in the pursuit of a variety of values, some material, some not. Thus dividing freedom into spheres is both arbitrary and ultimately destructive. There is no economic freedom and non-economic freedom. There is only freedom.

Foundation for Economic Education, June 8, 2012

Chapter 44.
The Inherently Humble Libertarian

You would think that the advocates of a philosophy of political economy that embraces spontaneous social order, bottom-up rule-making based on peaceful voluntary exchange, and even competing polycentric law (i.e., statelessness) would be safe from the charge of conceit. How conceited can someone be who forswears compelling other people to live in certain ways, expressing a willingness — no, an eagerness — to leave that to peaceful cooperation among free individuals? Making what social theorist F.A. Hayek called the social "knowledge problem" a centerpiece of one's worldview is hardly the mark of arrogance. Quite the contrary.

Yet critics of the libertarian philosophy throw the charge of know-it-allness at its exponents all the time. It's the go-to criticism. When counterarguments fail, accuse the libertarian of hubris.

I'm talking about substance, not style. Regrettably, someone could display arrogance while insisting that neither he nor anyone else could possibly know enough to plan other people's lives. However off-putting that style, it does not change the fact that the *position* embodies a fundamental humility. There are inherent limits to any individual's knowledge, and therefore government social engineering, which requires the use of aggressive force, must fail.

To put it succinctly, libertarianism has humility baked in at the most fundamental level.

Humility is not to be conflated with radical doubt, however. One can be humble while also believing it is possible to know things. And some things, including the nature and market implications of human action, can be known conceptually. One can know, for example, that intelligently planning an economy or even a particular market is beyond anyone's, including one's own, capacities. The same can be said of more modest schemes to modify market outcomes through government intervention. One can acknowledge the limits of reason à la Hayek without being a skeptic or rejecting reason as impotent. (Don't all skeptics make covert knowledge claims?) After all, it is reason that discovers its own limits.

Some libertarians and classical liberals have tried to defend liberty on the grounds that we can't really know anything, but this is a nonstarter. For example, libertarian economist Milton Friedman, in his 1991 *Liberty* article, "Say 'No' to Intolerance," wrote,

> I have no right to coerce someone else, because I cannot be sure that I am right and he is wrong. If we see someone doing something wrong, someone starting to sin (to use a theological term) let alone just make a simple mistake, how do we justify not initiating coercion? Are we not sinning if we don't stop him? ... How do I justify letting him sin? I believe that the ... answer is, can I be sure he's sinning? Can I be sure that I am right and he is wrong? That I know what sin is?

Strangely, this implies that if we could know right from wrong, we *would* be justified in interfering with people's wrongful but nonaggressive conduct. Only ignorance protects freedom. Yet am I not allowed to stop a murderer because "I cannot be sure that I am right [about the nature of murder] and he is wrong"? Skepticism, in other words, cannot get us to the nonaggression obligation or anywhere else.

We can know things, important things, that do get us to what I call the nonaggression obligation. Among the things we can know is that no individual or group of individuals can successfully plan an economy or society in the interests of all, or intelligently alter the outcomes of free social cooperation, because in principle they cannot have access to all that is now known or will be discovered by the people they intend to move about like so many chess pieces. That, of course, is an allusion to Adam Smith's insight about the "man of system" in *The Theory of Moral Sentiments*:

> The man of system, on the contrary, is apt to be very wise in his own conceit; and is often so enamoured with the supposed beauty of his own ideal plan of government, that he cannot suffer the smallest deviation from any part of it. He goes on to establish it completely and in all its parts, without any regard either to the great interests, or to the strong prejudices which may oppose it. He seems to imagine that he can arrange the different members of a great society with as much ease as the hand arranges the different pieces upon a chess-board. He does not consider that the pieces upon the chess-board have no other principle of motion besides that which the hand impresses upon them; but that, in the great chess-board of human society, every single piece has a principle of motion of its own, altogether different from that which the legislature might chuse to impress upon it. If those two principles coincide and act in the same direction, the game of human society will go on easily and harmoniously, and is very likely to be happy and successful. If they are opposite or different, the game will go on miserably, and the society must be at all times in the highest degree of disorder.

So who, at the deepest level, is full of conceit? Those who respect individual liberty, understanding that free association, like the justice on which it is based, has good consequences, or those who call on the state to interfere violently with free association because they presume to know which outcomes are superior to those they imagine would emerge through peaceful cooperation.

Future of Freedom Foundation, February 13, 2015

Chapter 45.
The Poison Called Nationalism

"Forward, the Light Brigade!"
Was there a man dismay'd?
Not tho' the soldier knew
Someone had blunder'd:
Theirs not to make reply,
Theirs not to reason why,
Theirs but to do and die:
Into the valley of Death
Rode the six hundred

"The Charge of the Light Brigade," Alfred, Lord Tennyson

The reason for the venom directed at those of us who question American sniper Chris Kyle's status as a hero can be put into one word: nationalism.

Nationalism is a poison. It attacks the mind, short-circuits thinking, and makes self-destruction look appealing. Nationalism sows the seeds of hate and war. It makes the title *warrior* an honorific instead of the pejorative it ought to be.

We see naked ugly nationalism in many defenses of Kyle. Defenders appear to have but one operating principle: if Kyle was an American military man and the people he killed were not Americans, then he was a hero. Full stop. No other facts are relevant. It matters not that Kyle was a cog in an imperial military machine that waged a war of aggression on behalf of the ruling elite's geopolitical and economic interests, that he did his killing on foreign soil, and that no Iraqi had come to the United States seeking to harm him or other Americans. (Contrary to what Kyle defenders seem to believe, not one Iraqi was among the 19 hijackers on 9/11, although had that been otherwise, the murder of millions of other Iraqis and the displacement of millions more would not have been justified.) All that apparently matters to Kyle fans is that this man was born in America, joined the American military, and faithfully obeyed orders to kill people he called savages.

That is what nationalism does to a human being.

The ugliness of nationalism is often perceptible even to those who harbor it and commit terrible acts as a result. So they rationalize. They don't openly cheer the killing of Iraqis because they are Iraqis (or Arabs or Muslims); rather they plead preemptive self-defense: if we don't kill them, they will kill us. Kyle and his comrades were defending America and Americans' freedom, his defenders say.

But if you've seen *American Sniper*, the movie based on Kyle's book, you heard Kyle's wife, Taya, reject that claim. I'm surprised that this bit of dialogue has been ignored (to my knowledge) in the voluminous writing about the movie. As Kyle gets ready for yet another tour in Iraq, his unhappy wife asks why he is going back. "For you," he says, and by extension, for America.

"No you're not," she fires back.

He also invokes the welfare of the Iraqis, telling his wife that being away from home for another long stretch would not be a problem because their family could spare the time and the Iraqis could not. She didn't buy that line either. She is deeply disturbed that her husband would rather try to fix Iraq (as though he and his comrades could do that through military force) than look after his own family.

It's curious that Taya Kyle (if this scene actually took place) had a clearer picture of the world than Kyle's vitriolic nationalist defenders, who praise the sniper for following orders without question. (One even approvingly alluded to Tennyson's poem.)

If not for nationalism, such contortions — the conjuring of imaginary threats, the conceit in aspiring to save a society one knows absolutely nothing about, the twisting of the warrior's ways into virtues — would be unnecessary. Things could be called what they are. Someone who swore an oath that *in practical terms* obliged him to kill whomever the current White House occupant told him to kill, "asking [in Herbert Spencer's words] nothing about the justice of [the] cause," would be called a cold-blooded contract killer rather than a hero.

Nationalism, to judge by how nationalists conduct themselves, is an unswerving religious-like devotion to the nation, construed as a quasi-mystical entity — "America" — that cannot be wrong and so has the authority to command reverence and obedience. The nation transcends particular political officeholders, but the government, or state, is integral to the entity. The nation (country) cannot be imagined without the state. It would not be the same thing. When an American nationalist thinks of *his country*, he thinks not merely of a land mass with distinctive features, the people (a diverse group indeed), its multifaceted culture, and its history (a mixed bag) because that list does not fully capture what he means by *America*.

For him the government represents and expresses the will and sentiment of the nation. (To be sure, a nationalist can think that the people have erred in picking their "leaders," in which case the nation is misrepresented and has to be "taken back.") The power of compartmentalization allows some people who think of themselves as individualists while seeing the nation in these corporate terms.

Let's remember that this quasi-mystical entity is what it is only because of countless contingent events effected by flawed human beings. The United States did not begin with 50 states, of course. Had events gone differently, it might have included some or all of Canada and none of what was once part of Mexico. It might have been without the Florida territory and the 828,000 square miles that constituted the Louisiana Purchase. The current boundaries were the result of (often bloody) human action but not entirely of human design. So it was with other nations. At one time, there were no nations as we think of them today.

"Forgetting, I would even go so far as to say historical error, is a crucial factor in the creation of a nation," Ernest Renan said in his famous 1882 lecture, "What Is a Nation?," "which is why progress in historical studies often constitutes a danger for [the principle of] nationality. Indeed, historical enquiry brings to light deeds of violence which took place at the origin of all political formations. ... Unity is always effected by means of brutality."

This integral relationship between nation and state is why nationalists reject claims that one can love one's country while despising the government. That's impossible by their definition of country. To oppose the government *is* to oppose the country. You may oppose a particular president, but don't dare oppose the military. Now, you can try to redefine *country* to make it something properly lovable, but you won't persuade a nationalist.

It's no accident that governments never fail to call on their flocks to "love their country," by which they mean: be willing to make any sacrifice on its behalf, with "sacrifice" defined by politicians. Instilling nationalism is always the primary mission of government and its schools because, as Ernst Gellner wrote in *Nations and Nationalism*, "It is nationalism which engenders nations, and not the other way round."

That mission is behind the near-compulsory recitations of the Pledge of Allegiance (written by an avowed Christian collectivist), salutes to "the troops" for "their service" on any and every occasion, and the playing of the national anthem and other nationalist songs at sporting events. It's what's behind the repeated, compulsive assurances that "America is the greatest country on earth." The ruling elite understands that love of country will inevitably find its application in fealty to the government, no matter what dissenters may say.

Some wish to distinguish nationalism from patriotism, but I don't think this works. *Patriot* has a lineage that includes the Greek words for "fatherland," *patris*; "of one's fathers," *patrios*; and "father," *pater*. This indicates the country's parental relationship to the citizen. It can't simply mean "land of one's fathers" because people believe they should feel patriotic about lands their fathers never set foot in. We're back to that quasi-mystical entity, America. Hence my definition of *patriot*: one who, no matter the difficulties, places power above party.

I understand the love of the place one knew as a child. I understand the love of home, of family, of community, of neighbors, and of people with whom one has shared experiences and beliefs. I understand the love of virtuous principles as expressed in historical documents (such as the Declaration of Independence). That kind of love does not ignite hate for the Other or create admiration for the warrior who enjoys killing the Other on order. That takes the poison of nationalism and an obsession with the nation it creates.

Future of Freedom Foundation, February 6, 2015

Chapter 46.
Do Ends Justify Means?

I — and most other people, I assume — grew up being taught that the end doesn't justify the means. Basically, this is an injunction not to rationalize one's own behavior while using other people as mere means to one's ends.

Most people apply that principle day to day. If you want an item on a supermarket shelf and someone is standing in the way, few of us would think it right to shove that person aside. Why not? It won't do to say that the person might fight back. Would things change if an elderly, frail person were there? It also won't do to say that other people might observe your conduct, perhaps leading to a fight, or an arrest, or at least a loss of reputation. Nor will it do to say that in normal circumstances waiting for the person to move would cost little in time and convenience. How much time and inconvenience would be required to make shoving an attractive option? The question answers itself.

A utilitarian (or any other sort of consequentialist) might say that greater good, happiness, or utility would be better achieved by waiting than by shoving. That is, the harm to the other person would exceed the benefits to you. But since interpersonal comparisons of subjective utility are impossible — not only is there no unit of measurement, in principle there's nothing to measure — that claim has no content. As J.J.C. Smart, a utilitarian, put it, "[T]he utilitarian is reduced to an intuitive weighing of various consequences with their probabilities. It is impossible to justify such intuitions rationally, and we have here a serious weakness in utilitarianism." Philosopher A.J. Ayer had a similar insight, "[Jeremy] Bentham's process of 'sober calculation' turns out to be a myth." Bentham himself was aware of this problem.

If "goods" are incommensurable, then one of them cannot be said to be "greater" than others. Thus acting for the "greater good" is without meaning. "[T]his lack of commensurability eliminates all possibility of reference for the expression 'greater good' as the consequentialist uses this expression," natural-law philosopher Germain Grisez writes.

So why wouldn't we shove the elderly, frail person aside even if we were certain to be unobserved? We abstain from that "efficient" means to an unobjectionable and perhaps worthy end because we sense that it would be injustice and that injustice is to be avoided. We don't calculate that committing the injustice would *in this case* be contrary to our own self-interest (what would you think of someone who actually did that?), nor do we even determine that shoving the person aside would ill-serve that person's interests. Rather, we know that the act would be wrong because it is wrong to use another person as a mere means to our ends. (In a sense we're all the "children of Athens," a reference to the ethical writings of the ancient Greek philosophers.)

So why is the principle that the end does not justify the means absent from most discussion of government policy? Why are political measures routinely defended on the sole basis that they will bring about some good consequence that supposedly outweighs the costs (from the perspective of those who propose them)? This happens all the time. A tariff is justified by the help it is thought to give to a struggling domestic industry. A price control is justified as a way to keep the price of some product affordable. A mandate that employers or insurance companies (nominally) pay for women's contraception is justified in terms of women's health or of reducing the number of abortions. Torture is justified as a source of useful information. Obliteration bombing is justified as a way to shorten a war.

In all these cases and more, those who proffer the government policy seem to think that all they need do is identify a consequence as the "greater good" and the discussion is over. The end justifies the means. That may indicate one of two things. The proponent of the measure may think that the objective of the policy is more important than whatever those who are forced to pay for it must forgo as a result. Or the proponent may be oblivious of the costs entirely, as though there were none.

But, first of all, there are always costs to — and therefore victims of — any government action. Government is force, and "coercive intervention ... signifies *per se* that the individual or individuals coerced would not have done what they are now doing were it not for the intervention," economist Murray Rothbard wrote in *Power and Market*. A tariff forces consumers to pay more for products, leaving them less money to spend on other people's products. That's two sets of victims. A price control will drive marginal producers out of business, creating shortages. A contraception mandate will cost *someone* money, no matter how often the products and services are called "free." Etc.

All those who are forced to bear the costs are treated by the government and the special-interest groups it empowers as *mere means* to other people's ends; that is, they are treated as less than human and as unworthy of consideration.

The proponents of such measures never tell us why the benefits they aim for are more important than the benefits other people would have to do without. But of course they couldn't tell us: The benefits are incommensurable.

Furthermore, apart from the material loss, the victims' progressive loss of freedom is real both in the immediate instance as well as with respect to the precedent set for future government action (the slippery slope).

Intervention begets intervention as policymakers try to clean up the mess their previous actions created.

As Grisez put it,

> The economic advantages and disadvantages of a proposed public project can be quantified. But people also want freedom of speech and of religion, equal protection of the laws, privacy, and other goods which block certain choices, *yet which cannot be costed out.* Cost-benefit analysis can tell one the most effective way of attaining certain objectives, assuming one accepts the objectives and has no concerns about the means and the side effects of the means required to attain them. But such analysis cannot tell one whether the objectives one seeks are objectives one ought to seek, or whether nonquantifiable factors should be ignored. [Emphasis added.]

Means and ends of course are intimately related. The end determines the array of relevant means. But that is not the end of the story. In selecting from that array, considerations apart from the end are highly relevant — such as the injunction never to use another person as a mere means. To ignore those considerations is to mock human dignity and countenance the slave principle.

That's basic to how we ordinarily think about morality. But politicians and those who leech off their power flout this insight as a matter of course.

Foundation for Economic Education, April 26, 2012

Chapter 47.
Free-Market Socialism

Libertarians are individualists. But since *individualist* has many senses, that statement isn't terribly informative.

Does it mean that libertarians are social nonconformists on principle? Not at all. Some few libertarians may aspire to be, but most would see that as undesirable because it would obstruct their most important objectives. Lots of libertarian men have no problem wearing a jacket and tie, or shoes, socks, and a shirt, on occasions when that attire is generally expected.

Besides, if it's bizarre to do what other people do *only* because other people do it, isn't it also bizarre to do the opposite of what other people do *only* because it's the opposite? Both types are in effect taking orders.

Virtually all libertarians observe most of the customs of their societies, just as they conform to language conventions if for no other reason than they wish to be understood. I don't know a libertarian who would regard this as tyranny. In fact, as one's appreciation of the libertarian philosophy deepens, so does one's understanding of the crucial behavior-shaping role played by the evolution of customs and rules — the true law — that have nothing whatever to do with the state. Indeed, these help form our very idea of *society*.

Libertarians are individualists in other respects, however. They are methodological individualists, which means that when they think about social and economic processes, they begin with the fact that only individuals act. That's shorthand for: only individuals have preferences, values, intentions, purposes, aspirations, expectations, dreams, and a raft of other related things. In truth these words don't actually refer to things we *have*, but rather to things we *do*. Strictly speaking, we don't *have* preferences; we prefer. We don't *have* values; we value. We don't *have* purposes; we act purposively. And so on. I'm reminded here of Thomas Szasz's statement that *mind* isn't essentially a noun but a verb. (It follows that one cannot lose it.)

From here, it's a short step to the principle that the unit of morality is the individual person. Morality concerns what individuals should and should not do, and what sort of life is proper for rational social beings. Interpersonal morality addresses, among other things, when the use of force is permissible (if ever), and this leads to the ideas of rights, entitlements, and enforceable obligations, also attributes of individuals.

None of this disparages the importance of groups, ranging in size from two persons to great societies. But it does implicitly remind us that the dynamics of groups cannot be understood without first understanding their components. It is certainly reasonable to talk about a college class doing things. But misunderstanding will plague anyone who fails to realize that *class* here simply indicates a group of individuals in a certain relationship with one another, with a professor, with a particular institution, and with society at large. When we say, "The class left the room," we don't mean that some blob flowed through the door, but rather that the individuals who count as members of the class left the room.

That's an easy case which no one is apt to misunderstand. But other statements shroud, perhaps intentionally, basic methodological and moral individualism. When the news media attribute preferences and actions to "the United States" or "the U.S. government," clarity would be served by keeping in mind that specific individuals with interests, preferences, and the rest — individuals whose legitimate claim to act on our behalf may at least be dubious — perform the actions. Collective nouns are unproblematic as long as we remember what we are talking about.

Nothing about libertarianism commits its adherents to what critics call "atomistic individualism." That would be a curious descriptor for people who love trade and the division of labor, even among perfect strangers at great distances. That's why I long ago proposed an alternative: *molecular individualism*. Libertarians agree with the ancient Greek philosophers who emphasized the fundamental social nature of human beings. Baked into this concept is the idea that persons inescapably are reason-and-language-using beings. An atomistic individual would be less than fully human because fundamental potentialities would be left unactualized, owing to the absence of contact with other reason-and-language-using beings. Our ability to think beyond the most primitive level depends on language, which is by nature social.

The progressives' caricature of the libertarian as a rugged, self-sufficient, antisocial off-the-grid inhabitant of a mountain shack — a Ted Kaczynski sans letter bombs — is ludicrous.

Libertarians, to the extent that they grasp the fundamentals of their philosophy, care about social dynamics, which accounts for their fascination with economics, especially the Austrian school.

I don't mean to downplay anything I've just said when I point out that, in an important sense, the social whole is greater than the sum of its parts. Economies are not machines; they are people exchanging things. *We* are the economy the politicians and bureaucrats wish to control. Yet our continuing interaction spontaneously generates — in a bottom-up way — a vast and complex order of interrelated institutions that no individual or group could possibly grasp in any detail, much less design.

The mundane price system is a perfect if unappreciated example. Prices are critical to our well-being because they enable us to plan our day-to-day lives. They do so by providing signals to us not only as consumers but also as producers. Prices guide our decisions about what to produce for exchange, how much to produce, and by what means. The resulting profits and losses reveal successes and failures at serving consumers. Without prices we'd fly blind, as Ludwig von Mises famously showed in his demolition of central economic planning, that is, socialism. This is the upshot of the famous socialist-calculation debate, which F.A. Hayek also participated in.

Mises had other interesting things to say about the market process that go toward debunking the progressives' critique of libertarianism as hyper-individualist. For example, we meaningfully if metaphorically speak of the "free market's" channeling of resources from those who serve consumers poorly to those with the potential to do a better job of it. This is no reification of the market, which has no purposes — only people have purposes. An analysis of this channeling would refer to individual consumers' decisions to buy or abstain from buying goods offered on the market.

But no individual decided to put, say, the bookseller Borders out of business. In an important sense, we did it *collectively*, but not at a mass meeting with people giving speeches and voting on whether the owners of Borders should keep control of the company's assets. Rather, the demise of Borders and the transfer of its assets to others were the outcome of many individual decisions, which were not consciously coordinated. It's just happened that enough people had preferences inconsistent with the company's business plan. So the people who ran Borders were out, however much they objected. No force was used.

Think about it: When the marketplace is really free and competitive (rather than constricted by the state to protect privileged interests), it is *we* collectively who decide who controls the means of production. We don't do this in the legal sense, for example, by literally expropriating the assets of some people and transferring them to others. Yet that's the effect of free competition and individual liberty.

In other words, the *freed* market would give traditional leftists what they say they want: a society in which free, voluntary, and peaceful cooperation ultimately control the means of production for the good of all people.

What well-wisher of humanity could ask for anything more?

Future of Freedom Foundation, November 14, 2014

Chapter 48.
Individualist Collectivism

Is the free market an individualist or collectivist social arrangement? Don't answer too quickly. It's a trick question.

Most people — free-market friend and free-market foe alike — will answer "individualist." And that makes perfect sense. The free market describes a political/legal environment in which individuals are at liberty to engage in any peaceful activity, with only force (including trespass) and fraud prohibited. No one may aggressively interfere with another human being's peaceful projects. This environment leaves it to each person to define himself or herself through the pursuit of subjective preferences. If that's not individualism, what would be?

A popular line of attack against the free market is that it leaves people little or no say in important matters that affect their lives. It's an appropriate concern. Libertarianism is about controlling your own life. The question is, Which social system gives the individual more control? Clearly it's the free market (not to be confused with current corporatism) that allows far more control, even in the midst of "impersonal market forces." When competition is not limited by government privilege and other restrictions, the individual has a wide range of choices in consumption and production activities. If you don't like one offering, chances are there will be others. The key to choice is the absence of barriers to competitive entry — barriers like taxes, regulations, land-use restrictions, government-sponsored cartels, intellectual property, and more.

The control that an individual exercises in the market far exceeds the alleged influence he or she has in a political democracy, where no person's vote is likely to be decisive, and the benefits from any particular government action are concentrated on well-organized interest groups — while the costs are spread thinly, almost invisibly, throughout the population.

So where does collectivism figure in the free market? This is a dimension of the market that cannot be ignored without missing something essential. If I wanted to be especially provocative, I'd call this the collectivist or socialist dimension.

If social democrats dropped their prejudice against money-making and took a fresh look, they would be struck by how closely the freed market would approach what they say they want. Economist Ludwig von Mises held that the "market economy is a democracy in which every penny constitutes a vote. The wealth of the successful businessman is the result of a consumer plebiscite." It is true that someone with more money has more "votes" than someone with less money. But the person with less money can still obtain things he or she wants, which makes the market superior to political democracy, in which anyone who votes with the losing side gets nothing. That's where the democracy analogy breaks down in favor of the market. As the liberal legal scholar Bruno Leoni noted, in a democratic vote 50 percent plus one effectively equals 100 percent, while 50 percent minus one effectively equals 0. In the market minority tastes are catered to. It's never winner-takes-all.

Mises made one more point that should impress good-faith social democrats: "In the last analysis, all decisions are dependent on the will of the people as consumers." He also wrote, "If a businessman does not strictly obey the orders of the public as they are conveyed to him by the structure of market prices, he suffers losses, he goes bankrupt, and is thus *removed from his eminent position at the helm*. Other men who did better in satisfying the demand of the consumers replace him." [Emphasis added.]

In a free market (and even today within limits), we *collectively* decide who controls the means of production. A defiant individual hasn't a chance against the relentless consumers' verdict. Who was responsible for the bookseller Borders's bankruptcy? Individually, you or I could not have driven the chain from the market. But we did it collectively by our individual decisions about where and how to buy books. In effect we said, "Borders, we think there are better uses for your assets, so we want them transferred to someone else. And we prefer that your 10,700 employees produce something else, because other people are already satisfying our book-buying needs."

That sounds like the kind of collective decision-making the social democrats say they want. (Without corporate protectionism, consumer power would be even more pronounced than it is today.) Had our language evolved differently, the free market might today be known as *socialism*, since decisions about who controls the means of production would be made socially. The opposing position — which favors decision-making within the state — would properly be called *statism*. In fact, individualist anarchist Benjamin Tucker and the other radical pro-market anarchists of his era called themselves *socialists*.

In the free market, therefore, we have a beneficent combination of individualism and collectivism. Nobel laureate F.A. Hayek, in his essay "Individualism: True and False," alluded to this irony when he wrote, "What individualism teaches us is that society is greater than the individual only in so far as it is free. In so far as it is controlled or directed, it is limited to the powers of the individual minds which control or direct it."

Future of Freedom Foundation, December 7, 2012

Chapter 49.
Individualism, Collectivism,
and Other Murky Labels

Imagine the following person. He believes all individuals should be free to do anything that's peaceful and therefore favors private property, free global markets, freedom of contract, civil liberties, and all the related ideas that come under the label libertarianism (or liberalism). Obviously he is not a statist. But is he an individualist and a capitalist or a socialist and a collectivist?

It sounds like an easy question, but on closer inspection it's not. Much depends on the context, or the level of analysis at which the question is directed. An answer appropriate at the level of personal ethics may not be appropriate in a discussion of political economy. Take the word *individualist*. There are many senses in which the person described above could be called an individualist. If in his personal life he habitually and ultimately relies on himself to make decisions (although he seeks information and wisdom from others) and does not slavishly follow fashion, he could appropriately be called an individualist. He likewise is a *methodological* individualist if he believes that only individuals act and create; only individuals have intentions, values, and preferences. He understands that when a group acts, it's really just individuals acting in concert.

What about at the level of political economy? Is this person also an individualist in that context? Here the labels get murkier. He certainly is an individualist in the political-legal sense; that is, he favors a system in which individuals' titles to honestly acquired property are respected. Group ownership would have to be traceable to express or implicit contracts among collections of individuals. (But for a libertarian theory of nonstate public property, see Roderick Long's "A Plea for Public Property" and Elinor Ostrom's Nobel Prize-winning work on common pool resources.)

This seems to yield the conclusion that a libertarian is categorically an individualist. But not so fast. The term individualist, let's recall, was (and sometimes still is) a pejorative aimed at people of the libertarian persuasion. It was meant to stigmatize them as antisocial. The adjectives *rugged* and *atomistic* were later added to drive home the point. In some minds, "Unabomber" Theodore Kaczynski, who lived alone in a shack in the wilderness, was the quintessential individualist (except for the letter bombs).

But the libertarian philosophy is the furthest thing from antisocial. That would be a peculiar way indeed to describe a philosophy that embraces — with gusto! — the global division of labor and free trade across property, city, county, state, and national lines. (Yes, I left out planetary — for now.)

There are other senses in which *individualist* is far off the mark and in which *socialist* and even *collectivist* are closer. The Austrian tradition in economics has long emphasized that the chief advantage of the market process over central decision-making lies in the market's embodiment of a social, or collective, intelligence that is denied to any individual or small subgroup. This doesn't mean that a collective mind literally emerges, only that the social process and the price system combine in such a way that the whole is greater than the sum of its parts. The market "knows" more than any of us do alone. (The same point can be made for a broader context. The philosopher Ludwig Wittgenstein argued that language itself, without which there is little or no thought, is essentially social.)

Further, Ludwig von Mises often emphasized that in a freed market, consumers collectively, not individual business people, actually *determine* who owns the means of production and what will be produced. When you trace out the implications of this, things get interesting. Consumers constantly make this determination through their buying and abstention from buying, but the outcome is never the intended result of conscious decision-making. Business people may legally own their capital and producers' goods, but if — in a genuinely competitive market — consumers don't like what those owners do with those assets, they face bankruptcy and loss of control. It is a *social*, or *collective*, process. As Mises wrote in *Human Action*,

> The direction of all economic affairs is in the market society a task of entrepreneurs. Theirs is the control of production. They are at the helm and steer the ship. A superficial observer would believe that they are supreme. But they are not. They are bound to obey unconditionally the captain's orders. *The captain is the consumer.* Neither the entrepreneurs nor the farmers nor the capitalists determine what has to be produced. The consumers do that. If a businessman does not strictly obey the orders of the public as they are conveyed to him by the structure of market prices, he suffers losses, he goes bankrupt, and is thus *removed from his eminent position at the helm.* Other men who did better in satisfying the demand of the consumers replace him. [Emphasis added.]

Isn't that social, or collective, control of the means of the production? Does that make libertarians socialists or collectivists? This fact about the market is worth passing along to our good-faith opponents who decry any system that does not allow the mass of people a say in matters than affect them. The irony is that the free market accomplishes this, while state socialist systems do not. But it is necessary to stress that Mises's point applies fully *only* under laissez faire — meaning a free market *without coercively provided privileges of any kind.* Historically, government intervention in the market has aimed to shelter the privileged (owners of land and capital who benefited from political favoritism like patents, licensing, and land enclosure) from the demands of regular people — consumers and workers — the very ones whose voices are most effective in a truly free market. That is why the struggle for freedom has always been a struggle *against privilege*.

In summary, the great political debate is not between individualists and collectivists, but between those who see the coercive state as the locus of authority and those who see voluntary society as that locus. Liberals from Adam Smith to Herbert Spencer to F.A. Hayek emphasized the benefits of free, spontaneous social (market) processes (including the common law) and how those processes are disrupted by the state. Advocates of the supremacy of state over society are properly called *statists*. Wouldn't it follow that advocates of the supremacy of society over state should be called *socialists*? In this regard, I recall that the libertarian James Dale Davidson, founder of the National Taxpayers Union, long ago wrote a book (*The Squeeze*, as I remember) that called for a "socialization of rules." By that he meant that the rules and customs of everyday life should be generated, bottom up, by society, not imposed, top down, by legislators.

Be assured, I am not suggesting that libertarians start calling themselves socialists. I *am* saying that a reconsideration of labels can clarify understanding. Nevertheless, as a historical matter I think Mises was mistaken when he wrote, "The notion of socialism as conceived and defined by all socialists implies the absence of a market for factors of production and of prices of such factors." This can't be true because some earlier American advocates of laissez faire — of what was dubbed *consistent Manchesterism* — called themselves *socialists* for a time, most prominently, Benjamin R. Tucker, editor of *Liberty* magazine (1881–1908). In the view of Tucker and his allies (and earlier liberal thinkers like Herbert Spencer's mentor Thomas Hodgskin), capitalism meant government interference in the market (tariffs, the banking cartel, patents, and the land monopoly) on behalf of the owners of capital and to the detriment of the rest of society. Their alternative was a completely free and competitive market void of privilege; only that system would restore to workers the just earnings taken through anticompetitive government intervention. In 1884 Tucker wrote in "Socialism: What It Is":

> Socialism says that what's one man's meat must no longer be another's poison; that no man shall be able to add to his riches except by labor; that in adding to his riches by labor alone no man makes another man poorer; that on the contrary every man thus adding to his riches makes every other man richer; that increase and concentration of wealth through labor tend to increase, cheapen, and vary production; that every increase of capital in the hands of the laborer tends, in the absence of legal monopoly, to put more products, better products, cheaper products,

and a greater variety of products within the reach of every man who works; and that this fact means the physical, mental, and moral perfecting of mankind, and the realization of human fraternity. Is that not glorious? Shall a word that means all that be cast aside simply because some have tried to wed it with authority?

When you include in the labor category what entrepreneurs do, as Tucker and Hodgskin did, this description of a free society is virtually indistinguishable from those offered by Frédéric Bastiat, Ludwig von Mises, and Leonard Read, founder of the Foundation for Economic Education.

Today *socialism* means only State, not social, control. But for many people here and abroad, *capitalism* means not laissez faire, but rather corporatism, or what the great libertarian Albert Jay Nock called the "Merchant-state." It behooves us to make sure our labels communicate clearly. Otherwise we will never bring the mass of people to the cause of liberty.

Foundation for Economic Education, August 31, 2012

Chapter 50.
Hayek on Individualism

F.A. Hayek's essay "Individualism: True and False" (chapter one of *Individualism and Economic Order*) overflows with insights that belong in any brief on behalf of a free society. As the title suggests, Hayek wished to distinguish two markedly different philosophies associated with the label *individualism*: one that rejected "rationalism" and one that embraced it. (As we'll see, by *rationalism* Hayek did not simply mean a commitment to reason.)

"One might even say," Hayek explained,

> that the former is a product of an acute consciousness of the limitations of the individual mind which induces an attitude of humility toward the impersonal and anonymous social processes by which individuals help to create things greater than they know, while the latter is the product of an exaggerated belief in the powers of individual reason and a consequent contempt for anything which has not been consciously designed by it or is not fully intelligible to it.

Thus for Hayek the crucial difference is over whether societies (institutions) are largely spontaneous, emergent, and organic or designed. His great concern was that rationalistic individualism, in awe of the mind's ability to engineer solutions, too readily leads to the centralization of power and totalitarianism.

This essay has not been without controversy even among fans of Hayek. He has been criticized for drawing too sharp a distinction between the liberal rationalists and liberal empiricists and for being arbitrarily pro-British and anti-French in dividing the true from the false individualists. I happily duck those controversies here and focus instead on points that are both less controversial among liberals and, in my view, indispensable to the full case for freedom. (In his book *Classical Liberalism and the Austrian School*, the great intellectual historian Ralph Raico criticized Hayek's derogation of the French liberals. "Some might uncharitably suspect Hayek of a terminal Anglophilia which tended to blind him to some obvious facts," Raico wrote.)

The first point I draw attention to comes in Hayek's discussion of Adam Smith's view of mankind. Smith's "chief concern," Hayek wrote,

> was not so much with what man might occasionally achieve when he was at his best but that *he should have as little opportunity as possible to do harm when*

he was at his worst. It would scarcely be too much to claim that the main merit of the individualism which he and his contemporaries advocated is that it is a system under which *bad men can do least harm.* It is a social system which does not depend for its functioning on our finding good men for running it, or on all men becoming better than they now are, but which makes use of men in all their given variety and complexity, sometimes good and sometimes bad, sometimes intelligent and more often stupid. Their aim was a system under which it should be possible to grant freedom to all, instead of restricting it … to "the good and the wise." [Emphasis added.]

Keep this in mind the next time someone proclaims that a muscular State, unconstrained by strict rules, is needed to prevent flawed human beings from harming others. Then ask: What will keep the flawed — and *privileged* — human beings who have access to the violent power of the state from harming others? Those who are familiar with Hayek's *The Road to Serfdom,* and especially his chapter "Why the Worst Get on Top," will know what Hayek is getting at.

Hayek also sought to correct a popular misconception about the early liberals' view of human motivation.

There can be no doubt, of course, that in the language of the great writers of the eighteenth century it was man's "self-love," or even his "selfish interests," which they represented as the "universal mover," and that by these terms they were referring primarily to a moral attitude, which they thought to be widely prevalent. These terms, however, did not mean egotism in the narrow sense of concern with only the immediate needs of one's proper person. The "self," for which alone people were supposed to care, did as a matter of course include their family and friends; and it would have made no difference to the argument if it had included anything for which people in fact did care.

When critics attack the alleged market ideal of the selfish maximizer, they tackle a straw man.

As important as this point regarding moral attitude is, Hayek found something more important in true individualism, namely:

the constitutional limitation of man's knowledge and interests, the fact that he *cannot* know more than a tiny part of the whole of society and that therefore all that can enter into his motives are the immediate effects which his actions will have in the sphere he knows. All the possible differences in men's moral attitudes amount to little, so far as the significance for social organization is concerned, compared with the fact that all man's mind can effectively comprehend are the facts of the narrow circle of which he is the center; that, whether he is completely selfish or the most perfect altruist, the human needs for which he *can* effectively care are an almost negligible fraction of the needs of all

186

members of society. The real question, therefore, is not whether man is, or ought to be, guided by selfish motives but whether we can allow him to be guided in his actions by those immediate consequences which he can know and care for or whether he ought to be made to do what seems appropriate to somebody else who is supposed to possess a fuller comprehension of the significance of these actions to society as a whole.

Of course, Hayek's true individualists — that is, the early economists — understood that *no one* possesses that fuller comprehension. Rulers can have no better grasp of the whole than do the ruled. However, rulers *lack* something that ruled individuals do not: knowledge of the subjects' own particular circumstances, interests, preferences, skills, and so on. Hence the liberal injunction that the state should leave peaceful people alone and the conviction that strict observance of that injunction serves the general good.

"What the economists understood for the first time," Hayek wrote, "was that the market as it had grown up was an effective way of making man take part in a process more complex and extended than he could comprehend and that it was through the market that he was made to contribute 'to ends which were no part of his purpose.'"

There's irony in individualism: "What individualism teaches us is that society is greater than the individual only in so far as it is free. In so far as it is controlled or directed, it is limited to the powers of the individual minds which control or direct it."

Foundation for Economic Education, June 15, 2012

Chapter 51.
Tackling Straw Men Is Easier
than Critiquing Libertarianism

Maybe I'm being unreasonable, but I think it behooves a critic to understand what he's criticizing. I realize that tackling straw men is much easier than dealing with challenging arguments, but that's no excuse for the shoddy work we find in John Edward Terrell's *New York Times* post, "Evolution and the American Myth of the Individual."

In his confused attempt to criticize libertarians, Terrell gets one thing right when he says, "The thought that it is both rational and natural for each of us to care *only* for ourselves, our own preservation, and our own achievements is a treacherous fabrication." [Emphasis added.]

Indeed it is. Unfortunately for Terrell's case, it's *his* treacherous fabrication.

Terrell targets the Enlightenment and Jean-Jacques Rousseau, which is doubly funny. Libertarians don't claim Rousseau as a forebear; he was an advocate of imposing the "general will" — ascertained through democratic procedures — on dissidents as a means of forcing them to be "free." Does that sound libertarian?

As for the Enlightenment, last I checked Adam Smith was a principal of the Scottish wing of that intellectual movement. And he never would have claimed that "it is both rational and natural for each of us to care only for ourselves, our own preservation, and our own achievements." (I'm not aware of French Enlightenment economists who thought that either.) Has Terrell never heard of Smith's *The Theory of Moral Sentiments*, published in 1859 — 17 years before *The Wealth of Nations* and revised throughout his life? Or is he in that group of scribblers who think *The Wealth of Nations* was all that Smith had to say about the human enterprise? (Of course, *The Wealth of Nations* also does not embrace the view that Terrell ascribes to libertarians.) For Terrell's edification, I'll point out that *The Theory of Moral Sentiments* is an extended discussion of "fellow-feeling," that is, our *natural* sympathy for other people.

Smith would laugh at any portrayal of the isolated, allegedly self-sufficient individual as the summit of human development. No less than the great Greek philosophers, Adam Smith understood how inherently social the individual person is. The self *itself* is a product of social life. People, he said, seek praise from their fellows and, importantly, aspire to be worthy of praise.

"What so great happiness as to be beloved, and to know that we deserve to be beloved? What so great misery as to be hated, and to know that we deserve to be hated?" Smith asked. The reason, he makes clear, is not merely that a good reputation produces material benefits. As he wrote on page one, "How selfish soever man may be supposed, there are evidently some principles in his nature, which interest him in the fortune of others, and render their happiness necessary to him, though he derives nothing from it except the pleasure of seeing it."

By coincidence, just before reading Terrell's post, I had listened to Russ Roberts's EconTalk interview with Vernon Smith, the Nobel laureate who is steeped in the economics tradition of Adam Smith and F.A. Hayek. The topic of discussion was *The Theory of Moral Sentiments*, which is entirely appropriate considering that Roberts and Vernon Smith are two of the small group of professional economists who are intimately familiar with the book. (Another is Dan Klein. Check out Roberts's book about *The Theory of Moral Sentiments*: *How Adam Smith Can Change Your Life: An Unexpected Guide to Human Nature and Happiness*.)

At one point in the interview, Vernon Smith notes enthusiastically,

> [Adam Smith] says, imagine a person, a member of the species being brought up entirely isolated. … He says that person can no more understand what it means for his mind to be deformed than for his face to be deformed. And Smith says — I'm paraphrasing — bring him into society and you give him the mirror he needed before. In other words, the looking glass in which we are able to see ourselves as others see us.

Thus society is indispensable for the proper development of the person (and reason).

Vernon Smith has also written (in the 1998 *Southern Economic Journal* article "The Two Faces of Adam Smith") that Adam Smith's two published works both describe

> one behavioral axiom, "the propensity to truck, barter, and exchange one thing for another," where the objects of trade I will interpret to include not only goods, but also gifts, assistance, and favors out of sympathy. … [W]hether it is goods or favors that are exchanged, they bestow gains from trade that humans seek relentlessly in all social transactions. Thus, Adam Smith's single axiom, broadly interpreted … is sufficient to characterize a major portion of the human social and cultural enterprise. It explains why human nature appears to be simultaneously self-regarding and other-regarding.

Does it sound as though either of the Smiths would be inclined to deny, as Terrell puts it, that "evolution has made us a powerfully social species, so much so that the essential precondition of human survival is and always has been the individual *plus* his or her relationships with others"?

Has Terrell not heard of Adam or Vernon Smith? Or Hayek or James Buchanan (two Nobel laureates, so their names have been in the papers)? Or Russ Roberts? Or Dan Klein? And while we're at it, let's drop the name Herbert Spencer. As Spencer wrote in *Social Statics* (1851):

> The increasing assertion of personal rights is an increasing demand that the external conditions needful to a complete unfolding of the individuality shall be respected. ...

> Yet must this higher individuation be joined with the greatest mutual dependence. Paradoxical though the assertion looks, the progress is at once toward complete separateness and complete union. But the separateness is of a kind consistent with the most complex combinations for fulfilling social wants; and the union is of a kind that does not hinder entire development of each personality. Civilization is evolving a state of things and a kind of character in which two apparently conflicting requirements are reconciled.

He anticipated "at once perfect individuation and perfect mutual dependence."

If Terrell has never encountered these thinkers, how much research could he have done before he opined about libertarianism? Why should we take him seriously?

I wish I could understand intellectuals who seem to form a priori notions about their opponents, do no empirical research to see if those notions hold up, and then go public with criticisms that should embarrass them badly. If I may say something in the spirit of *The Theory of Moral Sentiments*: I am embarrassed that a fellow member of the human race has written something so ridiculous.

What people like Terrell don't realize — or perhaps realize too well — is that the fundamental point in dispute is not whether the individual is a social animal or a creature best suited for an atomistic existence. No libertarian I know of subscribes to the latter notion. The point in dispute is whether proper social life should be founded on peaceful consensual cooperation or on compulsion. (See "What Social Animals Owe to Each Other" in this volume.)

Terrell asserts a dubious distinction between thinking of society as natural and thinking of society as merely a matter of convention. I say *dubious*, and of doubtful significance, because the conventionalist (David Hume, perhaps?) can believe that given their nature, only a social existence generated by *certain* conventions is appropriate for human beings.

But if for argument's sake we accept Terrell's distinction and his preference for naturalism, we still must ask: if society is natural, why must we be *compelled* (by government) to be social? Why is aggressive force — the initiation of violence, which robs persons of their dignity and self-determination — acceptable when free and spontaneous cooperation — voluntary exchange and mutual aid — ought to work reasonably well? Do the Terrells of the world believe that society would fail without violence? That, I submit, is bizarre.

Future of Freedom Foundation, December 5, 2014

Chapter 52.
The State Is No Friend of the Worker

In any election season we hear the usual political promises about raising wages. Democrats pledge to raise the minimum wage and assure equal pay for equal work for men and women. Republicans usually oppose those things, but their explanations are typically lame. ("The burden on small business would be increased too much.") Some Republicans endorse raising the minimum wage because they think opposition will cost them elections.

In addressing this issue, we who believe in freeing society from privilege as well as from regulation and taxes should be careful not to imply that we have free markets today. When we declare our opposition to minimum-wage or equal-pay-for-equal-work legislation, we must at the same time emphasize that the reigning corporate state compromises the market process in fundamental ways, usually to the detriment of workers. Therefore, not only should no new interference with the market be approved, but *all existing interference* should be repealed forthwith. If you omit that second part, you'll sound like an apologist for the corporatist status quo. Why would you want to do that?

The fact is that no politician, bureaucrat, economist, or pundit can say what anyone's labor is worth. That can only be fairly determined through the unadulterated competitive market process. Perhaps ironically (considering libertarians' individualism), it's a determination we make collectively and continuously as we enter the market and demonstrate our preferences for various kinds of services through our buying and abstaining.

If the market is free of competition-inhibiting government privileges and restrictions, we may assume that wages will roughly approximate worth according to the market participants' subjective valuations. In fact, only the market process can produce and reveal this information. This process isn't perfect; for one thing, preferences change and wage and price adjustments take time. Moreover, racial, ethnic, and sexual prejudice could result, for a time, in wage discrimination. Nothing happens instantaneously.

The surest way to eliminate wage discrimination is to keep government from impeding the competitive process with such devices as occupational licensing, permits, minimum product standards, so-called intellectual property, zoning, and other land-use restrictions. All government barriers to self-employment — and these can take implicit forms, such as patents and raising the cost of living through inflation, or burdening entrepreneurs with protectionist regulation — make workers vulnerable to exploitation. Being able to tell a boss, "Take this job and shove it," because alternatives, including self-employment, are available, is an effective way to establish the true market value of one's labor in the marketplace. With the collapsing price of what author Kevin Carson calls the "technologies of abundance" (think of information technology and digital machine tools), sophisticated small-scale enterprise — and the independence it represents — is more feasible than ever.

One thinker who understood how the worth of labor is determined in the market was the radical libertarian English writer Thomas Hodgskin (1787–1869). Hodgskin is often misunderstood. Wikipedia calls him a "socialist writer on political economy, critic of capitalism and defender of free trade and early trade unions." To the modern ear that will sound odd: a socialist critic of capitalism who defended free trade.

Hodgskin is usually labeled a Ricardian socialist, but Hodgskin criticized early classical economist David Ricardo while lauding Adam Smith. Moreover, *socialism* didn't always mean what it means today. In earlier times *socialist* was an umbrella term identifying those who thought workers were denied their full just reward under the prevailing political economy. The remedy for this injustice varied with particular socialists. Some advocated state control of the means of production; others wanted collective control without the state; and still others — libertarian and individualist anarchist Benjamin R. Tucker most prominently — favored private ownership and free competition under laissez faire.

What these self-styled socialists had in common was their conviction that *capitalism*, which was understood as a political economy of privilege for employers, cheated workers of their proper reward. By this definition, even an adherent of subjectivist and marginalist Austrian economics could have qualified as a socialist. (See "Austrian Exploitation Theory" in this volume.)

By the way, Hodgskin used the word *capitalist* disparagingly before Karl Marx ever wrote about capitalism. As philosopher and intellectual historian George H. Smith notes, Marx called the laissez-faireist Hodgskin "one of the most important modern English economists." It was not the first time the author of *Capital* complimented radical pro-market liberals. He credited class theory to French liberal historians. (Marx then proceeded to mangle their libertarian theory.)

As a libertarian champion of labor against state-privileged capital, Hodgskin had much to say about how just wages should be determined. In his 1825 book, *Labor Defended Against the Claims of Capital*, he first noted that many goods are the product of joint efforts, which would seem to make it difficult to reward individual workers properly. He wrote:

Though the defective nature of the claims of capital may now be satisfactorily proved, the question as to the wages of labour is by no means decided. Political economists, indeed, who have insisted very strongly on the necessity of giving security to property, and have ably demonstrated how much that security promotes general happiness, will not hesitate to agree with me when I say that whatever labour produces ought to belong to it. They have always embraced the maxim of permitting those to "reap who sow," and they have maintained that the labour of a man's body and the work of his hands are to be considered as exclusively his own. I take it for granted, therefore, that they will henceforth maintain that the whole produce of labour ought to belong to the labourer. But though this, as a general proposition, is quite evident, and quite true, there is a difficulty, in its practical application, which no individual can surmount. There is no principle or rule, as far as I know, for dividing the produce of joint labour among the different individuals who concur in production, but the judgment of the individuals themselves; that judgment depending on the value men may set on different species of labour can never be known, nor can any rule be given for its application by any single person. As well might a man say what others shall hate or what they shall like.

Whatever division of labour exists, and the further it is carried the more evident does this truth become, scarcely any individual completes of himself any species of produce. Almost any product of art and skill is the result of joint and combined labour. So dependent is man on man, and so much does this dependence increase as society advances, that hardly any labour of any single individual, however much it may contribute to the whole produce of society, is of the least value but as forming a part of the great social task. In the manufacture of a piece of cloth, the spinner, the weaver, the bleacher and the dyer are all different persons. All of them except the first is dependent for his supply of materials on him, and of what use would his thread be unless the others took it from him, and each performed that part of the task which is necessary to complete the cloth? Wherever the spinner purchases the cotton or wool, the price which he can obtain for his thread, over and above what he paid for the raw material, is the reward of his labour. But it is quite plain that the sum the weaver will be disposed to give for the thread will depend on his view of its utility. Wherever the division of labour is introduced, therefore, the judgment of other men intervenes before the labourer can realise his earnings, and there is no longer any thing which we can call the natural reward of individual labour. Each labourer produces only some part of a whole, and each part having no value or utility of itself, there is nothing on which the labourer can seize, and say: "This is my product, this will I keep to myself." Between the commencement of any joint operation, such as that of making cloth, and the division of its product among the different persons whose combined exertions have produced it, the judgment of men must intervene several times, and the question is, how much of this joint product should go to each of the individuals whose united labourers produce it?

Observe Hodgskin's Austrian-style subjectivism: How much someone is willing to pay for a product "will depend on his view of its utility." (The way this fits with his labor theory of value is an interesting matter that we cannot take up here.)

How then does he propose that the wage problem be solved? Here's how:

> I know no way of deciding this but by leaving it to be settled by the unfettered judgments of the labourers themselves. If all kinds of labour were perfectly free, if no unfounded prejudice invested some parts, and perhaps the least useful, of the social task with great honour, while other parts are very improperly branded with disgrace, there would be no difficulty on this point, and the wages of individual labour would be justly settled by what Dr [Adam] Smith calls the "higgling of the market."

Thus free competition among industrious individuals, who ultimately are trying to serve consumers, is the only way to reveal the worth of labor services and products. Worth is defined as the capacity to serve consumers. This is both just and efficient. There is no way for a legislator or bureaucrat to divine the correct minimum wage or to decide if "equal work" is being paid equally. Only the market process can discover this information.

"Unfortunately," Hodgskin added, "labour is not, in general, free." What keeps it from being free? The state, which serves special interests.

Importantly, Hodgskin emphasized that *labor* includes "mental exertion," that is, the work of entrepreneurs and managers:

> Far be it, therefore, from the manual labourer, while he claims the reward due to his own productive powers, to deny its appropriate reward to any other species of labour, whether it be of the head or the hands. The labour and skill of the contriver, or of the man who arranges and adapts a whole, are as necessary as the labour and skill of him who executes only a part, and they must be paid accordingly.

Perhaps Marx should have read his Hodgskin more closely, and those who would legislate the level of wages today should read him for the first time. So-called progressives who look to the state to set wages do a disservice to those who fare worst in the corporate state because while progressives work on behalf of measures that must price vulnerable marginal workers out of the market, truly radical reforms are overlooked.

Rather than empowering our rulers further, let's empower individuals by freeing the market.

Future of Freedom Foundation, December 5, 2014

Chapter 53.
Work!

I hear therefore with joy whatever is beginning to be said of the dignity and necessity of labor to every citizen. There is virtue yet in the hoe and the spade, for learned as well as for unlearned hands. And labor is everywhere welcome; always we are invited to work. — Ralph Waldo Emerson, "The American Scholar," 1837

Work! — Maynard G. Krebs, *The Many Loves of Dobie Gillis*, television, circa 1960

From the start, Americans have had a love-hate relationship with work. We tend to rhapsodize about labor, but at least in our personal lives, we praise labor-saving devices and condemn "make-work" schemes. (Unfortunately, public policy is another matter.) Emerson and other pillars of American culture — whom for these purposes I will call the moralists — associated work with dignity and purpose. Historian Thaddeus Russell teaches us that when the slaves were freed from the Southern plantations, they were pounded with the gospel of work. "Slaves generally considered work to be only a means to wealth, but after emancipation, Americans told them that work — even thankless, nonremunerative work — was a virtue in itself," Russell writes in *A Renegade History of the United States*. He reports that the Freedman's Bureau admonished the former slaves, "You must be industrious and frugal. It is feared that some will act from the mistaken notion that Freedom means liberty to be idle. This class of persons, known to the law as vagrants, must at once correct this mistake." Russell notes that "thousands of black men were rounded up for refusing to work."

The message was that work is not just an honest and proper way to obtain the necessities of life without mooching off others. The activity in itself is a source of goodness, even saintliness, and should be engaged in unceasingly, taking time out only for eating, sleeping, other bodily functions, and tending to one's familial duties. One didn't work to live; one lived to work.

Whites had been subjected to the same harangue for ages: work was a reward in itself, apart from remuneration, because "idle hands are the devil's playground."

We must be clear that the message was not merely that work could be a source of satisfaction apart from the money. The message amounted to a vilification of leisure, indeed, of consumption. (Some conservatives seem to hold this view today.)

In a good illustration of the "Bootleggers and Baptists" phenomenon, the moralists were joined in their labor evangelism by employers, who needed uncomplaining workers willing to spend long hours in unpleasant factories. People preferred leisure and looked for every opportunity to indulge in it. Hence, "Saint Monday," which, as Russell notes, Benjamin Franklin sneered at because it "is as duly kept by our working people as Sunday; the only difference is that instead of employing their time cheaply in church, they are wasting it expensively in the alehouse."

We get a different picture of labor from the economists, however. The classical economists and the Austrians (at least from Ludwig von Mises onward) stressed the unpleasantness — the "disutility" and even sad necessity — of labor. Adam Smith and other early economists equated work with "toil," which is not a word overflowing with positive connotations. In *The Wealth of Nations*, Smith wrote,

> The real price of every thing, what every thing really costs to the man who wants to acquire it, is the toil and trouble of acquiring it. What every thing is really worth to the man who has acquired it and who wants to dispose of it, or exchange it for something else, is the toil and trouble which it can save to himself, and which it can impose upon other people. What is bought with money or with goods is purchased by labour, as much as what we acquire by the toil of our own body. That money, or those goods, indeed, save us this toil.

The 19th-century French liberal economist Frédéric Bastiat carried on this tradition by emphasizing that exchange arises out of a wish to be spared labor. One accepts the terms of an exchange only if obtaining the desired good in other ways would be more arduous.

For Bastiat and other early economists, exchange was the foundation of society. "Society is purely and solely a continual series of exchanges," the late-18th-early-19th-century French liberal economist Destutt de Tracy wrote. It follows that the penchant for economizing effort — the preference for leisure — is a beneficent feature of human nature. (The science-fiction writer Robert Heinlein has a character, Lazarus Long, I believe, who praises the lazy person who invented the wheelbarrow.)

Further, Bastiat explained, technological advancement is valued precisely because it substitutes the free services of nature for human toil. In his uncompleted magnum opus, *Economic Harmonies*, he wrote, "It is characteristic of progress (and, indeed, this is what we mean by progress) to transform onerous utility into gratuitous utility; to decrease [exchange-]value without decreasing utility; and to enable all men, for fewer pains or at smaller cost, to obtain the same satisfactions."

By onerous utility, he meant utility bought with sweat and strain; by gratuitous utility, he meant utility provided by nature free of charge. When ingenuity is applied to the making of a good, "its production has in large measure been turned over to Nature. It is obtained for less expenditure of human effort; less service is performed as it passes from hand to hand." Needless to say, this is a good thing. Of course, some of the freed-up time will be devoted to producing other goods that were unaffordable yesterday, but some will be devoted to consumption or leisure. The proportion set aside for leisure will likely increase as living standards rise (assuming government interference doesn't deny workers their rewards for higher productivity).

> The goal of all men, in all their activities, is to reduce the amount of effort in relation to the end desired and, in order to accomplish this end, to incorporate in their labor a constantly increasing proportion of the forces of Nature. ... [T]hey invent tools or machines, they enlist the chemical and mechanical forces of the elements, they divide their labors, and they unite their efforts. How to do more with less, is the eternal question asked in all times, in all places, in all situations, in all things.

(Bastiat elaborated on this in his remarkable chapter 8, "Private Property and Common Wealth," which was the subject of "Bastiat on the Socialization of Wealth" in this volume.)

Bastiat agreed with Adam Smith, who wrote, "Consumption is the sole end and purpose of all production." Hence the economists rejected the moralists' view that production — labor — is an end in itself.

We see this same lack of enthusiasm for work in John Stuart Mill, an influential classical economist as well as a philosopher. In 1849 Thomas Carlyle published an article lamenting that the end of slavery in Great Britain meant that white people couldn't make sure that blacks worked enough (for *whites*). (He presented this in "Occasional Discourse on the Negro Question," *Fraser's Magazine for Town and Country*, December 1849.) Indeed, this is why Carlyle dubbed economics, which was premised on free labor, "the dismal science."

Mill wrote an anonymous response ("The Negro Question") in the following issue. He protested Carlyle's suggestion that blacks were meant to serve white people. Mill then turned to "the gospel of work," praised by Carlyle, "which, to my mind, justly deserves the name of a cant." Mill attacked the idea that work is an end in itself, rather than merely a means.

> While we talk only of work, and not of its object, we are far from the root of the matter; or, if it may be called the root, it is a root without flower or fruit. ... In opposition to the "gospel of work," I would assert the gospel of leisure, and maintain that human beings cannot rise to the finer attributes of their nature compatibly with a life filled with labor ... the exhausting, stiffening, stupefying toil of many kinds of agricultural and

manufacturing laborers. To reduce very greatly the quantity of work required to carry on existence is as needful as to distribute it more equally; and the progress of science, and the increasing ascendancy of justice and good sense, tend to this result.

In Mises and Murray Rothbard we find similar views: work is to be economized. Mises devoted an entire chapter in *Socialism* to refuting the state socialists' claim that work is unpleasant only because of the market economy and that it would be blissful if private property were abolished and the market were replaced with state central planning. Under any system, Mises wrote, labor may afford a small (and insignificant, he thought) measure of direct satisfaction, but that soon passes. Yet people must keep working to obtain its indirect satisfactions, the goods it enables them to buy.

Mises may overstate his case here, as did his mentor, Carl Menger, in the other direction (in 1871, mind you): "The occupations of by far the great majority of men afford enjoyment, are thus themselves true satisfactions of needs, and would be practiced, although perhaps in smaller measure or in a modified manner, even if men were not forced by lack of means to exert their powers."

Mises mocked the state socialists by putting scare quotes around the words *joy of labor*, asking, "If work gives satisfaction per se why is the worker paid? Why does he not reward the employer for the pleasure which the employer gives him by allowing him to work?"

What people often take for the joy of labor, he said, was actually the satisfaction of finishing a task, the "pleasure in being free of work rather than pleasure in the work itself." Mises quoted the medieval monks who appended to the manuscript copies they had just painstakingly produced by hand, "*Laus tibi sit Christe, quoniam liber explicit iste*" (which he translated inexactly as "Praise the Lord because the work is completed").

For Rothbard, leisure is a "desirable good," a consumer good, which people will forgo only if at the margin the fruits of a unit of labor undertaken are preferred to the satisfaction that a unit of leisure would afford. Rothbard acknowledged that labor can be satisfying and wrote *Man, Economy, and State*:

> In cases where the labor itself provides positive satisfactions, however, these are intertwined with and cannot be separated from the prospect of obtaining the final product. Deprived of the final product, man will consider his labor senseless and useless, and the labor itself will no longer bring positive satisfactions. *Those activities which are engaged in purely for their own sake are not labor but are pure play, consumers' goods in themselves.* Play, as a consumers' good, is subject to the law of marginal utility as are all goods, and the time spent in play will be balanced against the utility to be derived from other obtainable goods. In the expenditure of any hour of labor, therefore, man weighs the disutility of the labor involved (including the leisure forgone plus any dissatisfaction stemming from the work itself)

against the utility of the contribution he will make in that hour to the production of desired goods (including future goods and any pleasure in the work itself), i.e., with the value of his marginal product. [Emphasis added.]

Rothbard's mentor, Mises, made a fundamental point about human action when he wrote, "Even if labor were a pure pleasure it would have to be used economically, since human life is limited in time, and human energy is not inexhaustible."

That being the case, I will reserve further thoughts on work for another time. Meanwhile, *Laus tibi sit Christe, quoniam liber explicit iste!*

Future of Freedom Foundation, March 7, 2014

Chapter 54.
Labor's "Right to a Free Market"

No issue has been more contentious in labor relations than the Employee Free Choice Act (EFCA), which has been introduced many times in Congress. It would have required the National Labor Relations Board (NLRB) to recognize a union when a majority of the employees in a unit appropriate for bargaining had signed valid authorizations. Under current federal law an NLRB-supervised election must be held and a majority must vote by *secret ballot* for the union before it can become government-certified. The union-backed EFCA would presumably make it easier to establish a union in a company, but opponents say worker intimidation would be encouraged with an open card-signing process versus a secret-ballot election.

The expected polarization can be seen in the conflicting claims. The AFL-CIO blog has called the EFCA

> maybe the most important labor law reform in nearly 50 years. …
> Currently, if employees present an employer with union authorization
> cards signed by a majority, the employer can demand a secret ballot
> election supervised by the National Labor Relations Board (NLRB). But
> the NLRB election process is broken because it enables employers to
> intimidate, coerce and harass workers and drag out the process
> indefinitely.

On the other side the Coalition for a Democratic Workplace, whose members include the U.S. Chamber of Commerce and the National Association of Manufacturers, has said,

> the EFCA would strip Americans of that right [to a federally supervised
> private ballot] and replace it with a system where your vote is no longer
> private, and it is made public to your employer, the union organizers and
> your co-workers. We believe the only way to guarantee worker protection
> from coercion and intimidation is through the continued use of a
> federally supervised private ballot election so that personal decisions
> about whether to join a union remain private.

What should free-market advocates say about this controversy? As might be expected, in a corporatist mixed economy such questions aren't as clear-cut as they appear. Of course the pro-business side opposes the EFCA, while the pro-labor side supports it. Both say they want to protect workers from intimidation. But looking deeper we see that the conflict is over how a *government agency*, the NLRB, should manage labor relations. Should libertarians be offering advice to interventionists on how to do a job that they shouldn't be doing in the first place?

This question leads us in a direction perhaps many of us have not gone before. Advocates of the market typically assume that federal labor legislation since the New Deal has put the government squarely on the side of unionism. Some seek countervailing intervention, such as a national right-to-work law, which would forbid employers from signing union-shop agreements even if they wanted to. (See "Right-to-Work Laws and the Modern Classical-Liberal Tradition" in this volume.)

Others go further and call for repeal of all labor laws, especially the Wagner Act, which established the NLRB during the New Deal.

But would such wholesale repeal really shift the pendulum away from labor? There's reason to doubt it. Wouldn't it be ironic if repeal of the labor laws *increased* workers' clout? What if, subtly, government regulation of employer-employee relations has tended to benefit *business* to the detriment of labor? That's counterintuitive, but let's see how it might be so.

We start by recalling what the Wagner Act and then the Taft-Hartley Amendments accomplished. The Wagner Act established a legal right of workers to be represented by a union if a majority in a bargaining unit wishes to be. As noted, the NLRB is empowered to *certify* unions that win elections conducted according to the government's procedures. The certified union becomes the exclusive bargaining agent, and the employer has no choice but to deal with it in good faith. All affected employees have to join, or at least have to pay dues relabeled "fees," except in right-to-work states, which Taft-Hartley later permitted.

This looks as though the government has tipped the scales for the unions, but it's not the full story. Labor laws also *restrict* — severely — how workers can organize and what a union can do after it is established. Before the NLRB, workers sometimes agitated for union recognition by striking spontaneously and engaging in other kinds of actions — both peaceful and violent. Many of those organizing tactics — even the peaceful ones — became illegal under the Wagner Act, which set out specific procedures for having a union government-certified, and Taft-Hartley. Thus wildcat strikes, sympathy strikes, and secondary boycotts — in themselves examples of freedom of non-association — became forbidden tactics. (Unsurprisingly, the ban on boycotts began as a wartime measure in 1942.) Also outlawed was minority unionism, in which a minority of workers could ignore the majority union and seek representation by another one.

Although the new regime conferred on workers the right to strike, the NLRB sets the rules and the U.S. president may impose a 60-day cooling-off period by invoking national security. The strike was more a permission than a right.

It's an old story: no government favor comes without strings. One way or another, you pay for what you get. When we realize that for years, beginning in the Progressive Era, America's corporate elite — through the National Civic Federation and the American Alliance for Labor Legislation — advocated labor laws, a story at variance from the standard one emerges. It appears that the New Deal and subsequent labor rules were not so much intended to empower workers but to divert unruly labor energies into safe, predictable forms more acceptable to the politicians and corporate establishment, which was always comfortable in partnership with the government. "Respectable" labor leaders could thereby be anointed and given seats at the boardroom table — as junior partners, of course. How better to legitimize the American Federation of Labor and de-legitimate the Industrial Workers of the World (or Wobblies), which saw (and still sees) the NLRB as co-opting workers?

As historian and libertarian Joseph Stromberg describes it, "The Wagner Labor Act of 1935, perhaps the most original of the New Deal measures[,] ... finally defined the position of labor within the syndicalist or corporatist system. After this the unions settled down to fit in the corporatist mold and enjoy their share of the economic pie."

Kevin Carson, a free-market political economist, sums up the situation neatly:

> Far from being a labor charter that empowered unions for the first time, FDR's labor regime had the same practical effect as telling the irregulars of Lexington and Concord, "Look, you guys come out from behind those rocks, put on these bright red uniforms, and march in parade ground formation like the Brits, and in return we'll set up a system of arbitration to guarantee you don't lose all the time."

This is not to say that organized labor got no favors from the government. Federal laws (the Norris-LaGuardia Act, for example) and court decisions immunized violent acts from prosecution and shielded unions from liability for the sanctioned actions of their members. This was a departure from common-law principles.

Further, I don't mean to say that business leaders have liked everything that has happened since the labor regime was installed; quite the contrary. But it *is* the case that many enlightened business leaders wanted to use government power to domesticate labor, to buy it off, and isolate the labor movement's unruly anarchists, syndicalists, socialists, and communists for the sake of industrial peace. Indeed, the whole welfare state can be seen in this light. The corporate elite was willingly to accept some government interference with private property in return for labor-relations management and other protections. (The Swope Plan, precursor to FDR's National Industrial Recovery Administration proposed by General Electric president Gerard Swope in 1931, is a case in point.) The business elite surely knew that once set up, the labor apparatus would not always go its way.

It should be obvious that government-managed labor organizing is no more deserving of support than government-managed trade or government-managed political campaigns. Laissez faire means that workers are free to use any tactics *short of violence* to press their case with employers. This would include peaceful unauthorized wildcat strikes, sympathy strikes, secondary boycotts, and other nonviolent activities now outlawed. Needless to say, violent interference with strikebreakers is illegitimate.

Similarly, employers would be free to use all peaceful tactics in opposing union organizing, including yellow-dog contracts and company unions (now illegal). Laissez faire would not sanction the horrors of the past: neither union violence against innocent persons and property nor police, military, or private violence against peaceful workers.

But if violence against the innocent is illegitimate, we can't ignore the larger context in which employer-employee relations take place in America — the cartelized corporatist, or neomercantilist, political economy, which at its most fundamental level privileges entrenched business interests through a variety of interventions that dampen new competition and hence reduce the demand for labor and otherwise restrict worker options. The result is a systemic bias — albeit not insurmountable — against independent centers of economic activity, whether from upstart entrepreneurs, worker-owned cooperatives, or employees merely seeking better working conditions. The same principle that would eliminate the labor laws would also devour those anticompetitive interventions.

As the editor of the old *Liberty* magazine, individualist Benjamin Tucker, put it:

> It is not enough, however true, to say that, "if a man has labor to sell, he must find some one with money to buy it"; it is necessary to add the much more important truth that, if a man has labor to sell, he has a right to a free market in which to sell it, — a market in which no one shall be prevented by restrictive laws from honestly obtaining the money to buy it. If the man with labor to sell has not this free market, then his liberty is violated and his property virtually taken from him.

Foundation for Economic Education, April 27, 2007

Chapter 55.
Right-to-Work Laws and the
Modern Classical-Liberal Tradition

It's not widely known, but an earlier generation of libertarians condemned so-called right-to-work laws as *anti*-market. For example, Milton Friedman, in *Capitalism and Freedom*, compared right-to-work to anti-discrimination laws. Ayn Rand also opposed right-to-work laws. The Spring 1966 issue of the libertarian student-run journal *New Individualist Review* carried Professor Hirschel Kasper's article, "What's Wrong with Right-to-Work Laws." *NIR* was edited by University of Chicago libertarians Ralph Raico, Joe Cobb, and Jim Powell. Among its editorial advisers were Friedman, F.A. Hayek, and Ben Rogge, a classical liberal long associated with the Foundation for Economic Education. (Of course this does not mean that any of these men necessarily agreed with Kasper, although [with one exception] that may not be an unreasonable inference, considering that *NIR* never published a pro-right-to-work article. The exception is Hayek, who wrote, curiously, in *The Constitution of Liberty* that "closed- and union-shop contracts … must be treated as contracts in restraint of trade and denied the protection of the law.")

Percy L. Greaves Jr., a student and friend of Ludwig von Mises and a close associate of FEE founder Leonard E. Read, also made the libertarian and Austrian-economics case against right-to-work laws. The essay was published in a *festschrift* to Mises, *On Freedom and Free Enterprise*, which was assembled in 1956 to honor the 50th anniversary of his doctorate. One may draw one's own conclusion about how Mises saw the issue, given Greaves's choice of topic in this context.

In light of the controversy surrounding the 2012 passage of a right-to-work law in Michigan, Greaves's lengthy argument is worth examining. For the record, no one was more fully devoted to laissez faire than Greaves, a dedicated promoter of Mises's work. (See his *Mises Made Easier*.) And he was no union sympathizer — or, to be precise, he had no sympathy for *compulsory* unions under the legal regime created by the National Labor Relations Act of 1935 (the Wagner Act).

But Greaves was consistent, and when he saw businesspeople asking states to pass right-to-work laws, which forbid employers from agreeing to make union membership a condition of employment, he objected. Let's first be clear about what these laws do. The 1947 Taft-Hartley Act, which amended the Wagner Act, contains provision 14(b), stating that Taft-Hartley should not "be construed as authorizing the execution or application of agreements requiring membership in a labor organization as a condition of employment in any State or Territory in which such execution or application is *prohibited* by State or Territorial law." [Emphasis added.]

Thus states may forbid a particular kind of contract between an employer and a union. (Under Wagner a majority of employees can authorize a union to represent them regardless of an employer's wishes, and employees who do not want to join must still pay fees — not "dues" — to the union for representation services since any conditions negotiated must by law apply all employees, members and nonmembers alike.)

Support for banning such voluntary agreements did not sit well with Greaves even if the ban was intended to counter an earlier government action. "The mass myopia of our age has been a reactionary reverence for government intervention," he wrote in "Is Further Intervention a Cure for Prior Intervention?" "When anything goes wrong, from a train wreck to a change in stock market prices, the craven crowds always clamor for just one more law."

He found "most astonishing" that businesspeople "seldom ... ask for a repeal of the laws which are so often the root of their troubles. In accordance with the religion of the day, they ask for new legal restrictions which they think will protect them from the ills produced by the interventional laws already on the statute books." (Here he invoked Mises's "critique of interventionism": Intervention creates problems that, unless the original intervention is repealed, beget further intervention, and so on.)

Greaves knew well that those "who advocate the so-called right-to-work laws [believe] these laws will remedy some of the sins of the federal labor laws that now grant special privileges to labor unions." He had no sympathy for the Wagner Act, but he wasn't buying the excuse: "Two wrongs never make a right. The economic answer is to repeal the bad intervention and not try to counterbalance it with another bad intervention. Such moves only provide the politicians with greater power over the entire economy." In other words, the end doesn't justify the means.

He continued, "Those who advocate a legal ban on union shops seldom realize that they are sealing their own doom and placing their future fate in the hands of legislators who are only too eager to assume control of all economic activity."

Greaves was closely involved in the issue. At the request of Sen. Robert A. Taft in 1946, he helped draft a precursor to Taft-Hartley. According to Greaves, union activity had caused the Wagner Act to fall out of favor with the public. Taft wanted an ameliorative bill that would win enough votes to override a veto by President Harry Truman — in other words, a watered-down bill. Then, Taft calculated, after the Republicans won the White House and Congress in 1948, they would pass a better law.

Greaves "opposed this thinking on the basis that it would be better not to have any new law at that time[, contending] that a successful veto of a better law would result in a growing public pressure for the repeal of the Wagner Act and the election of the party that espoused such a move. The senator was not willing to go that far." Greaves feared that "if the senator's plan were successful, the public would be persuaded that the then[-]evident economic distress flowing from union activity had been remedied and the next tide of public opinion might well be in the other direction."

Taft disagreed, and Greaves left the Senate committee. "Freedom … lost," Greaves wrote looking back, because once Taft-Hartley passed, the pressure on the Wagner Act disappeared.

"Somewhat the same situation is involved in the so-called right-to-work laws," he continued.

> If they are passed in a large number of states, they will temporarily relieve the present uneconomic evils that exist in federal labor laws. They will allay the fear among those people who see and comprehend the dire results now flowing from present union activities. … Actually, it might be both better economics and better expediency to let present laws go their limit, so that people might soon learn how bad they really are.

Greaves's prediction was accurate. Taft-Hartley passed, and talk about repealing Wagner ended. Over the years the National Labor Relations Board has managed labor relations unimpeded, often in outrageous ways.

"The so-called right-to-work laws are … a proposed middle-of-the-road compromise with free-market principles for expedient purposes," Greaves wrote. "They limit the right of free men to negotiate contracts for morally acceptable purposes and attempt to substitute the decisions of politicians for those that consumers would like to express in the market place."

Greaves's bottom line is that if Wagner is the root of the evil, one should work to repeal it rather than support new interventions. Short of that, in my view a better stopgap would have been to let states opt out of the Wagner regime. In other words, rather than prohibiting voluntary union-shop agreements between employers and unions, a state legislature could pass a bill simply declaring that the NLRB had no jurisdiction in that state.

Greaves could imagine sound reasons for an employer wishing to sign a union-shop agreement:

> The fact that many current labor union practices are injurious to the general welfare does not mean that all actions of all labor unions must of necessity be considered evil or uneconomic. There are many truly economic functions that labor unions can perform. In a free and moral society, unions would be solely voluntary groups organized to help their

members by helping them to increase their production and thereby their contributions to society. Their chief purpose would be to raise the standards of workmanship and production. They would then be a force for the general economic good of society as well as their members.

Here he echoes the views of Rand and Henry Hazlitt. Thus for Greaves, "If we can visualize such a situation, we will then be better able to understand why employers should be free to sign contracts to hire only such high type workers and why the so-called right-to-work laws would interfere with the main objective of social cooperation — the increased satisfactions of all the individual participants in the market."

To be sure, Greaves's analysis has serious deficiencies, particularly regarding the pervasiveness of corporatism. In opposing legal privileges for unions, he stated that "most employers have been stripped of the privileges they had legally obtained during the latter part of the [19th] century." This clearly was not the case. Big business continues to have myriad explicit and implicit privileges that would be unattainable in a freed market, as well as enduring benefits of earlier privileges.

But to his great credit, Greaves noted that it was government intervention on behalf of capitalists that "*produced the demand*" for countervailing pro-labor privileges: "Most such intervention was planned to help organized 'labor' and the other large groups that had *suffered when employers were in the saddle and obtaining favorable intervention for themselves.*" [Emphasis added.]

This insight putting the horse before the cart sets Greaves apart from many libertarian analysts. (On at least one occasion, Grover Cleveland thought similarly, even if it was not reflected in his actions. See "Forgotten Critic of Corporatism" in this volume.)

What Greaves and others overlooked, however, is that much of the business elite had long pushed for Wagner-style labor laws for the sake of industrial peace. The last thing they wanted was laissez faire for labor organizers. The New Deal, rather than being anti-business and pro-labor, actually *tamed* labor by bringing "responsible" union leaders to the conference table as junior partners. The Wagner-Taft-Hartley regime imposed *restrictions* on labor activity and required labor leaders to *police* their members' compliance with union contracts. The final Wagner Act had elements that big business disliked, but it was the business elite nonetheless that laid the groundwork for federal management of labor relations.

Radical labor activists, such as those in the Industrial Workers of the World, the Wobblies, wanted no part of labor law because it imposed rules on what they could do to get a better deal from employers. Older tactics, such as wildcat strikes, secondary boycotts, and sympathy strikes along the supply chain, were outlawed in the new labor regime. Cooling-off periods, compulsory arbitration, and other constraints were imposed. It's enough to make one wonder if employers would really want Wagner repealed.

Greaves was right when he said that the target of free-market advocates should be all laws that interfere with free association — including Wagner, Taft-Hartley, and right-to-work. As Hirschel Kasper wrote, "The argument here is not one of whether union security provisions are good or bad; the argument is whether there should be legislation which prohibits them." The nonaggression obligation says no.

Future of Freedom Foundation, December 14, 2012

Chapter 56.
Individualism, Trade Unions, and "Self-Governing Combinations"

Who do you imagine said this? "[Trade-unions] seem natural to the passing phase of social evolution, and may have beneficial functions under existing conditions."

If you guessed some wily labor leader or social democrat, you are wrong. British laissez-faire advocate Herbert Spencer (1820–1903) wrote those words in his *Principles of Sociology* (1896). Spencer was the most prominent and respected individualist philosopher of his time. To this day his voluminous scholarly and popular writing remains an important resource for adherents of the freedom philosophy.

Spencer's statement, then, may surprise some readers. It shouldn't. Our libertarian forebears put the plight of workers at the top of their concerns. In England feudalism had not entirely disappeared, many people had been pushed off the land, to which they had long-standing customary rights, through enclosure, and laissez faire was nowhere in evidence. Neomercantilism, or what libertarian Albert Jay Nock called the "Merchant-state," was the rule. For example, early in the Industrial Revolution worker "combinations" were outlawed in England and people were not free to leave their home parishes in search of better employment opportunities, something decried by Adam Smith. When these laws were finally repealed, workers were hampered by other state interventions, such as land engrossment, patents, government-backed banking cartels, and tariffs. To be sure, living standards improved, but to the extent that the government stifled free competition, workers were deprived of bargaining power and thus their full free-market reward.

Spencer is famous for setting out a theory of social evolution, according to which society was moving from the rigidly hierarchical "militant" type to the open, contract-based "industrial" type. Society was still in transition and had a long way to go.

Spencer began his discussion of unions by noting that worker guilds (like employers) historically preferred suppression of competition to the uncertainties of market rivalry. He criticized the hypocrisy of workers who applaud competition that lowered the price of bread, but oppose competition that lowered the price of labor. He also argued that agitation for higher

210

wages, if successful throughout the economy, would do workers no good because prices and hence the cost of living would rise as a consequence. (This analysis requires some assumptions that may not in fact hold.)

But he also noted that "under their original form as friendly societies — organizations for rendering mutual aid — [unions] were of course extremely beneficial; and in so far as they subserve this purpose down to the present time, they can scarcely be too much lauded."

Nevertheless Spencer asked: "Must we say that while ultimately failing in their proposed ends [higher wages], trade-unions do nothing else than inflict grave mischiefs in trying to achieve them?"

His response: "This is too sweeping a conclusion. ... There is an ultimate gain in moral and physical treatment if there is no ultimate gain in wages." For example:

> Judging from their harsh and cruel conduct in the past, it is tolerably certain that employers are now prevented from doing unfair things which they would else do. Conscious that trade-unions are ever ready to act, they are more prompt to raise wages when trade is flourishing than they would otherwise be; and when there come times of depression, they lower wages only when they cannot otherwise carry on their businesses.

> Knowing the power which unions can exert, masters are led to treat the individual members of them with more respect than they would otherwise do: the status of the workman is almost necessarily raised. Moreover, having a strong motive for keeping on good terms with the union, a master is more likely than he would else be to study the general convenience of his men, and to carry on his works in ways conducive to their health.

Spencer thought that unions are necessary because "everywhere aggression begets resistance and counter-aggression; and in our present transitional state, semi-militant and semi-industrial, trespasses have to be kept in check by the fear of retaliatory trespasses."

However, he was not satisfied with this state of affairs. Recall that he said that trade unions belong to "a passing phase of social evolution." Passing to what?

Spencer was attracted to alternatives to the standard "master-and-workman type of industrial organization" and discussed at length profit-sharing arrangements, pointing out both their advantages and disadvantages. But these too left him unsatisfied.

Thus he foresaw the emergence of "self-governing combinations of workers," which, while not without problems, would avoid most of the drawbacks of traditional firms:

> Evils like those arising from antagonistic interests [between master and workman], cannot arise where there are no antagonistic interests. Each cooperator exists in a double capacity. He is a unit in an incorporated body standing in the place of employer; and he is a worker employed by the incorporated body. Manifestly, when, instead of an employing master, alien to the workers, there is an employing master compounded of the workers, the mischiefs ordinarily caused by piece-work can no longer be caused.

He elaborated how cooperative organizations would encourage productivity, cut costs, and permit the division of larger profits. For instance:

> Resentment against a foreman, who ranks some above others, no longer finds any place. Overlooking to check idleness becomes superfluous: the idling almost disappears, and another cause of dissension ceases. Not only do the irritations which superintendence excites decrease, but the cost of it decreases also.

For Spencer, this would signify the pinnacle of social evolution:

> Here we reach a form in which the coerciveness has diminished to the smallest degree consistent with combined action. Each member is his own master in respect of the work he does; and is subject only to such rules, established by the majority of the members, as are needful for maintaining order. The transition from the compulsory cooperation of militancy to the voluntary cooperation of industrialism is completed. Under present arrangements it is incomplete. A wage-earner, while he voluntarily agrees to give so many hours work for so much pay, does not, during performance of his work, act in a purely voluntary way: he is coerced by the consciousness that discharge will follow if he idles, and is sometimes more manifestly coerced by an overlooker. But under the arrangement described, his activity becomes entirely voluntary.

"So long as the worker remains a wage-earner," Spencer concluded, "the marks of status do not wholly disappear. For so many hours daily he makes over his faculties to a master, or to a cooperative group, and is for the time owned by him or it. He is temporarily in the position of a slave, and his overlooker stands in the position of a slave-driver."

Spencer acknowledged that "the practicability of such a system depends on [personal] character," but he anticipated that the existing successful cooperatives "might be the germs of a spreading organization. ... [T]he growth would become increasingly rapid; since the master-and-workmen type of industrial organization could not withstand competition with this cooperative type, so much more productive and costing so much less in superintendence."

Of course, Spencer's prediction could — and should — be tested — by freeing the market and ending all state-based privileges, each one a remnant of the militant type of society. Libertarians should hope that Spencer is proven right, since individualists more than anyone will see the merit in any arrangement which minimizes the chance that one will be subjected to the arbitrary will of another — even in consensual relationships.

Foundation for Economic Education, May 18, 2012

Chapter 57.
The Myth of Market Failure

In the language of economics, a market failure is, as economist David Friedman writes, "a situation where each individual correctly chooses the action that best accomplishes his objectives, yet the result is worse, in terms of those same objectives, than if everyone had done something else." As a rule, the pursuit of individual good in the market brings no such negative result. On the rare occasions when rational individual actions lead to regret by those same individuals, the result is labeled "market failure."

When I say that market failure is a myth, I *don't* mean to deny that such regrettable situations can occur. I only mean to deny that they are peculiar to the market. They can occur in all sorts of contexts, including the political context — hence we need a broader, more accurate term. I propose "group-rationality failure." We might win some support for the free market if more people understood that this kind of failure is not unique to markets but rather is a feature of human action under certain special circumstances. Moreover, as we'll see, this is less of a problem in the market than elsewhere.

A popular example of market failure is the negative externality from pollution. It would seem rational for each producer to avoid the expense of reducing or eliminating harmful emissions by spewing them into the air, but the result is dirtier air for everyone. (If there were only one polluter, the harm would be insignificant.) But similar phenomena occur outside of the market context. Friedman gives an example from warfare:

> It is sometime in the 12th century, somewhere in Europe, and I am one of a line of men with spears, on foot, facing another bunch of men — on horseback with spears — moving rapidly in our direction. I make a rapid cost-benefit calculation. If we all stand, we might break their charge. If we run, we die. I should stand.

> The mistake I have just made is the word "we." I only control me, and I am only one spearman out of several thousand. If everybody else stands and I run, my running has little effect on whether their charge is stopped — and I won't be one of the men who dies stopping it. If everybody else runs and I stand, I die. So whether the rest of the line is going to run or stand, I should run. Everybody else in the line makes the same calculation. We all run and most of us die.

Economist Bryan Caplan has examples from the world of government and politics:

> Many economists who study politics decry the large negative externalities of voter ignorance. An economic illiterate who votes for protectionism hurts not just himself but also his fellow citizens. Other economists believe externalities in the budget process lead to wasteful spending. A congressman who lobbies for federal funds for his district improves his chances of reelection but hurts the financial health of the rest of the nation.

Or take this case: I tell a group of people I'll go to Washington, D.C., to lobby for a general tax cut if they help finance my effort. Each person wants lower taxes but calculates that he will get a tax cut whether or not he donates to the cause. So each abstains. Without the money, I don't go to Washington. No one's taxes are reduced.

And there is the famous "failure" from game theory, the prisoner's dilemma. In this case, two people arrested and accused of committing a crime are held in isolation and confronted with the option of squealing on the accomplice or remaining silent. Under the plea deal offered, each person's best possible scenario is to squeal while the accomplice remains silent. The second-best scenario is for both to remain silent. The problem is that, since neither can control what the other does and since they can't coordinate, neither can take the chance that the other will talk — under the plea deal, if one remains silent while the other talks, the first goes to prison for the maximum term while the stool pigeon goes free. Thus both find it rational to talk and (under the deal) serve less than the maximum. Yet had they both taken the greatest risk and remained silent, they would have served even less time.

My question is this: If this same kind of failure can occur in the market, government, battlefield, and law-enforcement contexts, why do we call it *market* failure? The name implies that this problem is unique to the market — but as we've seen, it most emphatically is not.

Such failure in the political realm was largely overlooked until the Public Choice school of political economy brought it to the world's attention. To justify government action, it was deemed sufficient to show that the market led to a suboptimal outcome. The Public Choice thinkers showed that this is an illegitimate argument because one could merely assume that the outcome of government action would be better than the market outcome. It might well be worse, and we have reason to believe it would be.

If group-rationality failure is ubiquitous, does that mean it can't serve as an argument for the market over the state? No, it does not. As Friedman says, while such failure can be used as an argument *against* laissez faire, it's an even stronger argument *for* laissez faire. How so? The key lies in the issue of externalities, that is, in the question of who reaps most of the benefits and bears most of the costs of actions: the particular actor or the public?

Friedman writes:

> In private markets, most of the time, an individual who makes a decision bears most, although not all, of the resulting costs, and receives most of the resulting benefits. In political markets that is rarely true. So we should expect that the market failure that results from A taking an action most of whose costs or benefits are born by B, C, and D should be the exception in the private market, the rule in the political market. It follows that shifting control over human activities from the private market to the political market is likely to *increase the problems associated with market failure, not decrease them.* [Emphasis added.]

Moreover, the failures that occur in the market are more easily solved:

> A market failure is also a profit opportunity. If the result of individuals acting rationally in their own interest is to make them worse off than if they acted in some other way, it follows that an entrepreneur who could somehow move them to the better outcome would produce a net benefit — some of which, with luck, he could pocket. Hence in a market society there is an incentive for private parties to find ways around the inefficiencies due to market failure.

Broadcast radio and television should have been impossible because no broadcaster could charge receivers of the signal, who would have every incentive to "free-ride." But some sharp entrepreneur motivated by the desire for profit came up with the idea of selling commercial time to soap makers. Problem solved.

A similar incentive is not typically found in government. On the contrary, the incentives work the other way. A government failure is often the excuse for bigger budgets and staff, and more power. According to conventional wisdom, market failure requires more government, while government failure requires more government.

Not only are group-rationality failures far less frequent in the market than in government, in the market such problems contain the seeds of their own solution, thanks to entrepreneurship and the profit motive. Hence, I propose that we stop talking about *market* failure.

Foundation for Economic Education, April 5, 2013

Chapter 58.
Economy or Catallaxy?

That its champions have always understood the free market, first and foremost, as the most basic form of social cooperation is evidenced by a dissatisfaction with the term *economy* itself. In volume 2 of *Law, Legislation, and Liberty*, economist F.A. Hayek claimed that we cannot properly comprehend the market order unless we

> free ourselves of the misleading associations suggested by its usual description as an "economy." An economy, in the strict sense of the word in which a household, a farm, or an enterprise can be called economies, consists of a complex of activities by which a given set of means is allocated in accordance with a *unitary plan* among the competing ends according to their relative importance. [Emphasis added.]

Of course, that's not what a "national (or world) economy" is.

This may seem like semantic trivia, but an examination of Hayek's point underscores an important and often overlooked aspect of the market order: its cooperative nature.

Unlike a household (or other economy), Hayek wrote,

> the market order serves no such single order of ends. What is commonly called a social or national economy is in this sense not a single economy but a network of many interlaced economies. ... The belief that the economic activities of the individual members of society are or ought to be part of one economy in the strict sense of the term, and that what is commonly described as the economy of a country or a society ought to be ordered and judged by the same criteria as an economy proper, is a chief source of error in this field. But, whenever we speak of the economy of a country, or of the world, we are employing a term which suggests that these systems ought to be run on socialist lines and directed according to a single plan so as to serve a unitary system of ends.

What Hayek is getting at is this: the market order consists of countless individuals each pursuing his or her own aspirations. While each person demonstrates his or her (changeable) ranking of ends through the choices made and actions taken, there is *no social ranking* of all the ends valued by all the individuals in the society. My desire, say, for a pizza dinner can't be placed on a social value scale in order to see what it takes precedence over and what takes precedence over it. That simply makes no sense. Society is not an organism with a preference scale, and preferences cannot be compared interpersonally because each person's preferences are subjective and ranked; no unit exists by which to measure them.

We can see why Hayek stressed this point. As he suggested, if people think of the market order as a unified economy, they will be more susceptible to central planning; that is, to a conscious scheme for allocating scarce resources among competing ends society-wide. But if market advocates emphasize that there is no single economy — but many, with a diversity of goals — people may be less prone to the central planner's mindset. "The cosmos of the market," Hayek wrote, "neither is nor could be governed by such a single scale of ends; it serves the multiplicity of separate and incommensurable ends of all its separate members."

If the market order is widely understood as consisting of many individuals pursuing through exchange a multiplicity of separate and incommensurable ends, its intrinsically cooperative nature would be harder to ignore and social engineering would be less attractive. After all, if individuals living in society wish to achieve their ends and if force is barred — that is, if these individuals are respected as ends in themselves and not merely means to others' ends — then cooperation is the order of the day. Hence, the value of the division of labor, specialization, and free exchange, which together raise living standards and make possible the lofty pursuits that would be impossible in the abject poverty of isolated existence.

What goes on in the market order (to the extent it is free) is *not* the allocation of scarce resources aimed at maximizing fictitious social utility, but rather an unending series of exchanges. It is cooperation writ large.

Because of Hayek's concern to avoid misunderstanding, he suggested that the word *economy* be restricted to the earlier sense noted above and that another word be used "to describe the system of numerous interrelated economies which constitute the market order." He proposed that since the word *catallactics* was used as far back as 1855 by Richard Whately and more recently by Ludwig von Mises to mean the science of exchange, "it would seem appropriate to adopt a corresponding term for the market order itself." This makes sense, for as Hayek pointed out, "the term 'catallactics' was derived from the Greek verb *katallattein* (or *katallassein*) which meant, significantly, not only 'to exchange' but also 'to admit into the community' and 'to change from enemy into friend.'" Thus he proposed the Anglicized *catallaxy* "to describe the order brought about by the mutual adjustment of many individual economies in a market."

This is especially appropriate because Mises contended that it was the prospect of gains from trade that made human beings *social* beings. Mises wrote in *Human Action*,

The fundamental facts that brought about cooperation, society, and civilization and transformed the animal man into a human being are the facts that work performed under the division of labor is more productive than isolated work and that man's reason is capable of recognizing this truth. But for these facts men would have forever remained deadly foes of one another, irreconcilable rivals in their endeavors to secure a portion of the scarce supply of means of sustenance provided by nature. Each man would have been forced to view all other men as his enemies; his craving for the satisfaction of his own appetites would have brought him into an implacable conflict with all his neighbors. No sympathy could possibly develop under such a state of affairs.

Mises and Hayek were not alone in seeking to revive terms related to *catallactics*. Nobel laureate James M. Buchanan, a founder of the Public Choice school of political economy, was also attracted to that term over *economics* because of its emphasis on exchange. He also liked *symbiotics*:

The connotation of the term is that the association is mutually beneficial to all parties. This conveys, more or less precisely, the idea that should be central to our definition [of the discipline]. It draws attention to a unique sort of relationship, that which involves the cooperative association of individuals, one with another, even when individual interests are different. ... I want them [economists] to concentrate on *exchange* rather than *choice*.

Mises, Hayek, and Buchanan were onto something important. In the popular mind, *economics* is a cold, detached study of the Economy, almost as though it were a machine that acts on society. In contrast, the catallaxy is where people who disagree about the value of things peacefully exchange goods and services in a never-ending cooperative effort to improve their lives. It is indeed a community where enemies may be changed into friends.

Future of Freedom Foundation, February 1, 2013

Chapter 59.
Stimulate the Catallaxy?

The periodic brouhahas over so-called economic stimulus packages got me thinking about how far off target most people are when they talk about "the economy." To hear the politicians and commentators tell it, the economy is a big machine located somewhere in Washington, D.C. That machine requires skilled operators, and elections are more or less occasions for choosing those operators. Sometimes the machine slows down and needs a stimulus — perhaps an infusion of cheap credit or government spending or even tax cuts. At other times it risks overheating and needs to be cooled down — perhaps higher interest rates or a tax increase.

This misapprehension is helped along by a good part of the economics profession, many of whose members aspire to be the operators or their advisers.

To state what should be obvious: an economy isn't really a machine. The term *economy* is an abstraction, even a metaphor, and we always get ourselves into trouble by taking metaphors literally. As Nobel laureate F.A. Hayek was fond of pointing out, the word economy has its roots in the Greek word for household. (Remember those home-economics courses?) Even though a household is composed of individuals, it can usefully be thought of as a unit in the sense that its financial affairs are largely arranged around a single set of ends. (There's a limit of course to how far that can be taken.) We go astray the moment we apply this description to larger collections of people. As soon as we begin talking about the city's, state's, nation's, or world's economy, we have severed our moorings from reality because those groupings do not have a single set of ends.

That is why Hayek preferred the word *catallaxy* to *economy*; it comes from the Greek word for exchange. A catallaxy, he wrote, is "not a single economy but a network of many interlaced economies" (*Law, Legislation, and Liberty*, volume 2).

Another economist and Nobel laureate who was sensitive to this matter was James Buchanan, one of the pillars of the Public Choice school of political economy. His concerns are collected in the Liberty Fund volume *What Should Economists Do?* In the title essay (originally an address given in 1963) Buchanan identified what can only be described as the central collectivist premise of most economics, namely: some entity larger than the individual — usually the nation — must allocate scarce resources.

Many heavyweights in 20th-century economics — not just socialists — regrettably let that premise stand, Buchanan pointed out: Lionel Robbins never identified the allocator; Frank Knight attributed economic activity to the "social organization"; and even Milton Friedman held that (Buchanan quoting) "economics is the study of how a particular society solves its economic problem." Not that those men did not realize that groups consist of individuals. But as economists, Buchanan feared, they too readily left the impression that economics deals with a collective's solution to an allocation problem. It's a short step from a collective to a machine.

That's not how Buchanan saw economics. In contrast to the view that the economy is a "*means* of accomplishing the basic economic functions that must be carried out in any society," he believed "the market or market organization is not a *means* toward the accomplishment of anything. It is, instead, the institutional embodiment of the voluntary exchange processes that are entered into by individuals in their several capacities." He added: "This is all that there is to it."

Contemplate how different this conception of economy is from the general impression. As Buchanan wrote,

> Individuals are observed to cooperate with one another, to reach agreements, to trade. The network of relationships that emerges or evolves out of this trading process, the institutional framework, is called "the market." It is a setting, an arena, in which we, as economists, as theorists (as onlookers), observe men attempting to accomplish their own purposes, whatever these may be.

In such a conception of economy, where is there room for words like *overheated*, *cooled down*, and *stimulus*?

In another essay in his book, "General Implications of Subjectivism in Economics," Buchanan flaunted his affinity with the Austrian school of Hayek and Ludwig von Mises. Here he wrote, "The principle that exposure to economics *should* convey is that of the spontaneous coordination [of individuals] which the market achieves. The central principle of economics is not the economizing process." And he warned that economics will "become applied mathematics or engineering" if its practitioners think it is.

Subjectivism in economics is the recognition that economic phenomena emerge from what human beings believe, think, and do, and not from data they may know nothing about or rarefied statistical aggregates and averages. Subjectivism is good insurance against seeing the economy as a machine and the government as its vital attendant. Or as Buchanan put it, "To the extent that subjectivism tends to concentrate attention on the interaction among persons and away from the 'economic problem,' an understanding of the principle of order is facilitated rather than retarded."

Subjectivism can be seen most starkly in the notion of costs. Much economic theorizing and bureaucratic meddling regard costs as objective. That perspective encourages social engineering. After all, if those who would move us about the national chessboard had to confess that they cannot know the costs of their maneuverings, they would have a harder time justifying their power.

But they *cannot* know those costs. "The costs that influence 'choice' are purely subjective and these exist only within the mind of the decision-maker," Buchanan wrote. When one confronts two alternatives, one is really confronting two mental projections of what the world *might* be like in the future. Either or both projections could be wrong. At best they are educated guesses. And since one of those imagined worlds will *never* be realized, the chooser will never know if he was wrong about that one. But that world forgone is the true cost of the alternative chosen because that's what the chooser gives up to achieve it. We often think of costs as money paid. But while money is indispensable for making calculations, it does not express the true opportunity cost of a choice. No one wants money for its own sake but only for what it can buy now or later.

An economy is *people* cooperating to better their situations. Thus a "stimulus package" is fundamentally objectionable not because of anything that may be in the bill. (Tax cuts are always welcome.) It is objectionable because of its rationale. Government should endeavor to stay out of the way of cooperative productive activity at all times, not just when various numbers are deemed too high or low.

Foundation for Economic Education, July 1, 2010

Chapter 60.
Loving Economics

"My love affair with economics began in the fall of 1979."

With those words, Peter Boettke begins his valentine to the economics discipline, that is, his book: *Living Economics: Yesterday, Today, and Tomorrow* (Independent Institute and Universidad Francisco Marroquin, 2012). Boettke, besides being a University Professor of Economics and Philosophy at George Mason University, the BB&T Professor for the Study of Capitalism, and vice president for research and director of the F.A. Hayek Program for Advanced Study in Philosophy, Politics, and Economics at GMU's Mercatus Center, is the indefatigable intellectual entrepreneur and promoter of Austrian, or subjectivist market-process, economics.

He continues: "The summer prior to that I had experienced the long lines for gasoline, and I was confused and frustrated by the experience for a variety of reasons. Economics erased my confusion and targeted my frustration on the cause of the shortages. I was hooked."

In an important sense, this book is autobiographical, the story of one man's odyssey through the world of economics and his efforts to "get the teaching and doing of economics back on track." But it couldn't help but also be a useful introduction to the economic way of thinking. Not that it is a beginner's book — it's not. But an interested lay reader who realizes that economics can be about the world and hence is something to be taken seriously will learn a great deal. One need not have a degree in economics (I don't) to profit from *Living Economics*.

This book is a useful discussion of why economics is valuable and how its potential has been squandered by several generations of distracted practitioners. If I had been asked to design the cover of this book, I would have depicted the old joke about the drunk who looks for his keys under the street light, not because that's where he lost them, but because that's where the light is. That joke perfectly fits the story Boettke tells about how economics ran off the rails.

Economics began as a verbal and logical description of the social forces that arise out of reasonable but fallible human beings engaging in exchanges for mutual benefit. However, the main practitioners in the 20th century became charmed by the method of physics and mathematics for fear that otherwise they would not be taken seriously as scientists. They thus jettisoned virtually everything that was not amenable to their formalism.

The first things to go were uncertainty, error, and competitive entrepreneurship, which led to a serious problem for the discipline, even if its practitioners did not see it: of what relevance are elegant mathematical descriptions of general equilibrium, with its assumptions of perfect knowledge and perfect coordination, if you have no theory of the forces that tend to *equilibrate* markets? Who cares about the "there" if you've got no map to get there? Even when the theory was provided (by Israel Kirzner building on Adam Smith, Carl Menger, Ludwig von Mises, and F.A. Hayek), it was unappreciated because it was not and could not be worked into the equations. (Of course, because of constant changes in preferences, knowledge, resources, and technologies, there is no "there" there.)

Boettke has a helpful way, borrowed from one of his many great teachers (Kenneth Boulding), to convey what he's getting at. He distinguishes "mainline" from "mainstream" economics. Mainline economics embodies insights first achieved in the Middle Ages, then elaborated by Scottish and French thinkers of the classical school, the Austrians beginning with Menger, and the school known as new "institutional economics."

"The core idea in this approach to economics," Boettke writes, "is that there are two fundamental observations of commercial society: (1) individual pursuit of ... self-interest, and (2) complex social order that aligns individual interests with the general interest."

In the mainline of economics, the "invisible hand postulate" reconciles self-interest with the general interest not by collapsing one to the other or by assuming super-human cognitive capabilities among the actors, but through the reconciliation process of exchange within specific institutional environments. It is the "higgling and bargaining" within the market economy, as Adam Smith argued, that produces social order.

The mainline also incorporates the notion, implicitly or explicitly, of entrepreneurial action in an open-ended world. People don't make decisions by robotically choosing among known ends and means, in light of known constraints, in order to maximize something called utility. Decision-making is not applied mathematics. On the contrary, partly ignorant and fallible people act in an uncertain world where unanticipated change poses unexpected choices among unforeseen alternatives subject to the acuteness or dullness of their alertness to opportunities. The individual, whose action is by nature creative and entrepreneurial, makes decisions on the basis not of "data" but of subjective considerations such as speculations about what the future would be under various scenarios. This sort of action cannot be modeled in the precise ways that those suffering "physics envy" would wish.

More or less self-interested human agents acting under such circumstances hardly hold out the promise of social order. But theory and history counterintuitively say otherwise. The action that takes place is *exchange for mutual benefit* guided by prices, mostly among individuals who don't know each other. "The market economy," Boettke reminds us, "is about cooperation in anonymity, cooperation with strangers."

And somehow it works. "Economics teaches us many things," Boettke writes, "but to me the most important is how social cooperation under the division of labor is realized." Or, as the French laissez-faire radicals put it in the early 19th century, without central direction "Paris gets fed." There is indeed an undesigned order, one that is, in Boettke's words, "intention driven but not intention limited."

But to get the order and harmony that mainline economics promises, the institutions have to be appropriate: property rights, market prices, and the discipline of profit and loss.

If the institutions promote social cooperation under the division of labor, then the gains from trade and innovation will be realized. But if the institutions, in effect, hinder social cooperation under the division of labor, then life will devolve into a struggle for daily existence. Economics, in other words, gives us the key intellectual framework for understanding how we can live better together.

In contrast to mainline economics stands mainstream economics. Boettke writes:

> Mainline is defined by a set of positive propositions about social order that were held in common from Adam Smith onward, but mainstream economics is a sociological concept related to what is currently fashionable among the scientific elite of the profession. Often the mainline and the mainstream dovetail, but at other times they deviate from one another.

It is here that we see the preoccupation with general equilibrium (and mathematics), whether it be the neoclassical (including Chicagoite) assumption that the economy is already in equilibrium or the Keynesian and socialist assumption that because of market failure, the real world does not live up to the blackboard model and thus the government must step in to remake reality accordingly. (Why we would want to simulate that static and nonentrepreneurial world of homogeneous products and price-takers remains a deep mystery.)

Throughout Boettke's book we find good advice for the student of society: *be humble*. Social processes are too complex to justify hubris and social engineering. He fruitfully contrasts two kinds of economists — the student of society and the savior. Beware the latter. "The mainline of economic teaching from Adam Smith to F.A. Hayek taught not only what economics can tell us but more importantly what it *cannot* tell us," Boettke writes. "There are real limits to economic analysis and efforts at economic control." Hence

Hayek's admonition, "The curious task of economics is to demonstrate to men how little they really know about what they imagine they can design." Yet Boettke quickly adds:

> But if we accept the judgment that economics cannot play the role of social engineering, we need not be content with economics being purely philosophical. Economics and political economy are capable of generating significant empirical information. The discipline can inform us about how alternative institutional frameworks will impact our ability to realize the gains from trade and innovation. If the institutional framework impedes trade and innovation, then those gains will go unrealized; if the institutional framework encourages those aspects of an economy, then those gains will be realized.

Hence the need for private property and strict limits on power: "Economists are tasked with speaking truth to power, not catering to power. The discipline, from Smith to Hayek, has taught us about the need to limit power to curb the predatory capabilities of mankind." Importantly he notes, "Governance without government can, and does, happen."

Of course, Boettke realizes, many practitioners will not want to hear such talk:

> The reorientation we are calling for, however, is one that would reduce the prestige and power of the economists in modern society. Entrepreneurial action is usually not set in motion when the reward for the innovation is a reduction in relative status. On the other hand, we have argued that if economists give up their privileged position in society, they might regain their "soul."

That's the broad outline of Boettke's thesis. He fills it in with fascinating explorations of the thought of people who have deeply influenced him, including Smith, Mises, Hayek, Kirzner, Boulding, James M. Buchanan, Gordon Tullock, Hans Sennholz, Murray Rothbard, Warren Samuels, Douglass North, Vincent and Elinor Ostrom, Don Lavoie, and Peter Berger. Boettke has the admirable capacity to learn from a diverse group of thinkers, and his book allows the rest of us to benefit from his broad contacts, as well as his discussions of mainstream economists like Keynes, Samuelson, and Stiglitz. Along the way, readers will become acquainted (or better acquainted) with such issues as the nature of human action, the socialist-calculation debate, market socialism, economic development, Public Choice, rules versus outcomes, and "the limits of expertise."

While it is clear that Mises, Hayek, Kirzner, and Rothbard are four of his biggest influences, Boettke can write with complete sincerity that "once we realize that it is not a label, but an approach you take and the positions you hold, then we have to admit that good economics and political economy are not the exclusive domain of those who are willing to label their work as Austrian."

I heartily recommend this book.

Future of Freedom Foundation, March 29, 2013

Chapter 61.
James M. Buchanan
and Spontaneous Order

Nobel laureate James M. Buchanan of George Mason University, who died at 93 in 2013, is best known for his pioneering work in Public Choice — or what he called "politics without romance" — and constitutional economics as a way to limit government power. He also made important contributions to subjectivist economics. His book *Cost and Choice* (1969) examined the evolution and implications of the theory of subjective opportunity cost, contrasting it with the objectivist theory of the classical and later economists. Buchanan thereby situated himself squarely in the tradition of Carl Menger, Ludwig von Mises, and F.A. Hayek.

Buchanan made another contribution of interest to students of Austrian economics — this time in a mere letter to the editor.

In 1982 the classical-liberal political theorist Norman Barry penned a bibliographic essay on "The Tradition of Spontaneous Order" (*Literature of Liberty*, Summer 1982). Spontaneous, or unplanned, order is of course an essential concept in the case for individual liberty and the free market. Although counterintuitive, it is indispensable to explaining how the activities of free people can be orderly without coercive central control. Barry's essay prompted Buchanan to write a brief note to the publication, "Order Defined in the Process of Its Emergence." This note reveals how radically subjectivist Buchanan was.

He began with Barry's observation that the orderly patterns that spontaneously emerge from free people's interaction "appear to be a product of some omniscient designing mind." For Buchanan this seemingly innocuous point "may have, inadvertently, 'given the game away,'" and, at the same time, made [freedom advocates'] didactic task more difficult."

How can that be?

The answer lies in the distinction between a self-sufficient order and one that aims at some external objective. Buchanan rejected the latter conception as a proper description of the market order.

> I want to argue that the "order" of the market emerges only from the process of voluntary exchange among the participating individuals. The "order" is, itself, defined as *the outcome of the process that generates it*. The "it,"

the allocation-distribution result, does not, and cannot, exist independently of the trading process. Absent this process, there is and can be no "order." [Emphasis added.]

What the market order "achieves," then, is not something that *even in theory* could be ascertained apart from the playing out of the real-world market process itself and then achieved by nonmarket means. If you want the resource arrangements the market would produce, you have no alternative but the market. This is what Hayek was getting at when he jousted with "market socialists" in phase two of the socialist-calculation debate in the 1930s. (Mises launched phase one in the 1920s by showing that without private property, free exchange, and market prices, economic calculation and hence state socialism were impossible in practical terms.) Advocates of central planning thought they could defeat Mises and Hayek by showing that the bureaucrats could simulate the market and achieve its results without private property in the means of production.

Buchanan went on to explore what it means to say that the "order generated by market interaction is … comparable to that order which might emerge from an omniscient, designing single mind." He suggested that "if pushed on this question, economists would say that if the designer could somehow know the utility functions of all participants, along with the constraints, such a mind could, by fiat, duplicate precisely the results that would emerge from the process of market adjustment."

The assumption here is that human beings are mere calculating utility maximizers.

"By implication," Buchanan continued, "individuals are presumed to carry around with them fully determined utility functions, and, in the market, they act always to maximize utilities subject to the constraints they confront."

But, as a few moments' thought should reveal, this is a terribly impoverished portrait of flesh-and-blood human beings. It is a picture of decision-making that is distinctly non-entrepreneurial — if it qualifies as decision-making at all. As we know from everyday experience, when we make decisions about an uncertain future, we are speculative, risk-taking entrepreneurs who face the prospect of discovering not only means but also *ends that we never imagined were there* to be discovered. Serendipity happens! This possibility of dispelling what economist Israel Kirzner calls "utter ignorance" is not captured in the formal utility-maximizing model.

"Individuals do not act so as to maximize utilities described in independently existing functions," Buchanan insisted. "They confront *genuine choices*, and the sequence of decisions taken may be conceptualized, ex post (after the choices), in terms of 'as if' functions that are maximized. But these 'as if' functions are, themselves, *generated in the choosing process*, not separately from such process." [Emphasis added.]

Thus, Buchanan wrote,

if viewed in this perspective, there is no means by which even the most idealized omniscient designer could duplicate the results of voluntary interchange. The potential participants *do not know until they enter the process* what their own choices will be. From this it follows that it is logically impossible for an omniscient designer to know, unless, of course, we are to preclude individual freedom of will. [Emphasis added.]

This is no mere hairsplitting, for the debate over whether there are alternative paths to the rational use of resources hangs in the balance. If "rational use" is something definable apart from decision-making through the market process, then in theory one might come up with an alternative method of achieving it. But if "rational use" is an idea that makes sense *only* in light of the choices free people make entrepreneurially as they encounter unforeseen, and unforeseeable, alternatives in the marketplace, there is no alternative path. Fundamentally, the market is not a mere means to independent ends.

"The point I seek to make in this note is at the same time simple and subtle," Buchanan concluded.

> It reduces to the distinction between end-state and process criteria, between consequentialist and nonconsequentialist, teleological and deontological principles. Although they may not agree with my argument, philosophers should recognize and understand the distinction more readily than economists. In economics, even among many of those who remain strong advocates of market and market-like organization, the "efficiency" that such market arrangements produce is independently conceptualized. Market arrangements then become "means," which may or may not be relatively best. Until and unless this teleological element is fully exorcised from basic economic theory, economists are likely to remain confused and their discourse confusing.

Future of Freedom Foundation, January 11, 2013

Chapter 62.
James M. Buchanan's
Subjectivist Economics

James M. Buchanan won the Nobel Prize in economics in 1986 for his pioneering work known as Public Choice. Less well known — but just as important to libertarians — is his thinking on the nature of economics itself. Considering his deep subjectivism and methodological individualism, Buchanan may be seen at least as a fellow traveler of the Austrian school of economics, and I commend his writings in this area to anyone interested in the tradition of Ludwig von Mises, F.A. Hayek, Murray Rothbard, and Israel Kirzner. Fortunately, Buchanan's writings on the nature and scope of economics were collected in a volume published by Liberty Fund some years ago, *What Should Economists Do?* I'll draw on those papers here.

"I want economists to quit concerning themselves with allocation problems *per se*, with *the problem*, as it has been traditionally defined," Buchanan wrote in his essay "What Should Economists Do?" "I want them to concentrate on *exchange* rather than *choice*."

Exchange of course requires at least two people. So for Buchanan economics doesn't begin with Robinson Crusoe *until* Friday arrives. In fact, Buchanan doesn't like the word *economics* for reasons similar to those Hayek gave. (The Greek word derives from the word for *household*, conceived as having a single set of ends and resource constraints; hence "home economics.") Buchanan preferred a term that Hayek and Mises used: *catallactics*. He also liked *symbiotics*:

> the connotation of the term is that the association is mutually beneficial to all parties. This conveys, more or less precisely, the idea that should be central to our definition. It draws attention to a unique sort of relationship, that which involves the cooperative association of individuals, one with another, even when individual interests are different.

Putting social cooperation at the center of the discipline — whatever it's called — is highly significant. If the economic problem to be solved is seen as allocating resources among competing uses, attention may easily move to central decision-making, with bureaucracies filled with economists and computers. The social calculus of utilitarianism becomes prominent. But if the spotlight is on *cooperation* among entrepreneurial persons, one's orientation is different. Central decision-making is quickly seen as *interference* with cooperation among free individuals.

"The mutuality of advantage that may be secured by different organisms as a result of cooperative arrangements, be these simple or complex, is the one important truth of our discipline," Buchanan wrote. "There is no comparable principle, and the important place that has been traditionally assigned to the maximization norm that is called the 'economic principle' reflects misguided emphasis."

Buchanan went to great lengths to debunk misconceptions about the most fundamental matters of economics, even among economists favorable to free markets. "The market or market organization is not a *means* toward the accomplishment of anything. It is, instead, the institutional embodiment of the voluntary exchange processes that are entered into by individuals in their several capacities," he wrote.

> The network of relationships that emerges or evolves out of this trading process, the institutional framework, is called "the market." It is a setting, an arena, in which we, as economists, as theorists (as onlookers), observe men attempting to accomplish their own purposes, whatever those may be. And it is about these attempts that our basic theory is exclusively concerned if we would only recognize it as such.

Note that Buchanan is saying that "the market" does not aim at anything, such as an optimal allocation of resources or the maximization of utility. People aim at things through exchange and cooperation, and the institutional outcome is what we call the market. (Similarly, I have insisted that "the market" does not ration resources, which is something even free-market economists regularly claim.) Properly conceived, economics cannot be about social welfare, since utility is not something that can be aggregated. Rather, it is individual and subjective, which means that costs (utility forgone) are also subjective. (Buchanan wrote about this earlier in *Cost and Choice*.)

"In this conception," he continued, "there is no explicit meaning of the term *efficiency* as applied to aggregative or composite results. It is contradictory to talk of the market as achieving 'national goals,' efficiently or inefficiently." Here, again, Buchanan corrects a misconception held by most free-market economists, who constantly tell us that markets are efficient.

Buchanan extended this thinking in at least two more essays, "General Implications of Subjectivism in Economics" and "Natural and Artifactual Man."

In the second of the papers, he described the "central difference" of the human being as having a sense of "becoming." "We, as human beings, ... know that we can, within limits, shape the form of being that we shall be between now and the time of death," he wrote. Reminding ourselves of this fact is important because "modern economic theory forces upon us patterns of thought that make elementary recognition of the whole 'becoming' part of our behavior very difficult to analyze and easy to neglect." That is another way of saying that human beings are inherently entrepreneurial; they are not simply acting to maximize utility within known constraints. They project pictures of the future they wish to realize as they encounter alternatives that may have never been foreseen.

As noted, Buchanan rejected talk of "national goals" and other collectivist notions, but he went beyond others who do the same:

> Traditionally, many of us who have been critical of such talk remark that "only individuals can have goals." But I am here advancing the more radical notion that not even individuals have well-defined and well-articulated objectives that exist independently of choices themselves.

> Out of all this there emerges a strong defense of individual liberty that cannot readily be advanced by the modern economist, influenced as he is by his utilitarian heritage.

> *Man wants liberty to become the man he wants to become.* He does so precisely because he does not know what man he will want to become in time. Let us remove once and for all the instrumental defense of liberty, the only one that can possibly be derived directly from orthodox economic analysis. Man does not want liberty in order to maximize his utility, or that of society of which he is a part. *He wants liberty to become the man he wants to become.*

Buchanan's body of work is not entirely immune from libertarian criticism. But at its core is something invaluable for the case for freedom. He was always someone from whom one could learn.

Future of Freedom Foundation, April 1, 2013

Chapter 63.
The Importance of
Subjectivism in Economics

After many years 19th-century French liberal economist Frédéric Bastiat remains a hero to libertarians. No mystery there. He made the case for freedom and punctured the arguments for state socialism with clarity and imagination. He spoke to lay readers with great effect.

Bastiat loved the market economy and badly wanted it to blossom in full — in France and everywhere else. When he described the blessings of freedom, his benevolence shined forth. Free markets can raise living standards and enable everyone to have better lives; stifling freedom is therefore unjust and tragic. The reverse of Bastiat's benevolence is his indignation at the deprivation that results from interference with the market process.

He began his magnum opus, *Economic Harmonies*, by pointing out the economic benefits of living in society:

> It is impossible not to be struck by the disproportion, truly incommensurable, that exists between the satisfactions [a] man derives from society and the satisfactions that he could provide for himself if he were reduced to his own resources. I make bold to say that in one day he consumes more things than he could produce himself in ten centuries.

> What makes the phenomenon stranger still is that the same thing holds true for all other men. Every one of the members of society has consumed a million times more than he could have produced; yet no one has robbed anyone else.

Bastiat was not naïve. He knew he was not in a fully free market. He was well aware of the existence of privilege: "Privilege implies someone to profit from it and someone to pay for it," he wrote. Those who pay are worse off than they would be in the free market. "I trust that the reader will not conclude from the preceding remarks that we are insensible to the social suffering of our fellow men. Although the suffering is less in the present imperfect state of our society than in the state of isolation, it does not follow that we do not seek wholeheartedly for further progress to make it less and less."

He wished to emphasize the importance of free exchange for human flourishing. In chapter four he wrote,

Exchange is political economy. It is society itself, for it is impossible to conceive of society without exchange, or exchange without society. ... For man, isolation means death. ...

By means of exchange, men attain the same *satisfaction* with less *effort*, because the mutual services they render one another yield them a larger proportion of gratuitous utility.

Therefore, the fewer obstacles an exchange encounters, the less effort it requires, the more readily men exchange.

How does trade deliver its benefits?

Exchange produces two phenomena: the joining of men's forces and the diversification of their occupations, or the division of labor.

It is very clear that in many cases the combined force of several men is superior to the sum of their individual separate forces. ...

Now, the joining of men's forces implies exchange. To gain their co-operation, they must have good reason to anticipate sharing in the satisfaction to be obtained. Each one by his efforts benefits the others and in turn benefits by their efforts according to the terms of the bargain, which is exchange.

But isn't something missing from this account?

Indeed, there is: the subjectivist Austrian insight that individuals gain from trade *per se*. For an exchange to take place, the two parties must assess the items traded *differently*, with each party preferring what he is to receive to what he is to give up. If that condition did not hold, no exchange would occur. There must be what economist Murray Rothbard called a *double inequality of value*. It's in the very logic of human action — which Ludwig von Mises christened *praxeology*. Bastiat, like his classical forebears Smith and Ricardo, erroneously believed (at least explicitly) that people trade *equal* values and that something is wrong when unequal values are exchanged.

Perhaps I am too hard on Bastiat. After all, he was writing before 1850. Pioneering Austrian economist Carl Menger did not publish *Principles of Economics* until 1871. Yet the Austrians were not the first to look at exchange strictly through subjectivist spectacles, that is, from the economic actors' points of view. The French philosopher Étienne Bonnot de Condillac (1715–1780) did so a hundred years before Bastiat wrote: "The very fact that an exchange takes place is proof that there must necessarily be profit in it for both the contracting parties; otherwise it would not be made. Hence, every exchange represents two gains for humanity."

Well, perhaps Bastiat was unaware of Condillac's argument. That is not the case. He reprinted the quote above in his book and responded:

> The explanation we owe to Condillac seems to me entirely insufficient and empirical, or rather it fails to explain anything at all. ...

> The exchange represents two gains, you say. The question is: Why and how? It results from the very fact that it takes place. But why does it take place? What motives have induced the two men to make it take place? Does the exchange have in it a mysterious virtue, inherently beneficial and incapable of explanation?

> We see how exchange ... adds to our satisfactions. ... [T]here is no trace of ... the double and empirical profit alleged by Condillac.

This is perplexing. Clearly, the necessary double inequality of value is not empirical or contingent. Contra Bastiat, the double inequality explains quite a lot, and his questions all have easy answers.

Yet more perplexing still is Bastiat's statement in the same chapter: "The profit of the one is the profit of the other." This seems to imply what he just denied.

Bastiat's failure to grasp this point had consequences for his debates with other economists. For example, he and his fellow "left-free-market" advocate Pierre-Joseph Proudhon engaged in a lengthy debate over whether interest on loans would exist in the free market or whether it was a privilege bestowed when government suppressed competition. Unfortunately, the debate suffered because neither Bastiat nor Proudhon fully and explicitly grasped the Condillac/Austrian point about the double inequality of value. As Roderick Long explains in his priceless commentary on the exchange:

> Each one trips up his defense of his own position through an inconsistent grasp of the Austrian principle of the "double inequality of value"; Proudhon embraces it, but fails to apply it consistently, while Bastiat implicitly relies on it, but explicitly rejects it. ...

> Proudhon's case against interest seems to depend crucially on his claim that all exchange must be of equivalent values; so pointing out the incoherence of this notion would be a telling reply. But *Bastiat cannot officially give this reply* (though he comes tantalisingly close over and over throughout the debate) because elsewhere — in his *Economic Harmonies* — Bastiat explicitly *rejects* the doctrine of double inequality of value.

How frustrating! Bastiat has so much to teach. But here is one blind spot that kept him from being even better.

Foundation for Economic Education, September 7, 2012

Chapter 64.
"What Sort of Despotism Democratic Nations Have to Fear"

I took the title from volume 2, section 4, chapter 6, of Alexis de Tocqueville's *Democracy in America* (1840). That chapter has been quoted many times in many places. But it seems like a good time to revisit Tocqueville's writing about democratic despotism.

He noted that despotism in a constitutional republic would be different from what it was in the Roman empire. How so? "[I]t would be more extensive and more mild; it would degrade men without tormenting them."

Specifically: "Above this race of men stands an immense and tutelary power, which takes upon itself alone to secure their gratifications and to watch over their fate. That power is absolute, minute, regular, provident, and mild. It would be like the authority of a parent if, like that authority, its object was to prepare men for manhood."

But that is not its object. Rather,

> it seeks, on the contrary, to keep them in perpetual childhood. ... For their happiness such a government willingly labors, but it chooses to be the sole agent and the only arbiter of that happiness; it provides for their security, foresees and supplies their necessities, facilitates their pleasures, manages their principal concerns, directs their industry, regulates the descent of property, and subdivides their inheritances: what remains, but to spare them all the care of thinking and all the trouble of living?

What remains, indeed? He went on with an almost spooky prophecy.

> After having thus successively taken each member of the community in its powerful grasp and fashioned him at will, the supreme power then extends its arm over the whole community. It covers the surface of society with a network of small complicated rules, minute and uniform, through which the most original minds and the most energetic characters cannot penetrate, to rise above the crowd. *The will of man is not shattered, but softened, bent, and guided; men are seldom forced by it to act, but they are constantly restrained from acting. Such a power does not destroy, but it prevents existence; it does not tyrannize, but it compresses, enervates, extinguishes, and stupefies a people, till each nation is reduced to nothing better than a flock of timid and industrious animals, of which the government is the shepherd.* [Emphasis added]

237

Tocqueville also saw the paradoxes of democratic despotism. Note how relevant they still are:

> I have always thought that servitude of the regular, quiet, and gentle kind which I have just described might be combined more easily than is commonly believed with some of the outward forms of freedom, and that it might even establish itself under the wing of the sovereignty of the people.

> Our contemporaries are constantly excited by two conflicting passions: they want to be led, and they wish to remain free. As they cannot destroy either the one or the other of these contrary propensities, they strive to satisfy them both at once. They devise a sole, tutelary, and all-powerful form of government, but elected by the people. They combine the principle of centralization and that of popular sovereignty; this gives them a respite: they console themselves for being in tutelage by the reflection that *they have chosen their own guardians*. Every man allows himself to be put in leading-strings, because he sees that it is not a person or a class of persons, but the people at large who hold the end of his chain. [Emphasis added.]

Tocqueville taught us that "it is especially dangerous to enslave men in the minor details of life. ... Subjection in minor affairs breaks out every day and is felt by the whole community indiscriminately. It does not drive men to resistance, but it crosses them at every turn, till they are led to surrender the exercise of their own will."

What would he have thought about government's laying the foundation for, say, controlling our medical decisions?

He concluded,

> Thus their spirit is gradually broken and their character enervated. ... It is indeed difficult to conceive how men who have entirely given up the habit of self-government should succeed in making a proper choice of those by whom they are to be governed; and no one will ever believe that a liberal, wise, and energetic government can spring from the suffrages of a subservient people.

> A constitution [which is] republican in its head and ultra-monarchical in all its other parts has always appeared to me to be a short-lived monster.

Tocqueville might have had his timing off, but with a fiscal crisis on the horizon — the product of a bloated welfare state, an aging population, and a lackluster economy mired in corporatism — the "monster" indeed is in trouble. With work, we might still be able to turn things around.

Foundation for Economic Education, April 2, 2010

Chapter 65.
Real Liberalism and the Law of Nature

> Our leaders invent nothing but new taxes, and conquer nothing but the pockets of their subjects. — Thomas Hodgskin

Is government the source of our rights? I fear that today many people would say yes. Not infrequently we hear it said that the government or the Constitution *grants* us freedom of speech or press or the right to own property. This offends the natural-law tradition that was essential to the genesis of classical liberalism (or just liberalism) and the vital welfare-enhancing institutions it spawned. While some prominent early liberals sought to overthrow natural law in favor of the seemingly more-scientific utilitarianism, the heart and soul of liberalism is — and remains — the natural law. The freedom philosophy would be impoverished without it.

British writer Thomas Hodgskin (1787–1869) understood this. He deserves to be better known than he is. Hodgskin was an early editor of *The Economist* and an important influence on Herbert Spencer, who also worked at that publication. Hodgskin is something of a puzzle for many people. He is often described as a Ricardian socialist, but the label is misleading. Having lived before the marginal revolution of economics, in which Carl Menger, founder of the Austrian school, and other economists provided an alternative to the Adam Smith/David Ricardo labor theory of value, Hodgskin did regard labor, rather than subjective utility, as the source of economic value. However his writings contain indications that he regarded utility as a fundamental economic phenomenon. He writes in *Labour Defended against the Claims of Capital*: "But it is quite plain that the sum the weaver will be disposed to give for the thread will depend on his view of its utility." Nevertheless, he thought that what people found useful had to be created by labor.

But calling him a socialist is bound to confuse. He was indeed a critic of "capitalism," by which he and others back then meant government intervention on behalf of capital to the prejudice of labor. But he was no advocate of state control of the means of production. On the contrary, he was influenced by the radical market economist J.B. Say and believed that violations of laissez faire, such as tariffs, exploited workers by depriving them of their full, market-derived product. Only in a fully free and openly competitive environment void of privilege could laborers achieve justice. (Hodgskin developed his sympathy for labor while in the navy, where he observed the cruelty toward sailors. He himself was disciplined and eventually court-martialed and discharged.) As libertarians David Hart and Walter Grinder write,

> The radical individualist Thomas Hodgskin … gives a clear example of the application of the libertarian nonaggression principle to the acquisition and exchange of property. He also implies that those who benefit from "artificial" property rights, that is, by force and state privilege, comprise a class antagonistic to the producing class.

How unfortunate that siding with workers against government intervention on behalf of business has come to be considered anti-libertarian! There was a time when one could write a book, as Hodgskin did, titled *Labour Defended against the Claims of Capital* without being thought a communist.

The work of Hodgskin that Hart and Grinder were referring to is *The Natural and Artificial Right of Property Contrasted* (1832), which he signed "A Labourer." The book is a series of letters to British statesman Lord Brougham on the moral and legal status of property. The books' introductory letter is a good indication of Hodgskin's natural-law approach to liberty and government, an approach that ought to be emphasized by liberals. (This is not to slight a concern with consequences. But it *is* to reject the notion that *only* consequences in the narrow sense matter.)

Hodgskin was alarmed that few among the general public or in Parliament understood that society was a natural phenomenon, rather than an artificial product of government. It was too-commonly thought that without a constant stream of new legislation, society would run down and turn chaotic. (Have we heard anything like that lately?) He wanted to set Lord Brougham straight on this point.

> With one or two exceptions, they [members of Parliament] are so ignorant that they have yet to learn the existence of any natural laws regulating society. They believe that it is held together by the statutes at large; and they know no other laws which influence its destiny than those decreed by themselves and interpreted by the judges.

But if no one understands the true nature of society, i.e., that it is essentially self-regulating, then how can a legislator know that he must keep from interfering with it? It's a question we could put to almost any member of Congress.

> Rapidly therefore as the gentlemen at Westminster work, making three or four hundred laws per year, repeating their tasks session after session — actively as they multiply restraints, or add patch after patch, they invariably find that the call for their labours is continually renewed. The more they botch and mend, the more numerous are the holes. *Knowing nothing of natural principles, they seem to fancy that society — the most glorious part*

of creation, if individual man be the noblest of animals — derives its life and strength only from them. They regard it as a baby, whom they must dandle and foster into healthy existence; but while they are scheming how to breed and clothe their pretty foundling — lo! it has become a giant, whom they can only control as far as he consents to wear their fetters. [Emphasis added.]

How little basic attitudes have changed in all these years.

Because we have continually altered our laws piecemeal, paying no regard to principles, or setting out from an erroneous one, that has never since been revised, we are now lost in a vast wilderness of fictions and absurdities. The law, instead of being [quoting Brougham himself] "the staff of honesty and the shield of innocence, is a two-edged sword of craft and oppression," which, but for the large shield of the public press which the law has in vain endeavoured to break, would hack society asunder.

Then Hodgskin approaches the heart of the issue.

To remedy these monstrous evils, vitiating the whole social compact we must begin at first principles. To stop the flowing of the volcanic and sulphureous stream, which, though shining and sparkling with promise, like the fertilizing waters of the earth, withers the heart of the land, we must go to the fountain head. Convinced, by the every day practices of our legislators, that they never study first principles, though they continually and vainly try to modify results, and convinced by the present state of the law that they cannot begin the study too soon, I propose to call your attention to one of those principles, THE RIGHT OF PROPERTY — some of the consequences of which are now undergoing investigation by two sets of commissioners.

He didn't show much confidence in members of Parliament. I note that Congress's rating in public-opinion polls is at historically low levels, although I suspect that unlike Hodgskin, Americans probably think Congress is not doing *enough*. Hodgskin, on the other hand, operated from something like a Public Choice, as opposed to the textbook public-interest, perspective.

I am aware, indeed, that nothing is more irksome to legislators than to stop them short in their career, by any demands for previous investigation. — It is so much easier and shorter to decree than inquire, and so much more flattering to self-love to dictate than examine, that both indolence and vanity combine to make the law-giver act before he understands. He takes no comprehensive view of society; he grubs forward under the influence of his passions and animal instincts, like the mole, and is quite as blind. If any of those instincts had for their object the welfare of society, I should join the crowd and huzza him on. Unfortunately for his pretentions, his instincts, his passions, his desires — like those of all animals — have no other object than the preservation and welfare of the individual. Till, therefore, some incarnation of social instincts be made manifest, I, for one, must insist that the legislator is bound to inquire into the natural laws which regulate society, before he tries to bind society down to his own short-sighted views. Self-interest, too, should now dictate inquiry: for mankind are every where becoming the critics of his actions; and he will command their respect and obedience, no longer than he guides his conduct by the natural principles to which society owes its rise, progress, and continued existence.

Our author had a sense of the "knowledge problem" that Nobel laureate F. A. called attention to. Unfortunately, legislators haven't yet caught up with either thinker. They still believe, for example, that they can construct a proper immigration policy that will let in only the "right kind" of people, for example, those who fit the future needs of the economy — as though politicians could predict the future needs of an economy.

> The progress of the past may cast its shadow before, so that you may have a rough notion that society is to go on increasing in people, in wealth, and in knowledge, as it has increased in past time; but what shape that increase is to take, how rapid is to be the progress, and what are to be the new relations, both among individuals and among nations, it will call into existence — what new trades, what new arts, may arise — what new habits, manners, customs, and opinions, will be formed — *what is the precise outline society will assume*, with all the fillings-in of the picture to the most minute touches; — *all these things*, to which laws ought to be adapted, *cannot possibly be known*: and inquiry into them, with a view of making laws to accord with them, must necessarily make the whole business of legislation appear in its true character to mankind — a mockery of their interests, and a fraud on their understandings. [Emphasis added.]

Hodgskin then cut to the chase, raising the issue at the center of his attention: property rights. See if he sounds like a socialist, as we commonly apply that label.

> Political organization depends very much on the mode in which property is distributed. Wherever the right of property is placed on a proper foundation, slavery, with all its hateful consequences, is unknown: — wherever this foundation is rotten, freedom cannot exist, nor justice be administered.

> But though the Westminster philosophers, and you also, agree with Mr. Locke, in attributing to the right of property the utmost importance, making it the basis of the political edifice, they differ from him, fundamentally and totally, as to the origin of this right. Mr. Locke lays it down, that the preservation of property is the object for which men unite into a commonwealth. For this purpose, they put themselves under government. Property therefore, according to Mr. Locke, existed

antecedently to government, and government was established for the protection of an antecedently existing right of property. [Emphasis added.]

But this conception of property as a natural right is not what holds sway, Hodgskin went on:

On the contrary, both Mr. [John Stuart] Mill and M. [Etienne] Dumont, describe the right of property to be the offspring of law. Mr. Mill says, "the end of government is *to make* a distribution of wealth," or create such a right. M. Dumont expressly says, that the right of property is altogether the work or creation of the legislator, or the law. This difference of opinion is pregnant with momentous consequences. If a right of property be a natural right, not created by legislation, if it be a principle of society, derived immediately and directly from the laws of the universe, all its results will be determined, at all times, by those laws; and the legislator ought to ascertain these results, before he dreams of making decrees, to enforce them. Before he takes any steps to protect the right of property, he must, on Mr. Locke's principles, find out in what it consists.

That would seem to be mere common sense. Since natural law operates whether we acknowledge it or not, social engineering that contravenes natural law must come to grief.

If, on the other hand, a right of property be altogether the creature and work of laws, as the legislator seems to suppose, he may at all times determine all its consequences. He will have no occasion to inquire into any circumstances foreign to his own enactments; he will only have to frame his decrees with logical accuracy from the principles he lays down.

The two approaches are mutually exclusive and mutually exhaustive. There's no middle way.

One system looks on the legislator as an ally, in enforcing the laws of nature, to do which he must know them; the other denies that there are any such laws, which in fact its authors do in express terms, and they look on enactments as determining the welfare and destiny of mankind. A more important difference of opinion cannot exist. Either principle lies at the very foundation of the whole political edifice. Mr. Locke's view is, in my opinion, more correct than Mr. [Jeremy] Bentham's, though at present among legislators, and those who aspire to be legislators, the latter is by far the most prevalent. Practical men universally adopt it; for they always decree, and never inquire into the laws of nature. The prevalence of Mr. Bentham's opinion, makes it necessary to illustrate and enforce that of Mr. Locke, in so far as it is limited to asserting that a right of property is not the offspring of legislation.

Natural-law liberals, such as Thomas Paine, saw government, at best, as a necessary evil. Not so the utilitarians, Hodgskin said.

> Messrs. Bentham and Mill, both being eager to exercise the power of legislation, represent it as a beneficent deity which curbs our naturally evil passions and desires (they adopting the doctrine of the priests, that the desires and passions of man are naturally evil) — which checks ambition, sees justice done, and encourages virtue. Delightful characteristics! which have the single fault of being contradicted by every page of history. Hitherto, it has been generally supposed that the whole world was given to the human race, with dominion over all other created things, for them to use and enjoy in every way, abstaining from nothing — restricted in nothing consistent with their own happiness — bound mutually to share the blessings provided for them, because mutual assistance begets mutual love — supplies physical wants easier and better, and promotes moral and intellectual improvement; — that the rights and duties of men grow out of the great scheme of creation, which is sometimes misinterpreted, and rarely understood, by human sagacity, — sometimes marred, and never mended, by human wisdom. But, now, in compliment to political power, and to Mr. Bentham's theory, that we may find an apology for our own infirm and base submission, we must believe that men had naturally no right to pick up cockles on the beach or gather berries from the hedge — no right to cultivate the earth, to invent and make comfortable clothing, to use instruments to provide more easily for their enjoyments — no right to improve and adorn their habitations — nay, no right to have habitations — no right to buy or sell, or move from place to place — till the benevolent and wise law-giver conferred all these rights on them.

If this be the basis of the political system, Hodgskin wanted no part of it.

> To me, this system appears as mischievous as it is absurd. The doctrines accord too well with the practice of law-givers, they cut too securely all the Gordian knots of legislation, not to be readily adopted by all those who, however discontented they may be with a distribution of power, in which no share falls to them, are anxious to become the tutelary guardians of the happiness of mankind. They lift legislation beyond our reach, and secure it from censure. Man, having naturally no rights, may be experimented on, imprisoned, expatriated or even exterminated, as the legislator pleases. Life and property being his gift, he may resume them at pleasure; and hence he never classes the executions and wholesale slaughters, he continually commands, with murder — nor the forcible appropriation of property he sanctions, under the name of taxes, tithes, &c., with larceny or high-way robbery. [Sir Robert] Filmer's doctrine of the divine right of kings was rational benevolence, compared to the monstrous assertion that [quoting Mill] "all right is factitious, and only exists by the will of the law-maker." But though this may be comfortable doctrine for legislators, it will not satisfy the people; and in spite of false

theories and unreasonable practices, events are now teaching mankind to place a just value on law-making. Day does not follow day, without increasing our knowledge of the consequences of actions; and it is fast becoming apparent, that the wise men, such as Cicero and Seneca, as Bacon and Locke, and as Burke and Smith, who have advocated a totally different system from that of Messrs. Bentham and Mill and their arrogant disciples, have not cast the seeds of their faith in nature, on a barren and ungrateful soil.

Where are those such as Thomas Hodgskin when we really need them?

Foundation for Economic Education, August 10, 2007

Chapter 66.
The Natural Right of Property

Thomas Hodgskin, whom I discussed in the last chapter, is an enigma — until his philosophy is seen in its entirety. He was an editor at *The Economist* of London from 1846 to 1855, during the period author Scott Gordon called "the high tide of laissez faire, yet [Gordon continued] he is considered a Ricardian socialist, was quoted and deferred to by Marx [and] described by Sidney and Beatrice Webb as Marx's master." How could any libertarian claim Hodgskin as a mentor?

"The connection will only be fully appreciated," Gordon added, "by those who have learned that the geometry of politics is non-Euclidean; straight lines, when extended, form complete circles, and parallels may meet and even cross." (The quotes are from Gordon's "The London *Economist* and the High Tide of Laissez Faire," *Journal of Political Economy*, December 1955.)

The radical edge that Hodgskin gave his laissez-faire advocacy confuses people whose thoughts come in prefabricated boxes. Today if someone sympathizes with labor's plight, he's bound to be labeled a collectivist, although earlier radical individualists located the source of that plight not in the free market but in the halls of government. This was better understood in the 19th and early 20th centuries, when the likes of Lysander Spooner, Benjamin Tucker, and Herbert Spencer held the libertarian vanguard.

Hodgskin, very simply, was a natural-law individualist who thought the government should grant no privileges to anyone, particularly capitalists, landowners, and clergy, who in his time were the chief beneficiaries of state appropriation and other interference with peaceful market activity. He embraced the "natural right of property" and opposed the "artificial right of property," which he attributed to the utilitarians' belief that legislation, not natural law, was the source rights. In other words, land and other objects acquired through original appropriation and honest, voluntary methods were legitimate property. All forced and fraudulent means of acquisition yielded illegitimate, artificial property that could only be sustained by government power. He called for the abolition of all forms of the artificial right of property and full flowering of the natural right.

Hodgskin was a passionately consistent adherent of the philosophy of John Locke and the laissez-faire, free-trade, anti-imperial Manchester school of Richard Cobden and Cobden Bright. His dubious ideas on the labor theory of value (held also by Adam Smith and David Ricardo) and the nature of capital would not withstand the later Austrian school of economics, and he criticized "capitalists." But this was always in the context of systematic government intervention, most egregiously the prohibition of unions, or "combinations." Indeed, his early disparaging use of the word *capitalist* was a clear assault on privilege. Laissez faire would eliminate "most of the misery which exists in the world," he said. He fully appreciated that owners of producer goods and entrepreneurs were laborers too, possessing the right to their full product like any other laborer. Unlike Marx, he did not believe that the exploitation of labor was inherent in market relations but rather was the result of departures from the free market.

As for his alleged Ricardian socialism, Murray Rothbard wrote:

> There is no question that Hodgskin's ultra labourism influenced Karl Marx, but his extreme labour theory of value does not make him a Ricardian, much less a socialist. In fact, Hodgskin was highly critical of [David] Ricardo and the Ricardian system, denounced Ricardo's abstract methodology and his theory of rent, and considered himself a Smithian rather than a Ricardian. [Adam] Smith's natural law and harmony-of-interest free market doctrine was also more congenial to Hodgskin. ... Furthermore, even at his most labourist in the 1820s, Thomas Hodgskin ... widened rather than narrowed the definition of "labour." Mental activity is as much "labour," he pointed out, as muscular exertion. ... Not only that: Hodgskin also pointed out cogently that the capitalist is also very often a manager, and therefore also a "labourer."

This gives context to such Hodgskin statements as: "There is then, I conclude, a natural right of property, founded on the fact that labour is necessary to produce whatever bears the name of wealth." If *socialism* means abolition or crippling of the market, Hodgskin was no socialist as we understand the term today.

Hodgskin's intellectual career was something remarkable. He wrote for the public and even helped run an institute designed to teach free-market economics. His idea of natural economic harmony — absent government intervention — reminds one of his contemporary Frédéric Bastiat, who called *The Economist* "a precious collection of facts, doctrine and experience mutually supporting each other." Hodgskin's "philosophical basis was natural law," Gordon wrote. "He may appear to be an anachronism in the mid-nineteenth century until one reflects upon the fact that this is precisely what laissez faire and the economic harmony doctrine were. They were a reaction against utilitarianism and a return to natural law."

Observe his independence of thought. When many thinkers of his day were under the sway of Thomas Malthus's pessimism about the ability of a growing population to feed itself, Hodgskin sounded like Adam Smith, Julian Simon, Peter Bauer, and Jane Jacobs rolled into one — although he had trouble finding a publisher for his views. "Hodgskin argued that an increase in population provides a larger market which permits a more extensive division of labor to be carried out. Also, large centers of population are a stimulus to the inventive and creative powers of men" (Gordon).

Again in Bastiat-like fashion, Hodgskin found the right of property in the very nature of human beings and the world. In his book *The Natural and Artificial Right of Property Contrasted* (1832), he stated:

> I look on a *right* of property — on the right of individuals, to have and to own, for their own separate and selfish use and enjoyment, the produce of their own industry, with power freely to dispose of the whole of that in the manner most agreeable to themselves — as essential to the welfare and even to the continued existence of society. If, therefore, I did not suppose, with Mr. Locke, that nature establishes such a right — if I were not prepared to shew that she not merely establishes, but also protects and preserves it, so far as never to suffer it to be violated with impunity — I should at once take refuge in Mr. Bentham's impious theory, and admit that the legislator who established and preserved a right of property, deserved little less adoration than the Divinity himself. Believing, however, that nature establishes such a right, I can neither join those who vituperate it as the source of all our social misery, nor those who claim for the legislator the high honour of being "the author of the finest triumph of humanity over itself."

In Hodgskin's view, this natural right is self-sufficient, needing no help from the legislator.

> A savage, stronger than the labourer or more cunning, may undoubtedly take the fruit of his industry from him by force or fraud; but antecedently to the use of force or fraud, and antecedently to all legislation, nature bestows on every individual what his labour produces, just as she gives him his own body. She bestows the wish and the power to produce, she couples them with the expectation of enjoying that which is produced, and she confirms in the labourer's possession, if no wrong be practised, as long as he wishes to possess, whatever he makes or produces. All these are natural circumstances — the existence of any other person than the labourer not being necessary to the full accomplishment of them. The enjoyment is secured by the individual's own means. No contract, no legislation, is required. Whatever is made by human industry, is naturally appropriated as made, and belongs to the maker. In substance, I would feign hope, there is no difference between this statement and that of Mr. Locke; but I wish to mark, stronger than I think he has done, the fact, that, antecedently to all legislation, and to any possible interference by the legislator, nature establishes a law of appropriation by bestowing, as she creates individuality, the produce of labour on the labourer.

He goes so far to say that the right of property is embedded in the very idea of individuality. The latter would be meaningless without the former.

Mr. Locke says, that every man has a property in his own person; in fact, individuality — which is signified by the word *own* — cannot be disjoined from the person. Each individual learns his own shape and form, and even the existence of his limbs and body, from seeing and feeling them. These constitute his notion of *personal* identity, both for himself and others; and it is impossible to conceive — it is in fact a contradiction to say — that a man's limbs and body do not belong to himself: for the words himself, self, and his body, signify the same material thing.

As we learn the existence of our own bodies from seeing and feeling them, and as we see and feel the bodies of others, we have precisely similar grounds for believing in the individuality or identity of other persons, as for believing in our own identity. The ideas expressed by the words mine and thine, as applied to the produce of labour, are simply then an extended form of the ideas of personal identity and individuality.

The idea of property occurs to us naturally and early on as we act in the world. We don't need the legislator to instruct us in its nature or its intricacies. The individual's reason is capable of grasping the concept.

As nature gives to labour whatever it produces — as we extend the idea of personal individuality to what is produced by every individual — not merely is a right of property established by nature, we see also that she takes means to make known the existence of that right. It is as impossible for men not to have a notion of a right of property, as it is for them to want [lack] the idea of personal identity. ... Ideas of property are truly instinctive, and are acquired by children long before they ever hear of law. If they do not belong to the mind, as the legs and the tongue belong to the body, like the habit of walking or speaking, they are so early acquired, and so continually present to us that they appear innate.

Through production and commerce people would increasingly improve their material condition and the condition of those around them. The hitch is that some wish to prosper not through productive effort but through appropriation of the fruits of other people's labor. The most efficient way is through the power of government, which has nothing it hasn't first taken from some producer.

The first and chief violation of the right of property, which pervades and disturbs all the natural relations of ownership, confusing, and perplexing the ideas of all men as to the source of the right of property, and what is their own, of which so many actions stigmatized by the law as crimes, are the necessary consequences, and the natural corrections, — the parent theft from which flow all other thefts, is that of the legislator, who, not being a labourer, can make no disposition of any property whatever, without appropriating what does not naturally belong to him.

That is the source of the artificial right of property.

> One of the first objects then of the law, subordinate to the great principle of preserving its unconstrained dominion over our minds and bodies, is to bestow a sufficient revenue on the government. Who can enumerate the statutes imposing and exacting taxes? Who can describe the disgusting servility with which all classes submit to be fleeced by the demands of the tax-gatherer, on all sorts of false pretences, when his demands cannot be fraudulently evaded? Who is acquainted with all the restrictions placed on honest and praiseworthy enterprise; the penalties inflicted on upright and honourable exertions; — what pen is equal to the task of accurately describing all the vexations, and the continual misery, heaped on all the industrious classes of the community, under the pretext that it is necessary to raise a revenue for the government?

This was written in 1832. Hodgskin never experienced the Congress, the Internal Revenue Service, or the U.S. income tax. Would he be surprised if he visited us today?

> Nature may annihilate, but she never tortures. ... Not so the legislator. He has inflicted on mankind for ages the miseries of revenue laws, — greater than those of pestilence and famine, and sometimes producing both these calamities, without our learning the lesson which nature seems to have intended to teach, viz. the means of avoiding this perpetual calamity. Revenue laws meet us at every turn. They embitter our meals, and disturb our sleep. They excite dishonesty, and check enterprise. They impede division of labour, and create division of interest. They sow strife and enmity amongst townsmen and brethren.

Locke's commonwealth, says Hodgskin, has not lived up to its theory.

> The natural right of property far from being protected, is systematically violated, and both government and law seem to exist chiefly or solely, in order to protect and organize the most efficacious means of protecting the violation. ...

> The important and yet perhaps trite fact to which I wish by these remarks to direct your attention is, that law and governments are intended, and always have been intended, to establish and protect a right of property, different from that which, in common with Mr. Locke, I say is ordained by nature. The right of property created and protected by the law, is the artificial or legal right of property, as contra-distinguished from the natural right of property. It may be the theory that government ought to protect the natural right; in practice, government seems to exist only to violate it.

The more things change...

Foundation for Economic Education, August 17, 2007

Chapter 67.
Lost in Transcription

Following rules, such as the rules of language, of the market, or of just conduct, is more about "knowing how" than "knowing that." This is a lesson taught by many important thinkers, among them, Gilbert Ryle (who used these terms in the title of chapter 2 of *The Concept of Mind*), F.A. Hayek, and Ludwig Wittgenstein. On many matters we know more than we can say. Yet we are tempted to identify knowing with saying. It's a temptation best resisted. (Wittgenstein distinguished between knowing the height of a structure and knowing how a clarinet sounds. We use the same word *know*, but we don't mean the same thing. Do you know the height if you cannot say it?)

Language, economic activity, and law did not begin when someone published a grammar book, an economics text, or a political treatise that people then used to guide their actions. On the contrary, the books were written after the fact to codify what people had long been doing. And importantly, the books could never fully describe what people had been doing or would do in the future. At best they were imperfect codifications (abstractions) that couldn't possibly capture all the details involved in applying the rules to the varied circumstances of everyday life. In truth, they weren't rules — in the formal, self-conscious sense that we usually define that term — until the books were written. Yet they governed behavior.

"For not only do we not think of the rules of usage — of definitions, etc. — while using language, but when we are asked to give such rules, in most cases we aren't able to do so," Wittgenstein wrote. And elsewhere: "One learns the game by watching how others play. But we say that it is played according to such-and-such rules because an observer can read these rules off from the practice of the game — like a law of nature governing the play." Think how children learn something as complex as language and social roles.

Ryle put it this way:

> Rules of correct reasoning were first extracted by Aristotle, yet men knew how to avoid and detect fallacies before they learned his lessons, just as men since Aristotle, and including Aristotle, ordinarily conduct their arguments without making any internal reference to his formulae. They do not plan their arguments before constructing them. Indeed if they had

to plan what to think before thinking it they would never think at all; for this planning would itself be unplanned.

This fact about rules has important implications for the struggle for the free society. The belief that basic rules and social institutions are and can be the product of conscious design leads to the social engineer's conviction that society can be *redesigned* according to a detailed plan. (This is a species of rationalism.) That conviction easily leads to intolerance of those who won't go along with the plan. It's a short step to proposing that the uncooperative be liquidated — for the common good. (See Hayek's *The Road to Serfdom* in this regard.)

If in fact society cannot have been successfully designed, it follows that it cannot be successfully redesigned. Societies are too complex, and people will stubbornly cling to their tacit rules even in the face of draconian penalties. (Nation-builders, take heed.)

What might this tell us about the classical-liberal notion of individual rights? It seems to say that no society went from illiberal to liberal the day some political philosopher read his treatise of government to the assembled masses in the public square. By the time the treatise would have been written, the customs of ordinary people would already have been largely embodied in what we call natural rights. It is even possible — perhaps likely — that the formal expression of those rights got them wrong. Something was lost in the transcription.

This is largely what the legal philosopher John Hasnas is getting at in his remarkable 2005 paper "Toward a Theory of Empirical Natural Rights." The juxtaposition of "empirical" and "natural" only appears contradictory. Rather, it's a well-chosen oxymoron. What Hasnas sets out to do in this paper is to show how individual rights could "*evolve* in the state of nature"; that is, "in the absence of established government, [but] not in the absence of any mechanism of interpersonal governance."

How might that happen? In the state of nature problems need to be solved. A small number of people may use violence in attempting to live off the productive efforts of others. Besides that, disagreements over contracts and ownership arise among even the peaceful. In response, and contra Thomas Hobbes,

> Various methods of providing for mutual protection and for apprehending or discouraging aggressors are tried. ... Simultaneously, nonviolent alternatives for resolving interpersonal disputes among the productive members of the community are sought. ... Those [methods] that effectively resolve the disputes with the least disturbance to the peace of the community continue to be used and are accompanied by ever-increasing social pressure for disputants to employ them.

Over time, security arrangements and dispute settlement procedures that are well-enough adapted to social and material circumstances to reduce violence to generally acceptable levels become regularized. Members of the community learn what level of participation in or support for the security arrangements is required of them for the system to work and for them to receive its benefits.

Self-interest (and perhaps an Aristotelian sense that justice and other virtues are constitutive of self-interest) impel these developments. The overriding aim of the trial-and-error process is to minimize violence so the business of flourishing through social cooperation may proceed. Importantly, Hasnas adds, "As the members of the community conform their behavior to these practices, they begin to behave according to rules that specify the extent of their obligation to others, and, by implication, the extent to which they are free to act at their pleasure. Over time, these rules become invested with normative significance." Rights are thus born of problem-solving.

Now this is a nice theory, but what about practice? Hasnas illustrates the validity of his story by pointing to two "state of nature" episodes in history: Anglo-Saxon and early Norman England, and the rise of the Law Merchant in medieval Europe. In the first instance, "The process of negotiating settlements of potentially violent conflicts and repeating and eventually institutionalizing successful resolutions gradually produced a broad body of customary law that served as the basis for the England common law."

In the second, beginning in the 11th century, and in the absence of a transnational government, merchants from different cultures and language groups who were engaged in global commerce looked for a way to protect themselves from predation and conflict when away from home.

Merchants sought arrangements that provided the needed assurance. Many such arrangements were tried. Those that worked best were widely copied and eventually institutionalized in the Law Merchant. ... The merchant courts that evolved in this way eventually grew into a European system of commercial courts in which merchant judges quickly applied the tenets of the Law Merchant to resolve commercial disputes.

Hasnas notes that this nuanced body of law eventually provided the basis for modern systems of commercial law.

It is worth emphasizing that in both of Hasnas's examples, effective law that respected individual freedom was generated apart from the state and only later was absorbed — with state-serving distortions — into a formal governmental system. Today we think law is something only legislatures produce, but that is not the case. Strictly speaking, legislatures do not produce law at all. They issue decrees.

253

The "rights" that grew out of these spontaneous processes are recognizable as the rights to life, liberty, and property. Yet, Hasnas acknowledges, they did not perfectly match the natural rights of the political treatises. The empirical right to property is "a highly flexible, exception-laden one that invests individuals with the exclusive use and control of objects only to the extent that doing so facilitates a more peaceful life in society." Nevertheless, the process Hasnas describes gets us a long way down the road to freedom. Positive welfare rights did not arise because they would have created, not averted, social conflict.

No free society or law book will ever be able to describe rights and their application down to the minutest detail once and for all. As noted at the outset, rules are not of that nature. Conflict-resolution procedures that address particular disputes between particular parties as they arise will always be necessary, and such resolution will produce (or identify) additional law. The question is whether we want competition or monopoly in the production of law.

Foundation for Economic Education, August 22, 2008

Chapter 68.
The Rule of Lore

"This is a nation of laws not of men (and women)."

How often have we heard this said? It is accompanied by the claim that it's Congress's job to make the laws and the Supreme Court's job to interpret them, along with the Constitution. Or, to put it in the shorthand: judges should not make the law.

It seems like a tidy division of labor, but there is a certain problem — namely, that the line between making and interpreting law is exceedingly fine — if it exists at all. Indeed, interpreting the law is tantamount to making it. Interpretation is a creative act.

Since in our society it is men and women who write and interpret the laws (and the Constitution), the rule of law is necessarily the rule of men and women.

I realize this is a heretical thought among some advocates of individual freedom, but facts are facts and it's better to face them. A weak argument for liberty is harmful to the cause, so let's mount the best case we can.

Constitutions and laws do not speak for themselves. People must decide what they mean. This is by nature a controversial truth from which there is no escape. Seemingly clear language is often argued about for years, indeed decades and centuries. As I wrote in *America's Counter-Revolution: The Constitution Revisited*, "It's not as if the proper interpretation (whatever that may be) can be hardwired somehow to guarantee that legislators, presidents, and judges will act in certain ways, or that the public will demand it. At every point *people* will be making the interpretive decisions, including the decision over which interpretation is right."

Or as Ludwig Wittgenstein wrote in *Philosophical Investigations*, "Any interpretation still hangs in the air along with what it interprets, and cannot give it any support."

Legal scholar John Hasnas has taken up this matter in a paper explosively titled "The Myth of the Rule of Law" (*Wisconsin Law Review*, 1995).

Hasnas argues that laws can never be determinate because no language is exempt from interpretation. The First Amendment to the Constitution is about as plain as language gets, but after more than 200 years its meaning is still subject to disagreement. Or the Commerce Clause, which says Congress shall have the power to "regulate ... commerce among the several states," was initially *interpreted* as limited to interstate commerce, although that meaning is by no means obvious from the text. The framers were perfectly capable of writing "between citizens of different states" when they wanted to and as they did in Article III on the powers of the judiciary.

Thus to interpret law is to make law.

Moreover, in a legal system such as ours, Hasnas writes, there is inevitably a host of "incompatible, contradictory rules and principles. ... This means that a logically sound argument can be found for any legal conclusion." (Hasnas gives several examples.)

> Because the law is made up of contradictory rules that can generate any conclusion, what conclusion one finds will be determined by what conclusion one looks for, i.e., by the hypothesis one decides to test. This will invariably be the one that intuitively "feels" right, the one that is most congruent with one's antecedent, underlying political and moral beliefs. Thus, legal conclusions are always determined by the normative assumptions of the decisionmaker. ... [I]t is impossible to reach an objective decision based solely on the law. This is because the law is always open to interpretation and *there is no such thing as a normatively neutral interpretation.* The way one interprets the rules of law is always determined by one's underlying moral and political beliefs.

The upshot is that interpreting the law is an intrinsically political act.

Hasnas points out that the necessity for interpretation does not mean that the law will be acutely unstable. There is indeed a large degree of stability. The law changes over time, but not day to day. Yet, he writes,

> The stability of the law derives not from any feature of the law itself, but from the overwhelming uniformity of ideological background among those empowered to make legal decisions. ... [T]o assume that the law is stable because it is determinate is to reverse cause and effect. Rather, it is because the law is basically stable that it appears to be determinate. It is not the rule of law that gives us a stable legal system; it is the stability of the culturally shared values of the judiciary that gives rise and supports the *myth* of the rule of law.

Hasnas (who advocates competition in the production of law, which some would call anarchism) concludes, "The fact is that there is no such thing as a government of law and not people. The law is an amalgam of contradictory rules and counter-rules expressed in inherently vague language that can yield a legitimate legal argument for any desired conclusion."

This need not lead us to pessimism or cynicism. As Thomas Paine recognized, the fundamental order that defines any society — indeed, the order without which we would call a group of people a mob rather than a society — originated not with top-down legislation but from bottom-up custom, contract, and common-law processes. The great liberal legal scholar Bruno Leoni wrote in *Freedom and the Law* that a legislature is analogous to a central planner, with all the knowledge problems that plague it, while a common-law system is more like the free market, with far better access to the knowledge of time and place that is scattered throughout society and unavailable to a central authority. Better to progressively shrink the sphere in which legislators can operate so that people are free to govern themselves through voluntary exchange.

Advocates of liberty will ultimately carry the day not by invoking impossible standards like "the rule of law not of men," but rather by directly upholding the standard of freedom and justice.

Postscript: In *Theoretical Inquiries in Law* (2008), Hasnas developed his thesis further in "The Depoliticization of Law," where he writes, "Law can arise through a process of evolution. It can be a product of 'human action, but not the execution of any human design.' In such a case, those subject to law are indeed bound, but not by the will of any particular human beings. Although law is inherently coercive, it is not inherently a vehicle for domination. To the extent that the ideal of the rule of law consists of a vision of a society governed by 'laws but not men,' this conception of law places the ideal within reach."

Foundation for Economic Education, August 2, 2012

Chapter 69.
Sotomayor, Freedom, and the Law

The dreary Senate hearing on the nomination of Judge Sonia Sotomayor to the U.S. Supreme Court in 2009 left me so in the doldrums that my only chance for solace was to dig out my copy of *Freedom and the Law* (1961) by Bruno Leoni.

Leoni (1913–1967) was a professor of legal theory and a lawyer in Italy. He was also an eminent liberal scholar and champion of individual freedom, who served as president of the Mont Pelerin Society. *Freedom and the Law* has a provenance worth describing. In 1958 Leoni, F.A. Hayek, and Milton Friedman each gave a series of lectures at the Fifth Institute on Freedom and Competitive Enterprise at what is now Claremont McKenna College in California. To say this meeting was consequential would be a gross understatement. Hayek's lecturers were incorporated into *The Constitution of Liberty*. Friedman's grew into *Capitalism and Freedom*, and Leoni's were collected as *Freedom and the Law*.

Leoni's work was critical in helping to launch the multidisciplinary movement known as Law and Economics, in which these two areas of knowledge are applied to each other to achieve an otherwise impossible depth of understanding of society.

His work was highly relevant to the Judiciary Committee's hearing on Sotomayor. In speeches she suggested that because of sex and ethnicity, judges either can't or shouldn't try to be impartial in their rulings. Moreover, President Obama said he wanted a Court nominee with empathy based on life experience, as well as knowledge of the law. However, under questioning by adversarial senators, Sotomayor seemed to back away from both approaches. At one point, she said,

> They [judges] don't determine the law. Congress makes the laws. The job of a judge is to apply the law. And so it's not the heart that compels conclusions in cases. It's the law. The judge applies the law to the facts before that judge. ... I look at the law that's being cited. I look at how precedent informs it. I try to determine what those principles are of precedent to apply to the facts in the case before me and then do that. ... We apply law to facts. We don't apply feelings to facts.

This is clearly what the conservative senators wanted to hear, but observers of varying ideological stripes were disappointed that Sotomayor stooped to feeding the television audience such pablum. She more than implied that a judge's job is mechanistic: The facts plus the law plus precedent equals a ruling.

Nothing in human affairs is that simple. Judgment and interpretation are required every step of the way. This is why, contrary to popular fable, the line between the rule of law and the rule of men and women is so fine as to be nonexistent. (See "The Rule of Lore" in this volume.) Laws, which are intended to be applied to an unlimited number of unforeseeable future circumstances, do not speak for themselves. Human beings must interpret them. This does not mean language is inherently impenetrable. (I could hardly write if I believed that.) However, there is a broad middle ground between impenetrability and perfect clarity. As libertarian legal scholar Randy Barnett noted, "While I do not share [the] view of law as radically indeterminate, I sure think it is a whole lot more *under*determinate than Judge Sotomayor made it out to be in her testimony today."

If the law is underdeterminate — if there is scope for interpretation and more than one competing interpretation can be reasonable — what is an advocate of liberty to do?

Leoni offers us hope. Let's start at the beginning. Why do we care who is on the Supreme Court? We care because down the street from the Court is the legislation factory we call the U.S. Congress. It has virtually nothing to do but churn out bills. In fact, most "serious" pundits judge congresses by *how many* bills they churn out. All the incentives faced by members of Congress push in one direction: to *legislate* (that is, meddle in people's peaceful affairs).

Furthermore, we know that much of this legislation, since it interferes with what people want to do, will spawn litigation. Eventually some of these cases will wind up before the Supreme Court, the rulings of which will become the law of the land. Hence the interest in Supreme Court nominees.

Thus it would matter far less who is on the Supreme Court if there were little or no legislation.

But we need legislation, don't we?

Without legislation there would be no law, right?

Where did we get the idea that a group of undistinguished men and women — absurdly claiming to be our *representatives* and sitting in what is surely the ultimate ivory tower — should make blanket rules for everyone (except perhaps for themselves), regardless of time, place, and circumstance? It certainly has not protected liberty. Why don't more people realize how poorly this simpleminded procedure serves a complex society?

Most of us are badly in need of reminding that what is admirable about the Western legal tradition — that which has made our progress and prosperity possible — is the product not of legislatures but of something rather different. This fact compels us to distinguish *law* from *legislation*. As Hayek wrote in the first volume of *Law, Legislation, and Liberty*,

> Unlike law itself, which has never been "invented" in the same sense, the invention of legislation came relatively late in the history of mankind. ... Law in the sense of enforced rules of conduct is undoubtedly coeval with society; only the observance of common rules makes the peaceful existence of individuals in society possible. Long before man had developed language to the point where it enabled him to issue general commands, an individual would be accepted as a member of a group only so long as he conformed to its rules. ... To modern man ... the belief that all law governing human action is the product of legislation appears so obvious that the contention that law is older than law-making has almost the character of a paradox. Yet there can be no doubt that law existed for ages before it occurred to man that he could make or alter it.

Or as Leoni put it, "Fewer and fewer people now seem to realize that just as language and fashion are the products of the convergence of spontaneous actions and decisions on the part of a vast number of individuals, so the law too can, in theory, just as well be a product of a similar convergence in other fields."

He went on, "The paradoxical situation of our times is that we are governed by men, not, as the classical Aristotelian theory would contend, because we are not governed by laws [legislation], but because we *are*."

The question for Leoni was not how can we get good legislation and avoid bad legislation. The matter is much deeper: "It is a question of deciding whether individual freedom is compatible in principle with the present system centered on and almost completely identified with legislation."

He told us that in order to imagine an alternative to governance by legislatures, we need not visit Utopia. Rather, we may study Roman and English history: "Both the Romans and the English shared the idea that the law is something to be *discovered* more than to be *enacted* and that nobody is so powerful in his society as to be in a position to identify his own will with the will of the land." This was law that judges discerned when resolving specific disputes brought before them by specific individuals; it was law based on custom and the expectations it gave rise to.

Leoni listed three differences between judges in the sense just described and legislators:

1. "Judges or lawyers or others in a similar position are to intervene only when they are asked to do so by the people concerned, and their decision is to be reached and become effective, at least in civil matters, only through a continuous collaboration of the parties themselves and within its limits."

2. "The decision of judges is to be effective mainly in regard to the parties to the dispute, only occasionally in regard to third persons,

and practically never in regard to people who have no connection with the parties concerned."

3. "Such decisions on the part of judges and lawyers are very rarely to be reached without reference to the decisions of other judges and lawyers in similar cases and are therefore to be in indirect collaboration with all other parties concerned, both past and present."

Thus, "the authors of these decisions have no real power over other citizens beyond what those citizens themselves are prepared to give them by virtue of requesting a decision in a particular case."

Leoni drew important parallels between judge — discovered law and the free market on the one hand and legislation and central planning on the other: "A legal system centered on legislation resembles … a centralized economy in which all the relevant decisions are made by a handful of directors, whose knowledge of the whole situation is fatally limited and whose respect, if any, for the people's wishes is subject to that limitation."

He exposed the posturing of self-styled "representatives" with a refreshing bluntness not often encountered today:

> No solemn titles, no pompous ceremonies, no enthusiasm on the part of applauding masses can conceal the crude fact that both the legislators and the directors of a centralized economy are only particular individuals like you and me, ignorant of 99 percent of what is going on around them as far as the real transactions, agreements, attitudes, feelings, and convictions of people are concerned. … The mythology of our age is not religious, but political, and its chief myths seem to be "representation" of the people, on the one hand, and the charismatic pretension of political leaders to be in possession of the truth and to act accordingly, on the other.

Finally, to bring this back to now Justice Sotomayor, Leoni noted that judiciary law can become like legislation "whenever jurists or judges are entitled to decide ultimately a case." But isn't that what a Supreme Court is entitled to do when it makes law for everyone everywhere?

"In our time," Leoni wrote,

> the mechanism of the judiciary in certain countries where "supreme courts" are established results in the imposition of the personal views of the members of these courts, or of a majority of them, on all the other people concerned whenever there is a great deal of disagreement between the opinion of the former and the convictions of the latter.

Thus the assertion that the Supreme Court must not become a legislature is wishful thinking. It must and it will — no matter who sits on it.

So what's an advocate of liberty to do? Leoni concluded that we must limit legislatures to as few matters as possible. That in itself is a tall order. But it is a start in the right direction.

Foundation for Economic Education, July 17, 2009

Chapter 70.
Crime and Punishment
in a Free Society

Would a free society be a crime-free society? We have good reason to anticipate it.

Don't accuse me of utopianism. I don't foresee a future of new human beings who consistently respect the rights of others. Rather, I'm drawing attention to the distinction between *crime* and tort — between offenses against the state (or society) and offenses against individual persons or their justly held property. We're so used to this distinction, and the priority of the criminal law over tort law, that most of us don't realize that things used to be different. At one time, an "offense" that was *not* an act of force against an individual was not an offense at all.

What happened? In England, the early kings recognized that the administration of justice could be a cash cow. So they grabbed on and never let go. As a result, the emphasis shifted to punishment (fines and imprisonment) and away from restitution (making victims or their heirs as whole as possible).

Liberty-minded people should regret this change. Yet again, the ruling elite exploited the people. It needed wealth to buy war materiel and allegiance, so it took it by force from the laboring masses and corrupted the justice system in the process.

In *The Enterprise of Law*, economist Bruce Benson explains that before the royal preemption, customary law prevailed in England. One feature of this spontaneous order was that

> offenses are treated as torts (private wrongs and injuries) rather than crimes (offenses against the state or the "society"). A potential action by one person has to affect someone else before any question of legality can arise; any action that does not, such as what a person does alone or in voluntary cooperation with someone else but in a manner that clearly harms no one, is not likely to become the subject of a rule of conduct under customary law.

Benson also notes that

prosecutorial duties fall to the victim and his reciprocal protection association. Thus, the law provides for restitution to victims arrived at through clearly designed participatory adjudication procedures, in order to both provide incentives to pursue prosecution and to quell victims' desires for revenge.

In such a system of law, one was not likely to see "offenses" without true victims. Since cooperation through reciprocity is key to the success of customary law, the system is likely to be kept within narrow libertarian-ish limits.

This arrangement worked out fairly well — until would-be rulers, who needed money to finance wars of conquest and buy loyalty by dispensing favors, discovered that there was gold to be had in the administration of justice.

> Anglo-Saxon kings saw the justice process as a source of revenue, and violations of certain laws began to be referred to as violations of the "king's peace." Well before the Norman conquest [1066], outlawry began to involve not only liability to be killed with impunity but [quoting historians Frederick Pollack and Frederick Maitland] "forfeiture of goods to the king."

The idea of the "king's peace" started small but eventually expanded to all of society. The incentive was obvious. "Violations of the king's peace required payment to the king," Benson writes. As customary law was co-opted by the crown, the concept *felony*, arbitrariness in punishment, and imprisonment came to the administration of "justice." The people were not pleased with the shifting focus from victims to king and his cronies, so they had to be compelled to cooperate.

> For example, royal law imposed coercive rules declaring that the victim was a criminal if he obtained restitution before he brought the offender before a king's justice where the king could get his profits. This was not a strong enough inducement, so royal law created the crimes of "theftbote," making it a misdemeanor for a victim to accept the return of stolen property or to make other arrangements with a felon in exchange for an agreement not to prosecute.

Benson sums up:

> By the end of the reign of Edward I [1307], the basic institutions of government law had been established, and in many instances older custom had been altered or replaced by authoritarian rules to facilitate the transfer of wealth to relatively powerful groups. "Public interest" justifications for a government-dominated legal system and institutions *must* be viewed as *ex post* rationalizations rather than as *ex ante* explanations of their development.

Thus the criminal justice system as we know it is a product of state arrogation and a repudiation of individualism. This perverse approach to law was inherited by the representative democracies that succeeded the absolute monarchies in England and then America.

For reasons too obvious to need elaboration, a system of justice aimed at restitution makes eminently good sense. Someone is wronged, so the perpetrator should, to the extent possible, make things right. (In the case of murder, the victim's heirs would have a monetary claim against the killer; in the case of an heirless victim, the claim could be homesteaded by anyone who puts effort into identifying and prosecuting the killer.)

At the same time, the principle of restitution undercuts the case for punishment, correction, and deterrence as objectives of the justice system. The point isn't to make perpetrators suffer or to reform them or to make potential perpetrators think twice. What good are these for the present victim? Correction and deterrence may be natural byproducts of a system of restitution, but they are not proper objectives, for where could a right to do more than require restitution come from?

Violence is so destructive of the conditions required by a community that facilitates human flourishing that its use is justifiable only when necessary to protect innocent life or to make victims whole. Thus it cannot be legitimate to use force to punish, reform, or deter. (Private nonviolent acts — for example, shunning — can have a proper role here. Also, a perpetrator who poses a continuing threat might legitimately be confined for reasons of self-defense.)

Punishment is wrong, Auburn philosopher Roderick T. Long writes, because "after all, we do not think that those who violate others' rights accidentally should be made to suffer; but the only difference between a willing aggressor and an accidental aggressor lies in the contents of their thoughts — a matter over which the law has no legitimate jurisdiction." (To my knowledge, legal scholar Randy Barnett is the first libertarian of our era to lay out the case for a restitution-only system of justice.)

As legal philosopher Gary Chartier concludes in *Anarchy and Legal Order*, "Because there is no warrant for executions or punitive fines, and no warrant for restraint (which need not involve imprisonment) except as a matter of self-defense and the defense of others, there is no need for the distinctive institutions and practices of the criminal justice system."

In a free society, crimes against persons and property would be treated like torts. This would be a welcome change in a society that imprisons more people than any other, often for nonviolent and victimless "crimes."

Future of Freedom Foundation, December 6, 2013

Chapter 71.
Statecraft Is Not Soulcraft

I get nervous when presidential candidates — or their surrogates — take up subjects that are clearly none of their business. Actually, most of what they talk about is none of their business. But some things are so far over the line that hearing politicians discuss them gives me the creeps. Herbert Spencer, where are you when we need you?

Here are two examples.

In 2008 Michelle Obama said in a campaign speech on behalf of her husband that Barack Obama was the only person running for president who understood that before we can work on social problems we have to fix our souls.

Okay, I don't want my soul being diagnosed — much less fixed — by the government or society. I suspect I am not alone here. Politician, heal thyself and leave the rest of us alone. This may get chalked up as mere campaign rhetoric, but it worries me that politicians think we want to hear this stuff. I await the day when people stampede toward the doors whenever a candidate says something like this. (Better yet, when they don't attend the speeches.)

Democrats don't have a monopoly on over-the-line talk. In a speech at the Naval Academy titled "Service to America," Obama's opponent John McCain, said: "When healthy skepticism [about government] sours into corrosive cynicism our expectations of our government become reduced to the delivery of services. And to some people the expectations of liberty are reduced to the right to choose among competing brands of designer coffee. … What is lost is, in a word, citizenship."

So according to McCain, good citizens see the government as something other than a service provider. What would that be? A moral beacon, perhaps? I think he has this wrong. Noncynics see the government as a service provider. The rest of us see it as many early Americans saw it: as a distributor of privileges at the expense of the taxpayers, consumers, and laborers.

As for the expectations of liberty, no one who cares about freedom reduces it to the choice among coffee brands.

McCain went on to say: "Sacrifice for a cause greater than yourself, and you invest your life with the eminence of that cause, your self-respect assured. All lives are a struggle against selfishness."

This may shed light on the first McCain quotation. Did he propose that we see the nation — embodied in the government — as that cause greater than ourselves? He was not entirely clear. But he did echo John F. Kennedy's famous line: "Ask not what your country can do for you — ask what you can do for your country." Nobel laureate and economist Milton Friedman had the right response: "Neither half of the statement expresses a relation between the citizen and his government that is worthy of the ideals of free men in a free society."

McCain had an uncomfortably expansive sense of citizenship. It was not just about voting, he said.

> Citizenship thrives in the communal spaces where government is absent. Anywhere Americans come together to govern their lives and their communities — in families, churches, synagogues, museums, symphonies, the Little League, the Boy Scouts, the Girl Scouts, the Salvation Army or the VFW — they are exercising their citizenship.

That seems ominously pretentious. Why aren't people seen simply as living their private lives and interacting with others for mutual enrichment? Because McCain, like many others, apparently believed that the truly private life is the "selfish" existence of a hermit. In his speech he said, "There is no honor or happiness in just being strong enough to be left alone." And: "Self-reliance — not foisting our responsibilities off on others — is the ethic that made America great." McCain paid this tribute to self-reliance before warning that when it combines with an exaggerated skepticism about government, it transmogrifies into corrosive cynicism.

His use of the phrase *left alone* is ambiguous because there are two senses of the term: 1) literally left by oneself and 2) respected in one's freedom and choices. McCain conflates the two. Few people seek to be left alone literally. The vast majority engage in mutual aid and the division of labor — that is, social cooperation — whenever they're free to do so.

A similar point can be made about the term self-reliance. If McCain means literal self-reliance, then he is wrong; that's not what made American society what it is. (This is the atomistic-individual fallacy.) Again, mutual aid (as Tocqueville noted) and the division of labor were the keys to American success. But if by self-reliance he meant *independent of the state*, then he is right. Unfortunately, considering that Theodore Roosevelt and Abraham Lincoln were his heroes, McCain didn't appear to relish independence from the state.

Actually, I didn't really want to get into the specifics of McCain's musings on social and political obligation. The details are not the point. What bothers me is that someone who merely sought to run the executive branch of the government (or was it the country that he wanted to run?) thinks he should lecture you and me on matters of obligation and such. I think of George Will's 1980s ominously titled book *Statecraft as Soulcraft*. When a would-be president tells me that I should be committed to a cause greater than myself, I'm tempted to lock the doors.

It's talk like McCain's and (presumably) Obama's that propels me to the bookshelf that holds Herbert Spencer's *Social Statics* (1851) — and one chapter in particular, "The Right to Ignore the State," in which he wrote: "If every man has freedom to do all that he wills, provided he infringes not the equal freedom of any other man, then he is free to drop connection with the state — to relinquish its protection, and to refuse paying towards its support."

Wouldn't it be bliss to be able to ignore the self-styled leaders who wish to remake our characters and who, in that quest, would do anything to get their hands on power?

Foundation for Economic Education, April 4, 2008

Chapter 72.
Stigmatizing Resistance to Authority

In 1861 Samuel A. Cartwright, an American physician, described a mental illness he called *drapetomania*. The term derived from *drapetes*, Greek for *runaway* [*slave*], and *mania* for madness or frenzy.

Thus Cartwright defined *drapetomania* as "the disease causing negroes to run away [from captivity]."

"Its diagnostic symptom, the absconding from service, is well known to our planters and overseers," Cartwright wrote in a much-distributed paper delivered before the Medical Association of Louisiana. Yet this disorder was "unknown to our medical authorities."

Cartwright thought slave owners caused the illness by making "themselves too familiar with [their slaves], treating them as equals." Drapetomania could also be induced "if [the master] abuses the power which God has given him over his fellow-man, by being cruel to him, or punishing him in anger, or by neglecting to protect him from the wanton abuses of his fellow-servants and all others, or by denying him the usual comforts and necessaries of life."

Cartwright also had ideas about proper prevention and treatment:

> If his master or overseer be kind and gracious in his hearing towards him, without condescension, and at the sane [sic] time ministers to his physical wants, and protects him from abuses, the negro is spell-bound, and cannot run away. ...

> If any one or more of them, at any time, are inclined to raise their heads to a level with their master or overseer, humanity and *their own good* requires that they should be punished until they fall into that submissive state which was intended for them to occupy in all after-time. ... They have only to be kept in that state, and treated like children, with care, kindness, attention and humanity, to prevent and cure them from running away. [Emphasis added.]

The identification of drapetomania is not Cartwright's only achievement. He also "discovered" "dysaethesia aethiopica, or hebetude of mind and obtuse sensibility of body — a disease peculiar to negroes — called by overseers, 'rascality.'" Unlike drapetomania, dysaethesia afflicted mainly free blacks. "The disease is the natural offspring of negro liberty — the liberty to be idle, to wallow in filth, and to indulge in improper food and drinks."

Cartwright, I dare say, was a quack, ever ready to ascribe to disease behavior he found disturbing. A far more informative discussion of the conduct of slaves can be found in Thaddeus Russell's fascinating book, *A Renegade History of the United States.*

Have things changed much since Cartwright's day? You decide.

The Diagnostic and Statistical Manual of Mental Disorders (DSM-5) lists Oppositional Defiant Disorder (ODD) under "disorders usually first diagnosed infancy, childhood, or adolescence." According to the manual,

> The essential feature of Oppositional Defiant Disorder is a recurrent pattern of negativistic, defiant, disobedient, and hostile behavior toward authority figures that persist for at least six months. It is characterized by the frequent occurrence of at least four of the following behaviors: losing temper, arguing with adults, actively defying or refusing to comply with the requests or rules of adults, deliberately doing things that will annoy other people, blaming others for his or her own mistakes or misbehavior, being touchy or easily annoyed by others, being angry and resentful, or being spiteful and vindictive.

In diagnosing this disorder, children are marked on a curve. "To qualify for [ODD], the behaviors must occur *more frequently* than is typically observed in individuals of comparable age and developmental level." [Emphasis added.] The behaviors must also be seen to impair "social, academic, and occupational functioning."

The parallel with drapetomania is ominous. Children, after all, are in a form of captivity and as they get older may naturally resent having decisions made for them. They may especially dislike being confined most days in stifling government institutions allegedly dedicated to education ("public schools"). Some may rebel, becoming vexatious to the authorities.

Is that really a mental, or brain, disorder? PubMed Health, a website of the National Institutes of Health, discusses treatment and prevention in ways that suggest the answer is no. "The best treatment for the child is to *talk* with a mental health professional in individual and possibly family therapy. The parents should also learn how to manage the child's behavior," it says, adding, "Medications may also be helpful." [Emphasis added.]

As for prevention, it says, "Be consistent about rules and consequences at home. Don't make punishments too harsh or inconsistent. Model the right behaviors for your child. Abuse and neglect increase the chances that this condition will occur."

It seems strange that an illness can be treated by talk and prevented by good parenting. And how was four determined to be the minimum number of behaviors before diagnosis? Or six months as the minimum period? Odd, indeed.

While ODD is discussed with reference to children, one suspects it wouldn't take much to extend it to adults who "have trouble with authority." Surely one is not cured merely with the passing of adolescence. Adults are increasingly subject to oppressive government decision-making almost as much as children. Soviet psychiatry readily found this disorder in dissidents. Let's not forget that the alliance of psychiatry and state permits people innocent of any crime to be confined and/or drugged against their will if they are said to be a "danger" to self or others.

So we must ask: Do we have a disease here or rather what the late Thomas Szasz, the psychiatrist and libertarian critic of "the therapeutic state," called "the medicalization of everyday life." (Szasz's chief concern was commonly thought to be psychiatry, but in fact it was freedom and self-responsibility.)

It seems that the common denominator of what are called mental (or brain) disorders is *behavior that others wish to control because it bothers them*. Why assume such behavior is illness? Isn't this rather a category mistake? Why stigmatize a rebellious child with an ODD "diagnosis"?

In our scientific age, many people find *scientism*, the application of the concepts and techniques of the hard sciences to persons and economic/social phenomena, comforting. In truth it is dehumanization in the name of health.

Szasz wrote,

> People do not have to be told that malaria and melanoma are diseases. They know they are. But people have to be told, and are told over and over again, that alcoholism and depression are diseases. Why? Because people know that they are not diseases, that mental illnesses are not "like other illnesses," that mental hospitals are not like other hospitals, that the business of psychiatry is control and coercion, not care or cure. Accordingly, medicalizers engage in a never-ending task of "educating" people that nondiseases are diseases.

No one believes drapetomania is a disease anymore. Slaves had a good *reason* to run away. We all have reasons — not diseases — for "running away."

Foundation for Economic Education, April 20, 2012

About the Author

Sheldon Richman is the executive editor of The Libertarian Institute, senior fellow and chair of the trustees of the Center for a Stateless Society, and contributing editor at Antiwar.com.

He is the former senior editor at the Cato Institute and Institute for Humane Studies, former editor of *The Freeman*, published by the Foundation for Economic Education, and former vice president at the Future of Freedom Foundation.

Richman is also the author of *Coming to Palestine*, *America's Counter-Revolution: The Constitution Revisited*, *Separating School & State: How to Liberate America's Families*, *Your Money or Your Life: Why We Must Abolish the Income Tax*, and *Tethered Citizens: Time to Repeal the Welfare State*, and a contributor to *The Concise Encyclopedia of Economics*.

He keeps the blog Free Association at SheldonRichman.com.

Check out Sheldon Richman's great 2019 book, also published by The Libertarian Institute, titled *Coming to Palestine*. In this incredible volume of essays, collected over 30 years, Richman exposes the true history of Israeli dispossession of the Palestinians. *Coming to Palestine* turns the typical story most Americans have been told about Israel's founding on its head. It is a ringing endorsement of reason, freedom, peace, and toleration in Palestine and Israel.

Check out *Coming to Palestine* and our other great Libertarian Institute publications at https://libertarianinstitute.org/books/.

About the Libertarian Institute

The Libertarian Institute is a 501(c3) non-profit organization dedicated to promoting individual freedom and opposition to the permanent war state, the prison and police states, and corporate state.

All donations are fully tax-deductible.

EIN 83-2869616

The Libertarian Institute
612 W. 34th St.
Austin, TX 78705

https://libertarianinstitute.org/donate

Printed in Great Britain
by Amazon